ESSAYS
ON NEW TESTAMENT
THEMES

ESSAYS
ON NEW TESTAMENT
THEMES

ERNST KÄSEMANN

FORTRESS PRESS PHILADELPHIA

Translated by W. J. Montague from selections from the German *Exegetische Versuche und Besinnungen,* Erster Band, 2nd edition, Vandenhoeck und Ruprecht 1960.

TRANSLATION © SCM PRESS 1964

FIRST FORTRESS PRESS EDITION 1982

Library of Congress Cataloging in Publication Data

Kasemann, Ernst.
    Essays on New Testament themes.

    Translation of selections from: Exegetische Versuche und Besinnungen.
    Includes indexes.
    1. Bible. N.T.—Criticism, interpretation, etc.—Addresses, essays, lectures. I. Title.
BS2361.2.K32 1982   225.6   81–17351
ISBN 0–8006–1629–4   AACR2

9407J81   Printed in the United States of America   1–1629

CONTENTS

PREFACE TO THE ENGLISH EDITION

THIS translation of some of my essays into English I regard as an honour, but one which I cannot contemplate without some apprehension. Will it really help forward the dialogue which is unquestionably more necessary today in this ecumenical epoch than ever before? Or will my exegetical endeavours not rather increase the tensions which, whether secretly or openly, have determined our relationship for centuries—perhaps even been the essential element in it?

These essays (the German title calls them 'exegetical attempts') cannot simply be labelled 'continental' and then dismissed. They are, admittedly, typically German in their style, in their method of putting questions and in the nature of the solutions they offer; they are therefore radical and challenging, and diverge from the well-trodden paths. Having grown up in the theological tradition of the dialectical theology and in the exegetical tradition based on the presuppositions of historical and form-criticism, one feels almost a heretic in the face of the pietism which is everywhere gaining ground in New Testament scholarhip. What appears to us to be a genuine encounter with the freedom of the Gospel and the preservation of that freedom in the field of critical investigation appears to the contemporary world outside merely as lack of discipline. This world is acquainted with so many different criteria of what is Christian that it finds something far-fetched in our constant harping on *libertas christiana* as being the decisive mark of the disciples of Jesus and of their service to the world, certainly in our own time. In the last resort, even the representatives of radical biblical criticism do not seem to be clear that, paradoxically, their position presupposes and maintains the primacy of Scripture over the Church; nor that it is nevertheless at the same time raising in its own way what is probably the central theme of contemporary ecumenical discussions and, as the mouth-piece of the Reformation tradition, constructing a dam against the prevailing current.

There is, bound up with all this, a personal element. My

teachers impressed upon me by their example that the rigour of the demands made by scientific scholarship must never be tempered in the slightest degree. But I have never been able to think and write simply in a spirit of academic detachment. The only problems which I have felt as a challenge have been those which affected me personally and which had a direct bearing on the ministerial life within the Church. The exigencies of the Church's conflict with Nazism, the issue of which remains, unfortunately, in essence undecided, have confirmed me in the view that non-conforming thought and action are crying needs in Christendom today; and that in this context we must not be afraid of pursuing what may turn out to be détours or even false trails. Freedom cannot be defended without risk and experiment. Granted, experiments are almost always particularly vulnerable to the passage of time. They mark previous steps along some road which has not yet been explored to its end; their direction has to be very quickly corrected so long as it remains a completely open question whether the road is ever going to lead to the destination. From this it follows that I should not today see and formulate much that is in these essays in the same way as I once did. The most important thing about them seems to me to be not the correctness of the results I reached at that time, but the deeper understanding of the problem I was discussing; and I should be fully satisfied if I could at least enable my readers to share with me in my posing of the question and convince them of its necessity. All scholarship has a provocative character, in so far as it raises the question of truth. It is logically unavoidable tensions, considered in a realistic manner, which create the possibility of understanding and life, true though it undoubtedly is that they can also be their destruction. Further, there can be no fruitful common life without such tensions.

The fact that I now find myself at variance with my own past, with the school of theology in which I grew up and particularly with my teacher, Bultmann, is only marginally visible in these essays. The problem—which I feel to be the central problem of history as recorded fact (*Historie*)—of the relation of continuity and discontinuity also determines our own growth and matura-ation; and I no longer believe in a permanently valid self-under-standing, whether it be of epochs or of the life of the individual as it is exposed in self-criticism to the world about it. There is perhaps some connection between this view of mine and the fact that my generation has been subjected more rudely than earlier generations to upheavals the range of which, not by any means fully discernible as yet, forced us to find new angles of attack on our problems. On the other hand, I have never desired to repudiate my sense of gratitude for the inheritance which I received; thus, the game or adventure of challenge and the consequent abandonment of old positions is again repeated in this sphere. Only as we journey onward in a perpetual Exodus can we remain loyal both to truth and, surely, to our humanity also.

But if this is really so, then perhaps it is permissible to hope that my attempts at exegesis, which are bound to afford particularly extensive and strong provocation to the English reader, may nevertheless lead to a useful conversation. What I have had in mind here is not to arrive at generally received results and a monochrome similarity of approach, but at a community of experience based on a dialogue in which, both by concession and contradiction, we open ourselves to each other.

Finally, I should like to thank the SCM Press and Fortress Press for their interest in my work, and the translator, Canon Montague, for the great pains and care he has taken over the translation.

ERNST KÄSEMANN

Tübingen, October 1963

TRANSLATOR'S PREFACE

THE word 'Enthusiasm', with its derivatives, is used where it occurs in this translation in the same sense as in Bishop Butler's famous rebuke to John Wesley, or, more recently, in the title of the late Monsignor Ronald Knox's classic work. The German original is *die Schwärmerei*.

In translating the essay on 'The Problem of the Historical Jesus', I have been up against the well-known difficulty that, where English has the one word 'history', German has both *die Geschichte* and *die Historie*. I have usually tried to give the sense of the distinction by inserting the adjective 'mere' where the original had *die Historie*; at other times, the context has seemed to convey the distinction adequately.

New Testament citations are usually from the New English Bible, very occasionally from the Revised Version. Where it seemed necessary, in order to bring out some point made by the author, I have translated directly from the German.

The numbers at the top of each page are those of the pages of the German edition.

W.J.M.

ABBREVIATIONS

AGGW	Abhandlungen der Gesellschaft der Wissenschaften zu Göttingen
ATANT	Abhandlungen zur Theologie des Alten und Neuen Testaments, Zürich
ET	English translation
EvTh	*Evangelische Theologie*, Munich
FRLANT	Forschungen zur Religion und Literatur des Alten und Neuen Testaments, Göttingen
HNT	Handbuch zum Neuen Testament, ed. H. Lietzmann, Tübingen
KEKNT	Kritisch-exegetisch Kommentar über das Neue Testament, Göttingen
NTD	Das Neue Testament Deutsch, Göttingen
RGG	*Die Religion in Geschichte und Gegenwart*, Tübingen
SAH	Sitzungsberichte der Akademie der Wissenschaften, Heidelberg
TB	*Theologische Blätter*, Leipzig
TWNT	*Theologisches Wörterbuch zum Neuen Testament*, ed. G. Kittel, Stuttgart, 1932ff.
Strack-Billerbeck	H. L. Strack and P. Billerbeck, *Kommentar zum Neuen Testament aus Talmud und Midrasch*, Munich, 1922–56
ZNW	*Zeitschrift für die neutestamentliche Wissenschaft*, Giessen
ZTK	*Zeitschrift für Theologie und Kirche*, Tübingen

I

THE PROBLEM OF THE HISTORICAL JESUS[1]

I. THE PRESENT POSITION

IT is one of the marks of the upheaval in German work on the New Testament in this last generation that the old question about the Jesus of history has receded rather noticeably into the background. And yet, for about two hundred years before that, the advance of our discipline had been set in motion, impelled on its way and determined in its very essence by this same question. Basically, two factors were responsible when, after the First World War, the problem, if not completely solved, seemed at least to have come to a kind of full-stop. The break made with Liberalism by the Dialectical Theology and the parallel renewal of interest in the message of the Reformation combined to reveal the impoverishment and distortion of the Gospel which takes place wherever the question of the Jesus of history is treated as decisive for theology and preaching. At the same time, the work of the Form Critics was designed to show that the message of Jesus as given to us by the Synoptists is, for the most part, not authentic but was minted by the faith of the primitive Christian community in its various stages. Thus, from the fact that the genuine tradition about Jesus has only been transmitted to us embedded in the preaching of primitive Christianity and overlaid by it, the conclusion was drawn that the true bearer and moulder of the Gospel had been the Easter faith. For Bultmann, this judgment involved radical consequences. As early as his book *Jesus*[2] he was no longer relying exclusively on the material the authenticity of which his *History of the Synoptic Tradition*[3] had left unimpeached. He was simply concerned to uncover the earliest stratum of primitive Christian

---

[1] A lecture given at the reunion of Marburg old students on 20 October 1953' in Jugenheim. First published in *ZTK* 51, 1954, pp. 125–53.
[2] Berlin, 1926; ET, *Jesus and the Word*, London, 1935.
[3] ET of 3rd ed., Oxford, 1963. Originally in FRLANT 29, 1st ed., 1921; 2nd ed., 1931; 3rd ed., 1957 with 1958 supplement.

proclamation, in which the preaching of Jesus himself and its reflection in the kerygma of the community had in historical fact been interwoven; no doubt his own failure to draw a clear line between them was conscious and deliberate. Then, in his *Primitive Christianity in its Contemporary Setting*[1], he included his portrayal of Jesus within his account of late Judaism and, correspondingly, sketched New Testament Theology as a development of the primitive Christian message, thus making the preaching of Jesus appear the mere precondition of the latter. But this in turn means that Christian faith is here being understood as faith in the exalted Lord for which the Jesus of history as such is no longer considered of decisive importance.

There has not yet been any final and definite parting of the ways on this point. That this is so is in no small measure connected with the fact that any criticism would have to reckon with M. Kähler's book *Der sogenannte historische Jesus und der geschichtliche, biblische Christus*,[2] which still, after sixty years, is hardly dated and, in spite of many attacks and many possible reservations, has never really been refuted. In essence, Bultmann has merely, in his own way, underpinned and rendered more precise the thesis of this book. But the unmistakable embarrassment of apologetics, exposed to criticism both from the side of exegesis and from the side of systematic theology, has had a paralysing effect throughout a whole generation. This state of affairs is obviously approaching its end today. The old conflict is flaring up again and will probably result in the formation of distinct fronts such as we have hardly known since the War, in spite of all the tensions and differences of opinion which have existed among German New Testament scholars. Knowledge proceeds by antitheses and Bultmann's radicalism is provoking a reaction. But over and above this, we are all without exception concerned at present with the question of a proper understanding of history and historicity which is bound to find concrete, necessary and, indeed, archetypal expression for the theologian in the problem of the historical Jesus and of his significance for faith. Developing this in more detail, we find that present-day criticism hinges on three points. First, efforts

[1] London, 1956; ET of *Das Urchristentum im Rahmen der antiken Religionen*, Zürich, 1949.
[2] Leipzig, 1896; new ed. by E. Wolf, Munich, 1956.

are being made to show that the Synoptists contain much more authentic tradition than the other side is prepared to allow. Secondly, a case is being made out with particular vigour for the reliability, if not of the whole of the Passion and Easter tradition of the Gospels, at least of the most primitive elements in it. In both cases, the concern is to counteract any drastic separation, or even antithesis, of kerygma and tradition. Those who take this line are, fundamentally, trying to maintain that the kerygma includes the recital of facts as mediated by the tradition. And thus they arrive, thirdly, at the systematic conception of a 'salvation history' running parallel to universal history, embedded in it but yet separable from it, having its own laws and continuity and finding its vehicle in the history of faith and of the Church as the new divine creation.

The characteristic feature of our situation, then, is that the classic liberal question about the Jesus of history is increasingly regaining its theological importance; and that, paradoxically, this is happening at a time when liberalism is discredited over wide areas of Church life, and happening as a counter-blast to an historical and theological criticism which itself sprang from the soil of liberalism. This change of fronts is certainly among the most fascinating and fruitful phenomena in recent theological history. For two hundred years, critical research has been trying to free the Jesus of history from the fetters of the Church's dogma, only to find at the end that such an attempt was predestined to failure, and that we can learn nothing at all about the historical Jesus except through the medium of primitive Christian preaching and of the Church's dogma which is bound up with it; we can no longer detach him neatly and satisfactorily from the Christ of preaching and of faith. But at precisely the same moment, the very people who have hitherto been the opponents of the liberal quest of the historical Jesus are obviously going in fear and trembling lest the doors should for the first time be really opened to radical scepticism and lest, with the abandoning of any direct attack on the historical question, the historical reality of revelation itself should be endangered. This reality they themselves seek to defend by showing that the tradition is historically trustworthy. They are thus following in the footsteps of critics whose original intention in taking up the theme of history was precisely the reverse—to set it in opposition to dogma.

It would certainly not be a good thing to accept the stark fact of the surprising change of fronts so readily that we failed at least to inquire into this development, to see whether it might not perhaps have an inner necessity of its own. It might well be that each of the protagonists in this struggle was concerned, on his part, to pursue some interest which in fact ought not to be surrendered, and to this extent the two might be more than mere opponents; they might be partners in a genuine theological conversation. Such an assumption does not prejudge the issue as to the right and wrong in detail of the position we have provisionally adopted; it simply postulates the dialectic of two distinct standpoints. An over-emphasis on the one aspect is then met by a like over-emphasis on the other, and the change of posture by the first partner leads, provided that the conversation is conducted on a reasonable basis, to a corresponding change on the part of the other. Whether such an hypothesis is tenable can only be discovered from an examination of the underlying facts. We shall therefore next attempt to evaluate the significance of observable historical fact within the framework of the history which lies before us.

2. THE PROBLEM OF THE HISTORICAL ELEMENT IN OUR GOSPELS

Even the history which is recounted in the pages of the New Testament has become to us, who live nearly two thousand years later, *mere* history. In other words, we have no longer any immediate access to it, even if we take the most accurate and circumstantial conspectus of it which is possible. Over against those who were contemporary with it, we speak in another language, we think in other categories, we face other situations and decisions. In relation to it, we experience with peculiar force the sense that all history is conditioned by the fact of dying, and, as generation succeeds to generation, this sense emerges as discontinuity. Thus, if we desire to obtain knowledge of past history, we have to fall back on what has been narrated. History is only accessible to us through tradition and only comprehensible to us through interpretation. To be acquainted merely with what actually happened is of little use to us by itself. Both Rationalism and Supernaturalism have certainly striven hard on all sides to establish, in part or in sum, the credibility of the facts reported in the New Testament. But what has been the result of all these efforts, if the truth be told? Did not the Jesus of the Gospels become, under the hand of the Rationalists, a figure just like ourselves, thus showing how the wealth of portraits of Jesus assembled by A. Schweitzer corresponds to the multitude of possible viewpoints and beholders? And has not Supernaturalism succeeded only in depicting the miraculous aura of the θεῖος ἀνήρ, who can be accepted only by means of the *sacrificium intellectus*, which enthusiasts in their self-induced delusions and transports so readily offer? In neither case is there any gain for faith. For if, on the one hand, it was established that certain happenings *did* take place which could be fitted into the same category as the long succession of similar happenings elsewhere, on the other hand prodigies were brought to light which may still arouse curiosity but which can give no certainty of revelation. We have at this stage no need whatever to labour either the point that the whole history of religion abounds in miracles and prodigies, or the point that historical criticism is bound to call in question a great deal of what is alleged to have happened or, finally, the point that the passion for objective facts can be shown to have led time and again to unrestrained and highly subjective flights of fancy. It ought also to be clear to us that the Gospel history has not come any nearer to us when we have resolved it into bare facts. To fail to grasp this is the peculiar self-deception of all those who want to extract a salvation history in an objectively convincing form from universal history and who can yet rest their case at best on an abundance of remarkable occurrences. No one has ever been compelled (in the true sense) to make his decision between faith and unbelief, simply because someone else has succeeded in representing Jesus convincingly as a worker of miracles. And nothing is settled about the significance of the Resurrection tidings for me personally, simply because the evidence for the empty tomb has been shown to be reliable. The handing on of relatively probable facts does not as such provide any basis for genuinely historical communication and continuity.

It is obvious that primitive Christianity was well aware of this. We cannot otherwise explain why its Gospels were not written primarily as reportage and why its own kerygma actually overlays and conceals the figure of the historical Jesus, thus facing us as historians with incalculable difficulties and very often making any reconstruction quite impossible. The community did not inadvertently and senselessly amalgamate its own message with that of its Lord, much less did it merely repeat the latter. If it was indeed concerned not with the reproduction of a notable happening, but with that decision between faith and unbelief which was demanded of it, then it had no alternative but to act as it did. By the very fact of acting thus, it shows that this concern cannot be preserved and defended historically, that is, by the enumeration of bare facts within a causal nexus. By acting as it did the community bore (and still bears) witness to history as being living and contemporary. It interprets out of its own experience what for it has already become mere history and employs for this purpose the medium of its preaching. It is precisely by this method that the community rescues the facts of the past from being regarded only as prodigies and wonders. And in so doing it demonstrates that in its eyes Jesus is no mere miracle-worker, but the *Kyrios*, from whom it knows itself to receive both grace and obligation. To state the paradox as sharply as possible: the community takes so much trouble to maintain historical continuity with him who once trod this earth that it allows the historical events of this earthly life to pass for the most part into oblivion and replaces them by its own message. It is not only at this point in its history that the community does this. The same process is always being repeated in the course of Church history. Time and again, continuity with the past is preserved by shattering the received terminology, the received imagery, the received theology—in short, by shattering the tradition. We can early see this happening in the differing forms of the Palestinian and Hellenistic kerygmas. The variation in the New Testament message, which finds its strongest and most problematic form of expression in the transition from the preaching of Jesus to the preaching about Jesus, is anything but accidental and arbitrary. It plunges us into great difficulties. For not only does it compel us to raise the question of the significance of individuality for Christian preaching, but at the same time it is also the outward sign of radical historical changes and of new developments. There is an ever-present temptation, into which many have fallen, to infer from this variation the complete discontinuity of Christian history. The truth is that it is this variation which makes continuity possible at all. For mere history becomes significant history not through tradition as such but through interpretation, not through the simple establishment of facts but through the understanding of the events of the past which have become objectified and frozen into facts. The variation in the New Testament kerygma demonstrates that primitive Christendom held fast the profession of its faith throughout all changes of time and place, although these changes forced upon it the modification of received tradition. Mere history, the existence of which can only be prolonged with difficulty by its presence to human consciousness has, as such, no genuine historical significance, even if it is full of curiosities and wonders. At any rate, it has no more historical significance than a lunar landscape which itself is not without curiosities and wonders. Mere history only takes on genuine historical significance in so far as it can address both a question and an answer to our contemporary situation; in other words, by finding interpreters who hear and utter this question and answer. For this purpose primitive Christianity allows mere history no vehicle of expression other than the kerygma.

This truth must be seen to be of fundamental significance for the whole New Testament message. But it must, further, not be overlooked that the relationship of the individual writings to the life history of Jesus varies very considerably. Above all, we cannot help being struck by the fact that the Gospels alone present the tidings of the Christ within the framework of the story of the earthly life of Jesus. It is true that the other writings indicate from time to time that they are not wholly without information about this life. But basically it is only the event of Cross and Resurrection which has any real importance for them. For this reason the historical element in the story of Jesus has, in these other writings, shrunk almost to vanishing point. We might even say that it is present only as a shadow. For Cross and Resurrection are no longer regarded from the standpoint of the historian, but are expounded in their saving significance. Seen from this angle it will appear strange that we encounter in the New Testament *any* writings like the Gospels, which concern themselves with the earthly life of Jesus.

Yet even the Gospels themselves are far from displaying agreement in the way in which they relate themselves to the historical life of Jesus. It can hardly be doubted that the Synoptists intended in all good faith to give their readers authentic tradition about Jesus. But it is impossible to ascribe the same intention to the fourth Evangelist, at least in the same sense. The real violence done by John to the narrative material, his striking neglect of the Synoptic tradition, the quite different arrangement of the whole and, above all, the peculiar way in which he has constructed the discourses; all these compel us to suppose that such a reflective writer could not have been simply deceiving himself about the discrepancy between his mode of presentation and that of all other existing Church tradition, but that he willed and intended it. For this reason, it is now widely acknowledged that for him the merely historical only has interest and value to the extent to which it mirrors symbolically the recurring experiences of Christian faith. It provides him with the opportunity and the framework of writing for his own day the history of the *Christus praesens*. Mark, on the other hand, in Dibelius' excellent phrase, wrote the book of the secret epiphanies of Jesus. The words and deeds of the Christ, as W. Wrede has already established, appear here as an earnest of the glory of the Risen Lord, so that the life history of Jesus becomes almost the subject of a mystery play; the Son of God, who has come down to earth, lifts his incognito from time to time, until at Easter he allows it to drop away altogether. This earthly life is the battle which precedes the victory and can only be understood in the light of this victory. But if this is the case, then the historical life of Jesus is no longer the focus of Mark's attention. It merely provides the stage on which the God-man enters the lists against his enemies. The history of Jesus has become mythicized. Thus, when we inquire where in our Gospels a stronger emphasis is laid on the historical element, we are really left only with Matthew and Luke. What the situation in their case is, we shall have to discuss presently. But let us halt at this point to plot our series of findings.

We have been endeavouring to discover an answer to the problem of the position of the historical element in our Gospels. We owe the recognition of the existence of the problem to that radical criticism which, in the logic of its long and painful journey towards the ultimate datum of the Gospel tradition, arrived not, as it had hoped, at the historical Jesus but at the primitive Christian kerygma. In order to solve this problem, this criticism was finally compelled to give up the attempt to construct a life of Jesus out of the Synoptic Gospels. It did not take this step in order to throw itself anew into the arms of the Christological metaphysic of orthodoxy; but, by recognizing the necessity of re-formulating its original question, remained true to the impulse which gave it birth, and the historical method thus engendered. It does not deny the existence of the historical Jesus. But it recognizes that we can only gain access to this Jesus through the medium of the primitive Christian gospel and the primary effect of this gospel is not to open up the way for us but to bar it. The historical Jesus meets us in the New Testament, our only real and original documentation of him, *not* as he was in himself, *not* as an isolated individual, but as the Lord of the community which believes in him. Only in so far as, from the very outset, he was potentially and actually this Lord, does the story of his earthly life play any part in our Gospels. Anything else there was to him is completely overshadowed, so that we are no longer in a position to delineate with even approximate accuracy and completeness his portrait, his development, the actual course of his life: we are for the most part groping in absolute darkness so far as these are concerned. The significance of this Jesus for faith was so profound, that even in the very earliest days it almost entirely swallowed up his earthly history. The living experience of him which later generations enjoyed made the facts of his earthly life simply irrelevant, except in so far as they might serve to reflect the permanent experience. In such circumstances we must question whether the formula 'the historical Jesus' can be called at all appropriate or legitimate, because it is almost bound to awaken and nourish the illusion of a possible and satisfying reproduction of his 'life story'. The road of Liberalism had to be abandoned, because the hope of uncovering this 'life story' and of being able to correct the Church's dogma in the light of it proved a vain one. Anyone who tries to upset this verdict is seeking to rob us of the fruit and the meaning of all our research of the last two centuries and to conjure up once again the painful story of historical criticism, which would then have to be repeated in an even more drastic form. He is also failing to understand that the discovery of historical facts and their causal nexus

is not necessarily of help to us in our own historical situation but
that these must be interpreted before their relevance and their
challenge can be made plain. Mere history is petrified history,
whose historical significance cannot be brought to light simply by
verifying the facts and handing them on. On the contrary, the
passing on of the *bruta facta* can, as such, directly obstruct a proper
understanding of it. Only that man is in genuine continuity with
past history who allows it to place him in a new condition of
responsibility; this is not yet true of the man who is concerned
with its causality and teleology or who simply struggles on under
the burden of tradition. In theological terms, this means that only
in the decision between faith and unbelief can petrified history even
of the life of Jesus become once again living history. This is why
we only make contact with this life history of Jesus through the
kerygma of the community. The community neither could nor
would separate this life history from its own history. Therefore it
neither could nor would abstract from its Easter faith and distinguish between the earthly and the exalted Lord. By maintaining
the identity of the two, it demonstrated that any questioning
directed only towards the historical Jesus seemed to it to be pure
abstraction.

3. THE PROBLEM OF HISTORIFICATION (*Historisierung*) IN OUR GOSPELS

What has hitherto been said has a converse, which must on no
account be left out of our reckoning. For the decision taken by
primitive Christianity obviously does not permit us to choke off
the question about the Jesus of history, in spite of its dubious
status when raised in isolation and in spite of the difficulty of
finding an answer to it. No one may arbitrarily and with impunity
exempt himself from tackling the problems which have come down
to him from his fathers. The exponents of Liberal theology are,
over a wide area, no longer acknowledged as fathers today; but
this does not in any way alter the fact that they nevertheless do
stand in that relationship to us. Secular historical science will also
continue to confront us with this kind of question in some form
or other; and every New Testament scholar has in fact dealt with
it in his own particular way. But, most important of all, the New

Testament itself justifies us to this extent in asking the question, inasmuch as it is to the earthly Jesus that the Gospels ascribe their kerygma, wherever it actually originated, and thus they invest him unmistakably with pre-eminent authority. However strongly their conceptions of the history of Jesus may differ, however much the real life history of Jesus may be buried under their own proclamation, it is interest in this history which we have to thank, both for their genesis and for their form, which stands out in such peculiar relief against both the rest of the New Testament and the other literature of the time. In no case may we allow the exaggeration of insights which may be correct in themselves to exempt us from the dialectic obtaining here or to drive us to one-sided solutions. That would equally happen if we were to absolutize the irrefragable proposition that the Christian message is founded on the Easter faith. Such a proposition has its proper place and validity primarily in antithesis to the Liberal *Leben-Jesu-Forschung*. But it ought not to conceal a defeatist attitude which has already given up any attempt to penetrate the human individuality of Jesus, nor to appear to contest what the Evangelists would undoubtedly have maintained—namely, that the life history of Jesus has its relevance for faith. For if primitive Christianity identifies the humiliated with the exalted Lord, in so doing it is confessing that, in its presentation of his story, it is incapable of abstracting from its faith. At the same time, however, it is also making it clear that it is not minded to allow myth to take the place of history nor a heavenly being to take the place of the Man of Nazareth. In fact, the fight is already on against the docetism of the 'enthusiasts' and the *kenosis* doctrine of the historicizers. Primitive Christianity is obviously of the opinion that the earthly Jesus cannot be understood otherwise than from the far side of Easter, that is, in his majesty as Lord of the community and that, conversely, the event of Easter cannot be adequately comprehended if it is looked at apart from the earthly Jesus. The Gospel is always involved in a war on two fronts.

Certainly we must now determine exactly what the reasons were which lay behind this attitude. They will be most easily discovered by taking for our new point of departure some part of the tradition which must necessarily be regarded as unauthentic. For there a procedure has been adopted which we may call the 'historification' of the unhistorical. The dominating interest, whatever it may be, will be found to determine the form in which the historical element is presented. Matthew's infancy narrative seems to me particularly instructive. Two motifs stand out clearly here. On the one side, constant allusion is made to the fulfilment of the Scriptures in what is being narrated; on the other, a parallel with the Moses *haggadah* is being drawn, the sense of which is: as with the first Deliverer, so with the second. In both cases the birth of the child produces unrest on the part of the rulers, followed by consultation with wise men and the murder of children; in both cases there follows a wonderful deliverance in which Egypt becomes the land of refuge. From the study of the formation of tradition it can be established that the Moses legends have provided the tradition about Jesus with its characteristic features, while the comparative study of religion enables us to add that such a transfer of motifs is a frequent phenomenon and that we have before us a typical example of legendary overpainting and of mythologizing. However correct this analysis may be, we do not come up against the specifically theological problem until we ask ourselves what interest is being served by the combination of the already existing and originally mythical material with the story of Jesus. Here we can gain some help from the parallel of the proofs from prophecy in the very passages we have cited. Just as the Scriptures find their fulfilment in the events which are being portrayed, so the mythical scheme, taken up by Matthew, of the threat to the child and his miraculous deliverance marks him out as the future Saviour of the people of God—in concrete terms, the second and last Moses. Conversely, because Jesus is the future Saviour, the traditional and given scheme can be transferred to him and the events surrounding his birth and infancy must correspond to the stories already in existence concerning Moses. In this way an 'historification' of mythical material is arrived at. Its progress is rapid, in so far as Matthew has no longer any doubt that he is recapitulating genuine history. The process we have outlined takes on significance for us in that here we acknowledge unequivocally that the tradition concerning Jesus presupposes primitive Christian eschatology and has been shaped by it. It is not only here that this eschatology has conditioned the life story of Jesus as we have it in our Gospels. Matthew himself demonstrates this in a particularly impressive way, as some further examples may illustrate. The recital of the miracles takes place in his Gospel under the device of the compassion of God, which is revealing itself in the Last Days and at the same time visiting Israel in mercy. Matt. 9–10 offer us in more or less systematic fashion examples of what, in the answer to the Baptist's question in 11.5, are described as signs of the age of salvation. Our Evangelist is thus interested in the miracles of Jesus from the standpoint of his own particular eschatology. It emerges from the Sermon on the Mount that Matthew sees in Jesus the bringer of the Messianic Torah. We are to understand from this that Jesus is being consistently portrayed here as a rabbi and as founder of an eschatologically-orientated community life. This is by no means as self-evident a proposition as it may appear to us. Apart from the fact that an extraordinarily large number of logia cannot be regarded as authentic and that any portrait of Jesus based on them is thus rendered problematical, it is also a question how this picture of the rabbi can be reconciled with the knowledge of Jesus' divine Sonship. The answer is, that the bringer of the Messianic Torah is not just any rabbi, nor is his righteousness that of the scribes and Pharisees. Once again the Evangelist's eschatology has determined the shape he has given to the life story of Jesus. At this point we may mention the different twist which Matthew gives to the theory of 'hardening' put forward in Mark 4.12. Like Mark, he emphasizes that the parables are so slanted as to veil the truth. Like Mark, he sees in this veiling a judgment of God on those who shut their ears to the voice of the divine emissary. But Matthew now applies this quite concretely to the Jews. For while the disciples are portrayed throughout as those who understand (and thus not as in Mark), the Jesus of Matthew, from ch. 13 until his last clash with his adversaries in Jerusalem, is consistently executing judgment on Jewry by the very fact of speaking to them in veiled language, i.e. in parables. The eschatological trend of the proof from prophecy in the Passion story is obvious; that of the Easter narratives is still more obvious. We may sum up thus: the whole life history of Jesus as Matthew presents it is not only seen from the standpoint of eschatology, but basically shaped by it. It is precisely here that the story of Jesus has been interwoven with traditional material which can only be described as being in itself unhistorical, legendary and mythical.

But once we are clear about this, we can easily see that the position is the same in the Second and Fourth Gospels. Even Mark is not concerned in the last resort to depict Jesus as a miracle-worker, however much some of his details may give this impression. Rather, he sees in the earthly life of Jesus the glory of the risen Son of God bursting victoriously into the demon-controlled world and revealing equally to the earth and to the principalities and powers their eternal Lord. Because in Mark—and this is characteristic of the Gentile Christian outlook—the overcoming of the demonic forces forms the core of the eschatological event, the history of Jesus as outlined by him looks quite different from that given us by Matthew: and this accounts also for the pronounced shrinkage in the discourse material. In exactly the same way, there is a correspondence between the peculiarly Johannine eschatology, with its thoroughgoing elimination of the apocalyptic element, and the Johannine portrayal of the history of Jesus as the history of the *praesentia* of the Logos on earth; on this subject, I would at this point simply refer you to Bultmann's commentary on John.

The case of the Lucan corpus is more complicated. To begin with, we have the unusually significant and equally problematical situation that the story of Jesus is given a kind of extension in that of the Apostles. Such an undertaking could only be possible and meaningful for a writer at a time in which apocalyptic eschatology no longer controlled the whole of life, as it had done in primitive Christianity. You do not write the history of the Church, if you are expecting the end of the world to come any day. Acts thus shows clearly that, while the apocalyptic hope may still belong to the stock-in-trade of Christian doctrine, yet for Luke himself it no longer possesses any pivotal interest. If his Gospel creates at many points a quite different impression, this is to be placed to the account of the tradition which Luke has embraced and preserved. Primitive Christian eschatology is replaced by salvation history, which is characterized by an historically verifiable continuity and by a process of ever-extending development, as H. Conzelmann has demonstrated to particularly good effect in his *The Theology of St Luke*.[1] The preparation for this development is God's consistent action throughout the Old Testament and its culmination in the history of Jesus; the history of the Church is its unfolding

[1] *Die Mitte der Zeit*, Tübingen, 1954; ET, London, 1960.

and the Last Day is its final conclusion. The same conception is reflected in the way in which the various steps of Jesus' journey, and of the journey of the Church, are distinctly marked and directly control the divisions of the whole Lucan corpus. The outline of a chronological and geographical sequence determines this whole and gives it clarity of arrangement. But, in this careful ordering of what is immediately visible, we come to see the inward order created by the divine plan of salvation. It is not an accident that the Areopagus discourse speaks of God as the great Orderer of the cosmos and of the ages. Because Luke saw things in this light, he could and did become the first Christian historian to try to sketch out the great stages of the plan of salvation and to work consistently on that basis. His Gospel is indeed the first 'life of Jesus'. In it, consideration is given to the points of view of causality and teleology; and psychological insight, the composition of the historian and the particular slant of the writer who aims at edification are all equally discernible. It is true that the price Luke pays for all this is by no means small. His Jesus is the founder of the Christian religion; the Cross is a misunderstanding on the part of the Jews, who have not properly understood Old Testament prophecy, and the Resurrection is the necessary correction of this human error by the Great Disposer. The teaching of Jesus brings us a loftier ethic, the miracles are heavenly power bursting into the world, wonders which provide evidence of divine majesty. The story of Jesus becomes something absolutely in the past, namely, *initium Christianismi*—mere history indeed. As such, therefore, it can properly be tied to the history of the Apostles. To its own time—the era of the beginnings of early Catholicism—it appears as the sacred past, the epoch of great miracles, of right faith and of first love, a model of all that Church life should be and might be. This is the result of replacing primitive Christian eschatology by salvation history. Therefore even Luke confirms for us in his own way—that is, *e contrario*—that the mode in which the life history of Jesus is presented depends on the eschatology prevailing at the time. To put this in the form of an epigram (but an epigram which expresses the essential truth): if, in the other Gospels, the problem of history is a special form of the problem of eschatology, in Luke eschatology has become a special form of the problem of history.

4. THE SIGNIFICANCE OF THE HISTORICAL ELEMENT IN OUR GOSPELS

We have to ask at this point how this finding helps us to answer our particular questions. First, we have now come to see that our Gospels, with the necessary exception of Luke, are not in the least interested in the composition of a comprehensive biography of Jesus nor in investigating what has been reported about him to see how far it is reliable and how far it corresponds to historical reality. The story of his life is, for the Gospels, only a point where the eschatological events intersect and is only worthy of consideration as such; it receives its own peculiar life from these events and not from itself in isolation. This is supremely true of Jesus himself, in so far as he *is* the eschatological event. His historical existence is naturally presupposed and it enters the realm of the phenomenal to this extent, that his life on earth takes a human course. But as soon as he is portrayed as speaking and acting, this human course becomes an unbroken series of divine revelations and mighty acts, which has no common basis of comparison with any other human life and thus can no longer be comprehended within the category of the historical. All this finds its clearest expression in the fact that, while this human life runs, like any other, from birth to death, birth and death do not, however, appear as its beginning and its end; they do not appear as happenings within the ordinary course of nature but as events of salvation history. Because Luke has nevertheless attempted to contain this life within the category of historicity, he has ended up by making Jesus into a miracle-worker and the bringer of a new morality, the Cross into a misunderstanding on the part of the Jews and the Resurrection into the marvellous reanimation of a dead man.

But what meaning then has it for the other Evangelists, this life history which stands so deep within the shadow of the eschatological event, now almost swallowed up by it, now brought out again in strong relief; this life history which, in the first instance, prompted the very writing of the Gospels? It seems to me that it is not by accident that the New Testament's own answer is given in an eschatological key phrase, the ἐφ' ἅπαξ of which the two meanings—'once' and 'once for all'—merge in such a remarkable fashion. But this needs further explanation. A primary concern of the Gospels is unmistakably the particularity with which the eschatological event is bound to *this* man from Nazareth, to the arena of Palestine and to a concrete time with its special circumstances. For this eschatological event is not a new idea, nor is it the culminating point of a process of development, the significance of which can be explained by its causal connections and effects. Revelation ceases to be God's revelation once it has been brought within a causal nexus. It is what it is only when it is seen as an unconditioned happening. And it does not convey to me an idea or even a programme; it is an act which lays hold of me. In revelation, I do not primarily experience some *thing* or other, but my ultimate Lord, his word to me and his claim upon me. Because this is so, we can even reject revelation, while we may overlook facts but cannot meaningfully reject them. In the same way there is, in respect of revelation, a 'too late' of guilty procrastination which is not really the case in respect of an idea. Briefly, that particularity of revelation which is manifested in its unbreakable link with a concrete life history reflects the freedom of the God who acts and is the ground of our having a possibility of decision. In other words, revelation creates *kairos* which is a situation of grace or guilt, as the case may be. Because primitive Christianity experienced the earthly history of Jesus in this way as *kairos*, it wrote Gospels and did not after Easter simply let the life story of Jesus go by the board. Easter did not render this experience superfluous; on the contrary, it confirmed it. So far as it is desirable or possible to speak of a variation in faith before and after Easter, we can only say that out of the 'once' came the 'once for all' and out of the isolated encounter with Jesus, limited as it had been by death, came the presence of the exalted Lord, as described in the Fourth Gospel.

But this brings us to a second motive for keeping faith firmly tied to the life history of Jesus. It is more than strange that the Gospel of John treats of the abiding presence of the exalted Lord precisely within the framework of a history of the earthly Jesus. Admittedly, the Synoptists also describe the life of Jesus from the standpoint of the post-Easter community and its faith. They portray their Lord from the beginning as the Son of God, whereas this insight was only given to the Church after Easter. Thus, even

31

in the Synoptists, the story as presented by them is not 'once for all' in the sense that it excludes the experiences of those who come after. On the contrary, these people are expressly told that they can have the same experiences of Jesus. But this is not done with the same boldness which marks the procedure of the Fourth Evangelist. Indeed the Johannine symbolism, so often worked over, robs—there is no other word for it—what happened once upon a time of all intrinsic significance and only allows it any importance as a reflection of present experience. Even the events of Good Friday, Easter and Ascension Day are no longer clearly distinguished. We must admit that nowhere in the New Testament is the life story of Jesus so emptied of all real content as it already is here, where it seems to be almost a projection of the present back into the past. It is all the more astonishing that the Fourth Gospel can yet describe the story of the exalted Lord as one and the same with that of the earthly Lord. The explanation of this may well be summed up in the one key word 'condescension'. It is precisely the Fourth Gospel, originating in the age of the anti-docetic conflicts, which neither can nor will renounce the truth that revelation takes place on earth and in the flesh. Here it parts from Enthusiasm to which otherwise it approaches so suspiciously close. Whatever violence it may have done to biographical history, it found it neither possible nor desirable to abandon history altogether, because with history stands or falls not only the divine condescension of revelation but also earthly corporeality as the sphere of revelation. Revelation invades human history and takes its course within it. Thus it is possible for revelation to be over-looked, misunderstood, spurned, to be a cause of offence and tumult. The ambiguity of this particular history is preserved by the fact that it can and does become mere history, unless the *Christus praesens* is constantly re-entering the arena. But this ambiguity is the obverse of the divine condescension. The Evangelist expresses this last truth by writing the story of the exalted Lord and that of the humiliated Lord as one and the same story.

No concessions to John's kind of symbolism are as yet to be found in the Synoptists. They certainly bring out the relation of the Gospel story to the present experience of their readers, but see to it that what they narrate displays equally unmistakably the character of 'the past'. The contrast with the Fourth Gospel emerges most strongly with regard to the portrayal of the Passion and Resurrection. We must at least raise the question as to whether this is to be explained solely on the grounds of weaker powers of theological reflection. Rather, as it seems to me, a proper concern of faith is manifesting itself here also. For the more certainly history is determined by the possibilities and decisions of a given time, the less it can be resolved into a logical sequence of situations. Our possibilities and decisions are in historical reality always pre-destinated, and this through the events of the past, which bar certain possibilities and decisions to us, while opening up others. We are always finding ourselves in a *kairos* which overlaps the individual moment of decision. If the Synoptists differ from John in allowing considerable intrinsic importance to the past and are specially concerned to incapsulate the death and resurrection of Jesus within this past, this is surely because they want to draw attention to the *kairos* which began with Jesus, is determined by him and predestinates every subsequent situation and decision. They want, if I may so express it, to show that the *extra nos* of salvation is 'given' to faith. To cleave firmly to history is one way of giving expression to the *extra nos* of salvation. Yet Luke proves how dangerous this method is, by making the *kairos* into a mere epoch, predestination into the initial impulse of a development and the givenness of salvation to our faith into the accessibility of verifiable facts to our knowledge; and by making grace (which is our destiny, compelling every one of us to make the decision between faith and unbelief) into the validation of the Church as the organization of the *religio christiana*.

If these observations are in any way accurate, we conclude from them once again that it was in fact eschatological interests which led irresistibly to the setting out of the earthly history of Jesus in the Gospels. We conclude further that primitive Christianity was in any event not primarily interested in the *bruta facta* of the past as such, but was engaged in eliciting from the past the essence both of its faith and of its own history. And thirdly, it emerges that, as a result of this exercise, those concerned did not arrive at any monochrome outlook, but only at various partly inter-locking, partly contradictory answers. They were agreed only in one judgment: namely, that the life history of Jesus was con-stitutive for faith, because the earthly and the exalted Lord are identical. The Easter faith was the foundation of the Christian kerygma but was not the first or only source of its content. Rather, it was the Easter faith which took cognizance of the fact that God acted before we became believers, and which testified to this fact by incapsulating the earthly history of Jesus in its proclamation. How far are we obliged, or even able, to appropriate to ourselves the decision which was then taken? The immediate answer to this question is that we also cannot do away with the identity between the exalted and the earthly Lord without falling into docetism and depriving ourselves of the possibility of drawing a line between the Easter faith of the community and myth. Conversely, neither our sources nor the insights we have gained from what has gone before permit us to substitute the historical Jesus for the exalted Lord. Thus we are faced afresh with the problem which our Gospels grasped and solved in their own fashion. And the fact that they did not arrive at a unanimous viewpoint makes this a radical problem for us and shows that the clash over the historical Jesus has as its object a genuine theological problem.

5. THE EMBARRASSMENT OF HISTORICAL CRITICISM IN THE FACE OF OUR PROBLEM

It will be useful to reflect for a brief moment on the extent to which this problem has become a radical one for us. For our Gospels believed, in all good faith, that they possessed a tradition about the earthly Lord, which was reliable over wide stretches of its content. Historical criticism has shattered this good faith as far as we ourselves are concerned. We can no longer assume the general reliability of the Synoptic tradition about Jesus. Worse still, we cannot improve the situation merely by making corrections in the tradition in the light of historical criticism. With the work of the Form-Critics as a basis, our questioning has sharpened and widened until the obligation now laid upon us is to investigate and make credible not the possible unauthenticity of the individual unit of material but, on the contrary, its genuineness. The issue today is not whether criticism is right, but where it is to stop. If we usually prefer to discuss the former question, then this means that we are really closing our eyes to the fact that the Gospels offer us primarily the primitive Christian kerygma, and individual words and deeds of Jesus only as they are embedded in it; and also to the fact that this kind of criticism can only help us to arrive at corrections and modifications in the kerygma but never at a word or action of the earthly Jesus-himself. The inevitable consequence is a bewildering confusion of allegedly trustworthy portraits of Jesus: now he appears as a rabbi, now as a teacher of wisdom, now as a prophet; or again, as the man who thought of himself as the Son of Man or the Suffering Servant, who stood for an apocalyptic or a realized eschatology: or finally, as some sort of a mixture of all these. As far as the narratives of the miracles, of the Passion and of the Resurrection are concerned, every conceivable possibility is open to us, from complete scepticism through a cautious, milk-and-water kind of criticism to the greatest possible confidence. In practice, all these are defensible, once you are prepared to give credence to the tradition, because they are all actually contained in the tradition. Only, it is very difficult to arrive by this method at anything better than a judgment which may satisfy you personally but will still leave chaos all around. Only radical criticism can therefore do justice to the situation with which we are faced whether we like it or not, to the questions of principle which it raises and to the tasks which it sets us. By 'radical' in this context I naturally do not mean an uncontrolled passion for any and every extreme position, but a single-minded openness to the problems posed by the facts.

But even this kind of criticism finds itself in very great methodological difficulties because, apart from the parables, we possess absolutely no kind of formal criteria by which we can identify the authentic Jesus material. We do have such criteria for Palestinian and Hellenistic tradition, for the saying from Wisdom literature, for the prophetic utterance, for rabbinic doctrine, for prescriptions concerning the life of a community, for apocalyptic predictions and for anything else we like to name. Indeed, it is Form Criticism which has rendered us the best service here. But even Form Criticism leaves us in the lurch when we come to ask what are the formal characteristics of the authentic Jesus material. It cannot be otherwise, for Form Criticism is concerned with the *Sitz-im-Leben* of narrative forms and not with what we may call historical individuality. The only help it can give us here is that it can eliminate as unauthentic anything which must be ruled out of court because of its *Sitz-im-Leben*.

The case is not markedly different if we take as criteria the primitive Christian chronology or the actual content of what is set forth. True, we can reach some more or less satisfying position concerning the supplanting of the post-Easter enthusiasm by a Christian rabbinate and so on through the subsequent development up to and including early Catholicism, however obscure some of the details may remain. But it is just the earliest phase of all, upon the comparison of which with the Jesus tradition everything might well depend, which remains absolutely opaque to us, particularly as regards its soteriology and ecclesiology. From this there springs a never-ending conflict over such questions as whether or not Jesus founded a Church and instituted sacraments. The situation is made even more difficult by the fact that we cannot draw an exact line between Palestinian and Hellenistic Jewish Christianity, nor, conversely, can we simply identify the two. Correspondingly, we may adopt a highly sceptical attitude to Lohmeyer's attempted differentiation of Jerusalem and Galilee without, however, regarding the question it raises as being already settled. For the polity of the community will in fact have had a different look in the capital and in the province.

This state of affairs brings us up against a multitude of enigmas. How long had the rivalry between Hellenists and Palestinians (Acts 6) been going on? What part did Peter really play? How did he come to be supplanted by James? What is the significance of these things for the course of primitive Christian missionary history? As long as these problems are not even half solved, there is little prospect of arriving at a greater understanding of the principle on which the earliest sections of the Synoptic material were divided up and arranged; as might be illustrated from an analysis of Matt. 23, from the tradition about Peter, from the saying about the ransom, from the prayer at the end of Matt. 11, to say nothing of the Passion and Easter narrative. But I cannot go into too much detail, as we should then never finish. We can only sketch in a few bold strokes the embarrassment of critical research. It lies in this: while the historical credibility of the Synoptic tradition has become doubtful all along the line, yet at the same time we are still short of one essential requisite for the identification of the authentic Jesus material, namely, a conspectus of the very earliest stage of primitive Christian history; and also there is an almost complete lack of satisfactory and water-tight criteria for this material. In only one case do we have more or less safe ground under our feet; when there are no grounds either for deriving a tradition from Judaism or for ascribing it to primitive Christianity, and especially when Jewish Christianity has mitigated or modified the received tradition, as having found it too bold for its taste. We shall conclude by examining some material of this kind, although only in summary fashion. But in so doing we must realize beforehand that we shall not, from this angle of vision, gain any clear view of the connecting link between Jesus, his Palestinian environment and his later community. The frontiers here lie wide open to the most diverse hypotheses. However, it is even more important for us to gain some insight into what separated him from friends and foes alike.

6. THE DISTINCTIVE ELEMENT IN THE MISSION OF JESUS

In what follows I must renounce any attempt at completeness or at a detailed statement of my reasons for disagreeing with opinions that differ from my own. I shall content myself with setting out in the dogmatic form of a thesis what seems to me essential. All exegesis is agreed that the authenticity of the first, second and fourth antitheses in the Sermon on the Mount cannot be doubted. In fact, these words are among the most astonishing to be found anywhere in the Gospels. In their form, they elaborate the wording of the Torah as a rabbi interpreting the sense of the Scripture might have done. The determining factor however, is that the words ἐγὼ δὲ λέγω embody a claim to an authority which rivals and challenges that of Moses. But anyone who claims an authority rivalling and challenging Moses has *ipso facto* set himself above Moses; he has ceased to be a rabbi, for a rabbi's authority only comes to him as derived from Moses. Rabbis may oppose each other in debate by the use of the formula 'But *I* say'; but this is only a formal parallel, because, in the case we are discussing, it is not another rabbi but the Scriptures and Moses himself who constitute the other party. To this there are no Jewish parallels, nor indeed can there be. For the Jew who does what is done here has cut himself off from the community of Judaism—or else he brings the Messianic Torah and is therefore the Messiah. Even the

37

prophet does not stand alongside Moses but under him. The unheard-of implication of the saying testifies to its genuineness. It proves, secondly, that while Jesus may have made his appearance in the first place in the character of a rabbi or a prophet, nevertheless his claim far surpasses that of any rabbi or prophet; and thirdly, that he cannot be integrated into the background of the Jewish piety of his time. Certainly he was a Jew and made the assumptions of Jewish piety, but at the same time he shatters this framework with his claim. The only category which does justice to his claim (quite independently of whether he used it himself and required it of others) is that in which his disciples themselves placed him—namely, that of the Messiah.

This passage is not an isolated one so far as the Synoptists are concerned. The same dialectical relationship to the law, seeking the will of God and, in pursuit of it, shattering the letter of the law, is reflected in the attitude to the Sabbath commandment and the prescriptions for ceremonial purity. We can hardly say here that Jesus has left the law as such untouched and merely made its demands more radical. This is certainly Matthew's understanding of what happened. But the history of the Gospel is always at the same time a history of misunderstandings, as the Synoptists themselves frequently show us. And the majesty of Jesus is most plainly revealed when we see his first disciples already feeling that they must soften or correct his words, because otherwise they could not endure him. Most interesting in this connection is the pericope concerning the rubbing of the ears of corn in Mark 2.23ff. Only Mark has the sentence: 'The sabbath was made for man, not man for the sabbath'. All the Synoptists then go on to say that the Son of Man is Lord also of the sabbath. It is obvious that these two sayings clash, and equally obvious that it is only the first which really fits into the pattern of the exchanges, which have so far not been christologically orientated. Perhaps we ought to take note here that it is very questionable whether Jesus in his lifetime claimed for himself the title of 'Son of Man'. On this point Bultmann has made the admittedly very speculative suggestion that the predicate 'Son of Man' should be regarded as a mistaken translation from the Aramaic. He maintains that the original had 'child of man', that is, 'man', without qualification. He, too, considers that it is the former of the two sentences that has the correct bearing. We can clinch the argument by pointing out that the second saying—that about the freedom of the Son of Man—represents a distinct limitation and weakening of the first. But by now we have come very close to the hypothesis that the community embarked on this process of watering-down the saying because, while it might credit its Lord with the freedom he had assumed, it was not prepared to allow it to all men. Its members felt themselves more tightly bound by the law than he had been and, as the subsequent pericope about the healing on the sabbath shows, they exercised their freedom only in exceptional cases and not as a matter of principle; and certainly not in that spirit of unforced responsibility to God, which was Jesus' legacy to them. The greatness of his gift caused the community to take fright.

The same process may also be observed in the conflict over the law of purification. Again, Matthew obviously thought that Jesus was only attacking the rabbinate and Pharisaism with their heightening of the demands of the Torah. But the man who denies that impurity from external sources can penetrate into man's essential being is striking at the presuppositions and the plain verbal sense of the Torah and at the authority of Moses himself. Over and above that, he is striking at the presuppositions of the whole classical conception of cultus with its sacrificial and expiatory system. To put this in another way, he is removing the distinction (which is fundamental to the whole of ancient thought) between the *temenos*, the realm of the sacred, and the secular, and it is for this reason that he is able to consort with sinners. For Jesus, it is the heart of man which lets impurity loose upon the world. That the heart of man should become pure and free, this is the salvation of the world and the beginning of that sacrifice which is well-pleasing to God, the beginning of true worship, as the Pauline paraenesis in particular will expound. Finally, by this saying, Jesus destroys the basis of classical demonology which rests on the conception that man is threatened by the powers of the universe and thus at bottom fails to recognize the threat which is offered to the universe by man himself. It is true that throughout the Gospels there are reports of the healing of demoniacs by Jesus; and in the saying in Mark 3.27 (= Matt. 12.28), the authenticity of which can hardly be questioned, he claims for himself this kind of authority. It all depends in what sense he did this; whether as a magician, believing that the world is literally bedevilled (thus sub-scribing to a metaphysical dualism), or as one who knew the evil of the human heart and its demonic power and took possession of this heart for God. It is certain that Jesus did not put forward any metaphysical dualism—if he had done, how could he ever have been portrayed as a teacher of wisdom?—and was conscious of being sent, not to fight the devil but to minister to man. But the foregoing must suffice for the formulation of our first finding: Jesus felt himself in a position to override, with an unparalleled and sovereign freedom, the words of the Torah and the authority of Moses. This sovereign freedom not merely shakes the very foundations of Judaism and causes his death, but, further, it cuts the ground from under the feet of the ancient world-view with its antithesis of sacred and profane and its demonology.

In establishing this, it is impossible not to contract lively doubts about the widely current picture of the pious Jew, perhaps from the circle of the Anavim, studying the Scriptures day and night and finding described in them the pattern of his way as the Servant of God or the suffering Messiah. We have no reason to doubt that Jesus had the same familiarity with the Old Testament which we should assume in every pious Jew. But it is quite another question whether we should make this the decisive factor in his actions. There is much to be said on the other side. If this was so, then what was the cause of the highly credible break with his family and what drove him to be baptized by John (for this element in the tradition is undoubtedly reliable)? In any event, his relation-ship to the Torah and to Moses hardly seems to support this view. We have already established that Matthew and the tradition he inherited had their own reasons for depicting Jesus as a rabbi. But apart from the fact that it was not all that easy to become a rabbi and that, in any case, the rabbinate would have nothing to do with the Baptist's movement, there was never a rabbi who did not derive his authority from that of Moses. Also, most of the quotations from Scripture in the Gospels are undoubtedly out-crops of the theology of the community. Finally, it is striking that the Jesus of the Synoptists is noticeably different in at least two respects both from the image of the rabbi and from that of the model Jewish devotee. There is, first, the remarkable importance which the writers attach to representing him as a teacher of wisdom. It must be admitted from the outset that the authenticity of the material we have in mind here is particularly difficult to maintain, because in so much of it we are concerned with popular images and with proverbs. Nevertheless some of the sayings involved are so paradoxically formulated or juxtaposed that this very fact could be an argument for the genuineness. To name two examples: the logion Matt. 10.26f. and parallel, with its demand that what is heard in secret should be shouted from the house-tops, is traced back by Bultmann to a proverb which enjoins caution because secrets can so seldom be kept secret. If that is correct, the problem then arises as to why the warning has here been converted into a demand. Now if the sense of the saying were perhaps this, that in the Last Times caution must be thrown overboard, then that would square very well with the saying about not being anxious in Matt. 6.25ff. Here also the tradition of the Jewish belief in Providence is modified in a very odd fashion. Because we are now being called to thirst for the reign of God, we can, may, and must live without anxiety and be assured of God's loving care. They who, according to Matt. 10, exist as dying men in the aeon which is passing away, may and must be the ones who trust in God. To leave all is the obverse of receiving all. However this may be, the portrayal of the teacher of wisdom accords but ill with that of the rabbi, because the former lives by immediacy of contemplation, such as is familiar to us from the parables of Jesus, while the latter's existence is determined by meditation and by the bond which keeps him tied to Scripture.

We may concede that the full significance of this observation only becomes visible in the light of a second one. According to the saying in Matt. 12.28, which we have already cited, Jesus ascribes his conquest of the demons to the Spirit of God which fills him. We need not try to decide here whether this saying in its present form comes from Jesus himself. But what is certain is that he regarded himself as being inspired. This we can gather above all from the remarkable use of the word 'Amen' at the beginning of important logia, which has been so faithfully preserved by the Evangelists. 'Amen' is, of course, primarily a response. Even if we do not feel able to go as far as Schlatter, who, in the light of this, interpreted the words of Jesus as the repetition of what the divine Voice was saying to him, this prefix expresses an assurance which is much akin to the confirmation of an oath; and it signifies an extreme and immediate certainty, such as is conveyed by inspiration. Out of this certainty the antitheses of the Sermon on the Mount are pronounced, the Sabbath commandment and the law of purification are assailed; out of it, that dialectical relationship to the Scriptures originates, which is ready to pass by their literal meaning in order to seek in them the will of God; and out of it, the demand for intelligent love is set up and placed in opposition to the demand of the rabbinate for blind obedience. It is by this immediate assurance of knowing and proclaiming the will of God, which in him is combined with the direct and unsophisticated outlook of the teacher of wisdom and perhaps lies behind it, that Jesus is distinguished from the rabbis. It does not matter whether he used the actual words or not; he must have regarded himself as the instrument of that living Spirit of God, which Judaism expected to be the gift of the End.

It is thus very tempting to call him a prophet. But this will not do at all. No prophet could remove himself from the jurisdiction of Moses without thereby becoming a false prophet. Above all, no prophet could be credited with the eschatological significance which Jesus obviously ascribed to his own actions. A most enlightening passage in this connection seems to me to be the much puzzled over logion in Matt. 11.25f., according to which the kingdom of God suffers violence from the days of the Baptist until now and is hindered by men of violence. (This is, in my opinion, the only interpretation which makes sense.) Such a conception is strange enough. For in what sense can it be said that this happens to the kingdom of God? Luke had already asked himself this question and, being unable to answer it, had altered the sense. With his eye on the mission to the world, he makes Jesus proclaim that each man will be brought into the kingdom by force. Neither is Matthew really able to make anything of the saying. This is why he puts the sentence 'The law and the prophets are in force until John' (which Luke has in its original position before our logion) as a connecting link with the excursus on the Baptist's role as Elijah *redivivus*. The history of the saying shows that we are dealing with very primitive tradition, already unintelligible by the time of the Evangelists. Yet the content suggests quite unambiguously that the logion is authentic. For in it the Old Testament epoch of salvation history concludes with the Baptist, who himself already belongs to the new epoch and is not to be counted among the prophets. The situation in this epoch is that the kingdom of God has already dawned, but is still being obstructed. The Baptist has introduced it, and thus ushered in the turning-point of the aeons. Yet even he still stands in the shadow of him who now speaks and utters his 'until today'. Who but Jesus himself can look back in this way over the completed Old Testament epoch of salvation, not degrading the Baptist to the position of a mere forerunner as the whole Christian community and the whole New Testament were to do, but drawing him to his side and—an enormity to later Christian ears—presenting him as the initiator of the new aeon? But who then is this, who thus does justice to the Baptist and yet claims for himself a mission higher than that entrusted to John? Evidently, he who brings with his Gospel the kingdom itself; a kingdom which can yet be obstructed and snatched away, for the very reason that it appears in the defenceless form of the Gospel.

It was the belief of Jesus that, in his word, the *basileia* was coming to his hearers. Does this mean that he understood himself to be the Messiah? The only way of dealing briefly with this question is simply to express at this point one's own personal opinion. I personally am convinced that there can be no possible grounds for answering this question in the affirmative. I consider all passages in which any kind of Messianic prediction occurs to be kerygma shaped by the community. I do not feel able to admit as genuine even the saying in Mark 8.38, that the Son of Man will in the future be ashamed of the man who here and now is ashamed of him and his words. For this saying has preserved the peculiar character of the speech of the Palestinian Christian prophets, which utters maxims of holy law for the guidance of the community and attaches heavenly promise or divine curse in the eschatological future to the fulfilment or non-fulfilment here on earth of certain conditions. This means, then, that Jesus was not reckoning on the coming of a Son of Man other than himself, as Bultmann assumes. Indeed what would be the position of such a figure if the Baptist has already ushered in the turn of the aeons and yet, for his part, still stands in the shadow of Jesus? The predication 'Son of Man' must have reflected the Christology and the apocalyptic of post-Easter Christianity and from there must have found its way into the Jesus tradition which today includes so many pronouncements of Christian prophecy, originally uttered as the voice of the exalted Lord. But if this really was the case and Jesus never expressly laid claim to the Messiahship, it would be extraordinarily characteristic of him. He would have differentiated himself equally from late Jewish expectation and from the proclamation of his own community. He would not have produced a picture of the future but done what needed doing in the present; he would have placed not his person but his work in the forefront of his preaching. But his community would have shown that they understood the distinctive nature of his mission precisely by responding to his proclamation with their own acknowledgment of him as Messiah and Son of God.

Our investigation has led us to the conclusion that we must look for the distinctive element in the earthly Jesus in his preaching and interpret both his other activites and his destiny in the light of this preaching. Here we can do no more than touch lightly on the difficult problem of how far the preaching itself was determined by apocalyptic expectation. This problem is doubly difficult because it is unsafe to predicate authenticity of any passage where there is agreement with contemporary Judaism and/or the post-Easter community. However, we shall have to concede, against the exaggerations of Dodd and his advocacy of realized eschatology, that Jesus did speak of the kingdom of God as future; the only question is, in what sense? But this follows from the manner of the kingdom's manifestation: the *basileia* breaks through on earth in the word of Jesus, setting men in its presence and facing them with the decision between obedience and disobedience. Its power drives away the demons and any sacrifice is worth while in order to establish its dominion. Its badge is the love of those who can forgive because God forgives his enemies and who indeed must forgive if forgiveness is to be their own portion. Jesus did not preach realized eschatology, but, to use E. Haenchen's terminology, inaugurated eschatology. Confirmation of this is to be found above all in the parables, the clarity and self-containedness of which stand out sharply from the rabbinic parallels and reach a standard from which the compositions of the later community represent a declension. We can, however, only use them in support of our case if we are prepared to criticize in one respect the indispensable work of Jülicher on the subject, to which we are all so indebted; we must not isolate, as he does, the parables from the rest of Jesus' preaching in such a way as to make their interpretation depend on the *tertium comparationis* and nothing else. Otherwise we cannot really escape the moralization so frequently castigated in Jülicher; and ignorance of the situation to which they were directed will cause us very great embarrassment. But although we may be for the most part ignorant of the original circumstances in which the individual parables were spoken, we do know him who uttered them well enough to be aware of the eschatological orientation of his message and to realize that we may not abstract from it. For Jesus did not come to proclaim general religious or moral truths, but to tell of the *basileia* that had dawned and of how God was come near to man in grace and demand. He brought, and lived out, the liberty of the children of God, who only remain the Father's children and only remain free so long as they find in this Father their Lord.

7. CONCLUSION

What then is the general sense of this very superficial outline, the filling-in of which in any detailed or even approximately complete manner would far exceed the limits of a single lecture? Have I not arrived back on the road, the problematical nature of which I originally set myself to show? Have not some central points emerged, around which we might, if with the utmost caution and reserve, reconstruct something like a life of Jesus? I should reject such a view as being a misunderstanding. In writing a life of Jesus, we could not dispense with some account of his exterior and interior development. But we know nothing at all about the latter and next to nothing about the former, save only the way which led from Galilee to Jerusalem, from the preaching of the God who is near to us to the hatred of official Judaism and execution by the Romans. Only an uncontrolled imagination could have the self-confidence to weave out of these pitiful threads the fabric of a history in which cause and effect could be determined in detail.

But conversely, neither am I prepared to concede that, in the face of these facts, defeatism and scepticism must have the last word and lead us on to a complete disengagement of interest from the earthly Jesus. If this were to happen, we should either be failing to grasp the nature of the primitive Christian concern with the identity between the exalted and the humiliated Lord; or else we should be emptying that concern of any real content, as did the docetists. We should also be overlooking the fact that there are still pieces of the Synoptic tradition which the historian has to acknowledge as authentic if he wishes to remain an historian at all. My own concern is to show that, out of the obscurity of the life story of Jesus, certain characteristic traits in his preaching stand out in relatively sharp relief, and that primitive Christianity united its own message with these. The heart of our problem lies here: the exalted Lord has almost entirely swallowed up the image of the earthly Lord and yet the community maintains the identity of the exalted Lord with the earthly. The solution of this problem cannot, however, if our findings are right, be approached with any hope of success along the line of supposed historical *bruta facta* but only along the line of the connection and tension between the preaching of Jesus and that of his community. The question of the historical Jesus is, in its legitimate form, the question of the continuity of the Gospel within the discontinuity of the times and within the variation of the kerygma. We have to put this question to ourselves and to see within it the element of rightness in the liberal *Leben-Jesu-Forschung,* the presuppositions of whose questioning we no longer share. The preaching of the Church may be carried on anonymously; the important thing is not the person, but the message. But the Gospel itself cannot be anonymous, otherwise it leads to moralism and mysticism. The Gospel is tied to him, who, both before and after Easter, revealed himself to his own as the Lord, by setting them before the God who is near to them and thus translating them into the freedom and responsibility of faith. This he did once without any demonstrable credentials, even without claiming to be the Messiah, and yet he did it as having the authority of him whom the Fourth Gospel calls the only-begotten Son. He cannot be classified according to the categories either of psychology or of the comparative study of religion or, finally of general history. If he can be placed at all, it must be in terms of historical particularity. To this extent the problem of the historical Jesus is not our invention, but the riddle which he himself sets us.

The historian may establish the existence of this riddle, but he is unable to solve it. It is only solved by those who since the Cross and the Resurrection confess him as that which, in the days of his flesh, he never claimed to be and yet was—their Lord, and the bringer of the liberty of the children of God, which is the correlate of the kingdom of God. For to his particularity there corresponds the particularity of faith, for which the real history of Jesus is always happening afresh; it is now the history of the exalted Lord, but it does not cease to be the earthly history it once was, in which the call and the claim of the Gospel are encountered.

II

IS THE GOSPEL OBJECTIVE?[1]

In what follows I shall try to establish that the theologian may well take up, as something which is properly relevant to his own activity, the content of the cry of 'Non-objectifiability' which is raised against him by the natural scientists. We must, however, immediately define the limits of our task. The various theological disciplines will tackle the problem—a very complicated one in its own right—from various angles and will thus each be striving to reach a different point which it regards as the centre of gravity. Here we shall only be concerned to bring out, on the basis of historical considerations, what it is which compels the exegete in his work of interpreting his texts to have regard to the question of non-objectifiability. We shall elucidate by using three points as examples, in a way which is designed to be intelligible to the non-specialist.

I. MIRACLE

Over few subjects has there been such a bitter battle among the New Testament scholars of the last two centuries as over the miracle-stories of the Gospels. It was inevitable that in this sphere, as almost nowhere else, there should be a clash between super-naturalism and rationalism as manifestations respectively of traditional ecclesiastical orthodoxy and of the modern criticism of this orthodoxy and its tradition. We may say that today the battle is over, not perhaps as yet in the arena of church life, but certainly in the field of theological science. It has ended in the defeat of the concept of miracle which has been traditional in the Church; and this defeat has been brought about by attacks from two different quarters, between which there has been a constant

---

[1] Opening paper in the discussion between Natural Scientists and Theologians on 'Non-objectifiability' held in Göttingen on 7 February 1953. First published in *EvTh* 12, 1952–53, pp. 455–66, under the title 'Zum Thema der Nichtobjektivier-barkeit'.

and far from accidental interaction. First, miracle in general was offensive to the world view of the modern age and to the concept of nature and causality which was bound up with it. On the other side, historical research and the comparative study of religion led to the conclusion that the New Testament miracle stories (1) have been subject to a quite definite development, viz. that in the course of the tradition they have been multiplied and heightened, (2) have countless analogies (from which they cannot be isolated) in classical antiquity; (3) are narrated according to a fixed form, so that it is possible to speak with accuracy of a technique of the miracle story. Some examples may illustrate this.

The most characteristic example of (1) is perhaps the development which can be traced in the Easter narratives. About the year 55 Paul passes on in I Cor. 15.3–7 a tradition of catechetical instruction on the subject of the Resurrection events which he himself has received from the (Hellenistic?) Jewish Christian community and which therefore will go back at least as far as the early forties. In it the witnesses of the Resurrection are enumerated in a chronological order which is highly credible. But our Evangelists, for their part, have placed such remarkably little value on these important and historically almost irrefragable data that even the most important, such as the appearances before Peter, James and the five hundred, have not been thought worthy of any individual narration at all. This is all the more puzzling because the appearance to Peter was certainly fundamental to the awakening of the Easter faith, the one to James was at least of very great significance for the original community and that to the five hundred should perhaps be looked upon as the actual *terminus a quo* of the genesis of the Church. Even without the Pauline tradition of instruction to prove the point, we can assume that the accounts of these appearances could not simply have passed into oblivion. This means, however, that there can remain scarcely any other hypothesis for the historian than that more detailed narratives which were available were suppressed on dogmatic grounds, because they had ceased to correspond to the views of the second and third generations of Christians. We are following the same line of development when we not only observe a constant process of growth in the Easter narratives but also see that the older accounts of the Galilean appearance have been replaced in Luke and John by accounts of appearances in Jerusalem—the Resurrection has not happened out on the periphery of the world, but in the neighbourhood of the Jewish capital. Again, it is by a precisely similar process that the miracles of Jesus grow ever more impressive. In Mark, the little daughter of Jairus is still on her death-bed when her father seeks help; in Matthew, she is already dead. But according to John, who only narrates particularly striking miracles, Lazarus has already lain three days in the grave. The trend towards the crudely material, which in Luke portrays the Risen Lord as eating and drinking with his disciples, is unmistakable. The miracle is becoming more and more of a mere marvel.

(2) From the wealth of Jewish and Hellenistic parallels to the Gospel miracle-stories I have selected just two. There is a Jewish parallel to the Stilling of the Storm: 'It happened to a Gentile ship . . . and there was on board a Jewish child. Then there arose a great storm on the sea, which threatened to destroy them. . . . Then they said to that young Jew, "My son, stand up and call upon your God". The child immediately stood up and cried out . . . and the sea was quiet.' On the other hand, there is a wine miracle in the Dionysius-cult which corresponds to the miracle in the story of the wedding at Cana and which has in all probability been transferred to Jesus and so found its way into the Gospel narrative.

(3) The technique of the miracle-story, even before and outside the Christian sphere of influence, includes such motifs as, for example, the insistence on the long duration of the illness and the unsuccessful striving after healing, a transfusion of strength conveyed by physical contact, an action which demonstrates the success of the healing, and the precise marking of the end of the narrative—or the astonished cry of the witnesses which serves the same end. The adaptation of pagan motifs becomes particularly obvious when the woman with an issue of blood is healed through the mere grasping of the virtue-laden garment of Jesus, or healing power is ascribed in the setting of Acts to Peter's shadow or Paul's handkerchief.

From all that has so far been said, it follows that the great majority of the Gospel miracle-stories must be regarded as legends. The kind of incidents which in fact commend themselves as being historically credible are harmless episodes such as the healing of

Peter's mother-in-law from a fever, a pericope which was probably only handed down out of a biographical interest in Peter himself; the healing of so-called possessed persons; and those Easter events of I Cor. 15, the shape of which we can no longer discern, but which in any event did not satisfy the next Christian generation, perhaps because they were portrayed too much as 'visions'. All these happenings can easily be explained away and emptied of their significance in rationalistic fashion. Our view of the world need not be in the least degree disturbed by them and we can no longer employ them as objective proofs for the intervention of God in history. Indeed, even primitive Christianity was not always completely blind to this. Certainly there is no question but that in general it regarded the miracles recounted among its adherents as objective proofs of what it believed. But, just as unquestionably, we can see Paul and the Fourth Evangelist already criticizing this mode of thought. They were bound to do so because they saw that every miracle is ambivalent; it may equally well have been worked by God or the demons. Indeed, the adversaries of Jesus did in fact ascribe his miracles to satanic influence and thus disqualified them as evidence, as the Evangelists credibly report. For this reason Paul sees the proof of the Spirit and of power not in miracle, but in ministering obedience; and in the eyes of John (2.23ff.; 6.14f., 26f.) faith based only upon miracles does not count as genuine faith. We may justifiably conclude that Mark and Matthew were also aware at least of the necessity of some correction to the popular perspective; for the former represents all the miracles of Jesus as signposts to his Resurrection glory, the latter as evidences of the divine compassion working in and through him. Thus these Evangelists do not leave the miracles as isolated happenings in the realm of the merely contingent but integrate them into a wider context which is the real source of their validity.

We have seen that there is plenty of scope for destructive criticism. At this point the question is bound to arise as to whether, in the light of this kind of examination, the Gospel miracle-stories have been completely emptied of meaning. We should certainly give an affirmative answer if we felt able to speak of miracle purely in the traditional and prevailing ecclesiastical sense of a supernatural breach of the laws of causality. If that were the case, everything would depend on the historical authenticity of the narratives. Something which did not really happen—some sort of legend, perhaps—cannot touch the laws of causality. But, as we shall see, this modern conception of miracle cannot simply be equated with that of the New Testament nor even with that of the Hellenistic period in general. It cannot be so equated because, at least in antiquity (with which we are here concerned), nature and supernature, immanence and transcendence, heaven and earth, do not stand over against each other in a stark mutual exclusiveness, but are seen as continually touching, mingling and once again diverging. Consequently, causality in that world cannot in any way be orientated along the same line with what we like to call the laws of nature; it is rather the contingent force of things, men, demons and gods radiating out, encountering other forms and overcoming them or being overcome by them. The power of divinity is then in principle only one element in the concert or chaos of the forces—the strongest, the prevailing; perhaps the abnormal, but never the anomalous. It may do what is impossible to men but not what is intrinsically impossible. It arouses astonishment, shock, horror, but does not annihilate the earthly reality into which it has irrupted. Once we have this clear, we can see that the concept of miracle current in the ancient world was not orientated primarily, as ours is, towards the suspension of causality but towards the occurrence of an epiphany. In a miracle there is an encounter with the divinity and its power, which, in its self-manifestation is reaching out to take hold of me. It is not merely that *something* extraordinary is happening but that I encounter *someone,* be it deity or demon. This double possibility, that it may be deity or demon, belongs to the very nature of the encounter. Only one who is involved in such an encounter, not the neutral observer, can understand its significance. It requires something like interpretation or faith; the sum of its meaning cannot be reckoned at a glance. Where miracle is really understood as an epiphany, a relationship is being posited and demanded—we might call it a communication. In such a situation, we are not merely receiving instruction about something which might be considered in an objective and detached way; but, because a power is reaching out for us, we are being summoned to make a decision which may express itself either as faith or as unfaith (hardness of heart).

When, as early as the New Testament itself, miracles came to be understood as objective evidence designed to convince the neutral observer, the essential nature of miracle as an epiphany had already begun to be abandoned; the content of miracle had been emptied out, leaving only a mere marvel behind. It is true that the very fact that such a misinterpretation became possible is itself not without importance. It became possible first, because an epiphany is always the irruption of the heavenly into the sphere of earth and secondly, because a characteristic of miracle as epiphany is the experienced force of an overpowering particular happening. If this experience of the particularity of a numinous power is isolated from the other experience of an encounter which challenges us to decision, we come to look upon miracle as a thing with a detached and objective value of its own and can therefore regard it as a proof addressed to our reason. Mark sees the miracles as an earnest of the Resurrection glory, Matthew as evidence of the divine compassion encountered in Jesus; for Paul, the real miracle is the new obedience of the Christian; thus all three distinguish miracle from mere marvel. Together with John, they understand miracle as the outward sign of the grace of God which at once empowers and challenges us, as a question which cannot be separated from our answers, as an encounter which we may indeed experience but the reality of which we cannot simply establish by objective proof and the total significance of which we certainly cannot analyse without remainder. It is precisely for this reason that, according to Matt. 11.5f., the series of miraculous acts performed by Jesus finds its culmination in the preaching of the Gospel—something which is incomprehensible from the standpoint of our own secularized conception of miracle, orientated as it is towards the 'laws of nature'. In the same passage occurs the blessing pronounced on those who 'are not offended at me', a saying which we find equally incomprehensible. Miracles in the New Testament are in their deepest essence signs accompanying the Gospel, a self-manifestation in the sphere of our corporeality of the God who addresses us; as such, they are intelligible only to the believer and do not remove the offence given to the unbeliever. In its own particular way, historical criticism underlines this fact. By dissolving the historicity of the majority of the Gospel miracle-stories and by demonstrating the questionable status of the remainder, it forces us to acknowledge that in turn we are faced primarily with the preaching of primitive Christianity—the message of which is that in Jesus the divine love has taken the field and showed itself to be a life-giving power. Thus we are now being asked to accept not the breach of a law of nature, but the particularity of God's revelation; and to allow our existence to be determined by that communication to us of divine love and heavenly life which is thereby posited. At the same time we are being told that this communication is concerned not only with our *ratio* or interior life but with our whole being in its corporeality and therefore, because our corporeality constitutes our connection with the world, it is concerned with us in our total relationship to the world.

2. THE CANON

The phenomenon of biblical criticism has been a characteristic of Protestantism. This seems strange, for it is Protestantism which proclaims the sole sovereignty of Scripture and yet explains its own existence by reference to the same datum. For it is never permissible to speak of this sole sovereignty as a formal principle, although we have been doing just this for a long time now. This statement needs clarification. Unquestionably biblical criticism has always existed. When Matthew or Luke deliberately alter, for dogmatic reasons, the text of Mark which they have before them (as they do on a hundred occasions), we detect there the presence of a very early form of biblical criticism. Very soon it is joined by a second, stemming less from dogmatics than from historical-philological scholarship; we can probably see a good example of this in the variants contained in the Codex D version of Acts. From time to time both forms naturally combine in such a manner that scientific scholarship is enlisted in the service of a particular dogmatic theology, as is so often the case with Rationalist criticism. But it is not sufficient merely to make such observations. We shall have to be at least prepared to consider the suggestion that criticism became of prime importance with the Reformation. At this point it ceases to be an insignificant appendix of theology and attains a dimension of depth, hitherto unknown. The phrase 'sole sovereignty of Scripture' is certainly used critically and polemically, and especially so in the debate with the prevailing ecclesiastical tradition. But that was only possible because Scripture itself was not now seen primarily as ecclesiastical tradition, although the canon with its wealth of different writings certainly *is* that. Positively stated, that was only possible because the Scripture was now understood primarily in the light of its central content and of the message of which it is the deposit—that is, in the light of the Gospel. The dialectical relationship of Scripture and Gospel is a characteristic mark of the Reformation. Over against Enthusiasm, which tries to make itself master of the Gospel by going beyond Scripture, great weight is laid on Scripture. At the same time, over against the ecclesiastical traditionalism of the Catholic Church, great weight is laid on the Gospel, not least as a critical court of appeal by the judgment of which even Scripture itself must abide. This dialectic, however, does not only set up a disturbing tension; equally, it sets a lasting task. We can only maintain this dialectic by employing it in ever new and always relevant ways; that is, with a real understanding both of the Scripture itself and of its message for the present in which we live. It is necessary for us to see the history of Protestantism at any rate as, from one angle, the struggle to fulfil this task. Thus, there is always the obvious danger that the dialectic arrived at by the Reformers will dissolve into one of its two determing factors and, in so doing, surrender to one of its two defeated adversaries. Without wishing to make a mere snap judgment, we must say that Protestant orthodoxy is always most exposed to the danger of making a simple identification between Scripture and Gospel, thus setting up the canon in the place of the Gospel and relapsing into a new traditionalism; while the Enlightenment, conversely and as a counterblast, completely mislaid Scripture in its quest for the Gospel and arrived only at a general religious truth (which Scripture was seen as confirming) and thus delivered itself over to Enthusiasm.

The prime means which the Enlightenment employed to this end was historical criticism. This discipline did not, of course, spring first from the Reformation itself, but from humanism. But it would be a gross misunderstanding of events to miss the point that it was the particular role of the Reformation to make possible the radical application of historical criticism to the Bible. And this it did, not exclusively but pre-eminently, by setting Scripture and

Gospel in a dialectical relationship to each other so that, for example, Luther, beginning from this point of departure, found himself rejecting the Epistle of James. Similarly, it was the allegedly misunderstood Gospel that the Enlightenment undertook to discover from Scripture and unwearyingly attempted to construct out of Scripture until the end of Liberalism during the First World War. It is that which gives to its biblical criticism its particular pathos and at the same time its unique radicalism.

And so it can be said, paradoxically enough, but with that relative justification which the historian alone can establish, that the Enlightenment is the legitimate heir of the Reformation—not *materialiter* certainly, but *formaliter* and over against orthodoxy. The Reformation also acted as a liberating influence on historical criticism because it insisted on concerning itself with the literal sense of the biblical text and was thus compelled to give all possible encouragement to philology; and, finally, because it released the world and secular occupations from the *ordo* of the sacred precinct and faced them with their own proper task, which entailed an appropriate methodology. All this may serve to establish why we neither can nor will give up historical criticism. In spite of all its aberrations, it has proved itself to be an appropriate method of procedure. In consequence, we also are bound by its findings and are confident that any errors will be uncovered and corrected from within.

These findings are compelling us and our contemporaries to recognize, among other things, that the canon, looked at in the totality of its writings, does not present a unity of content. Because it represents the result of a late ecclesiastical process of selection and its limits were for a long time fluid, it is the precipitate of a highly complicated development, beginning with apocalyptic Judaism, ending with early Catholicism and affected in its course by profound crises. I would cite as illustrations the liberation (effected by its own missionary activity) of Jewish Christianity from the limits of Palestine, the reaction against this liberation in the shape of a legalistic Jewish Christianity, the assimilation of the local churches and their doctrine to the Hellenistic mystery religions and gnosis and the reaction against this in Pauline theology or in the adaptation of popular philosophy in the Pastoral Epistles. All these stages of development have left their mark on the

canon and consequently make it possible to look on Christianity
now as fervent apocalyptic, now as a mystery-religion, now as a
kind of popular philosophy, now as a religion of the law, now as
early Catholicism—that is, unless we choose, with some degree of
justification, to regard it simply as a conglomeration of all these
various elements. All these possibilities have in fact been realized
in the course of Church history and have, inevitably, been reproduced in Protestantism up to the present day. If my observations
are correct, nothing can be based on the canon as such. Those who
seek to maintain the identification of the Gospel with the canon
are delivering Christendom over to syncretism or, on the other
wing, to the hopeless conflict between the Confessions. It is true
that we must be equally careful not to go to the other extreme, of
which Church history gives us no fewer examples. A Christianity
which lets its binding relation to Scripture go by the board falls
of necessity a prey to Enthusiasm, if it does not altogether cease to
exist. Even if we no longer stood in a living continuity with the
Reformation, we should still have to adopt its dialectical deter-
mination of the relationship of Scripture and Gospel.

In this connection we can only rightly repeat the Reformation
solution—the sovereignty of Scripture—because and in so far as
in the Scripture we encounter the Gospel. The authority of the
Bible is the derived authority of the Gospel. In itself the Bible has
no authority other than that of a venerable and informative
historical document. There is no objective reason which we can
give to the neutral observer or the neutral spectator why we shall
not give it up altogether and replace it by other organs of tradition.
That is a decision of faith and as such must appear quite arbitrary
to any outsider, if the argument from antiquity be left aside. And
even this argument is questionable, because in this case the old is
by no means the same thing as the original. The acknowledgment
of Scripture is a decision of faith to this further extent: here it is a
piece of chequered and even contradictory history which is being
made the basis of obligation, not a dogma or an idea, which might
well raise the very dubious claim to timelessness and unambiguity.
Once again we are brought up against the fact of a particular
contingent happening to which the Church relates itself. And
once again this may not be interpreted in the sense of the acknowledgment of some wonder. The Bible is neither the Word of God

in an objective sense nor a doctrinal system, but the deposit left by the history and the preaching of primitive Christianity. The Church, which canonized it, yet maintains that it is just in this capacity that the Bible is the bearer of the Gospel. It maintains this because—and only in so far as—it sees that the consistent and self-authenticating history which is contained in the Bible is there presented under the aspect of the justification of the sinner. But because the Church's utterance here is witness and confession, we are being called by it to set ourselves and our own personal history within this event of the justification of the sinner. Thereby we are not merely led to a decision as to whether or not we will actively embrace this event but equally as to whether this confession of faith does lay hold in the appropriate fashion on the central truth of Scripture. We are, in other words—indeed, in New Testament language—driven to test the spirits even within Scripture itself. We cannot simply accept a dogma or a system of doctrine but are placed in a situation *vis-à-vis* Scripture which is, at the same time and inseparably, both responsibility and freedom. Only to such an attitude can the Word of God reveal itself in Scripture; and that Word, as biblical criticism makes plain, has no existence in the realm of the objective—that is, outside our act of decision.

3. THE GOSPEL

The quest for the Gospel has been seen during the last two centuries as, in essence, the quest for the historical Jesus. It is a rewarding exercise to trace briefly the course and the result of this quest. We are indebted for its inception to the Enlightenment. Earlier Church history was not in a position to embark on it in any systematic fashion, because the Church's Christology was dominated by the doctrine of the two natures. If we have a vision of the God-man striding over the earth it is possible for us to comprehend his path within the compass of an historical sketch, as the Synoptists, and above all Luke, very early did. But this history could describe only the places and the times traversed by Jesus, not Jesus himself; for him as the God-man there could be no standard of comparison or measurement, however relevantly such a standard might be applied to his individual deeds. The concern of the Enlightenment was with the history of the person Jesus himself and was exercised in a manner so radical that I have already described it as peculiar to the quest for the Gospel. It is the Gospel which is at stake for the Enlightenment. It sought to free the historical Jesus from the veils of christological dogma and expected, by so doing, to come upon the Gospel in its primitive form. Albert Schweitzer has given us a breath-taking account of the history of this attempt, with its continual fresh starts and ever-changing methods. It is not necessary to go into details on the subject here. All we need for our purpose is the finding: the attempt was a failure. It was precisely that radical criticism which stood, and stands, incontestably in methodological continuity with the Enlightenment, which arrived at this result. It found that at the very beginning, not of primitive Christianity, but of its preaching, there stands, sharply formulated, the Church's dogma as the expression of its faith; and that there is no access to the historical Jesus other than by way of the community's faith in the Risen Lord. This I must clarify yet further.

The Synoptic Gospels as we have them today are the product of a tradition which was at least forty years in process of formation and the material of which is composed of very small units. At first it was individual sayings and isolated stories which were handed on; later, these were collected together probably for preaching purposes; this made it possible for the Evangelists, in a third and final stage, to set the appearance of Jesus on earth within a framework of space and time. It is thus quite impossible to extract from our Gospels anything resembling an historical sequence or even a biographical development and all efforts of this kind were, and remained, flights of fancy. Anything which could be used for such a purpose belongs to the later stage of tradition, and for the most part to the Evangelists' technique of composition. But of the individual sayings and stories it must be said that from their first appearance they were used in the service of the community's preaching and were indeed preserved for this very reason. It was not historical but kerygmatic interest which handed them on. From this standpoint it becomes comprehensible that this tradition, or at least the overwhelming mass of it, cannot be called authentic. Only a few words of the Sermon on the Mount and of the conflict with the Pharisees, a number of parables and some scattered material of various kinds go back with any real degree of probability to the Jesus of history himself. Of his deeds, we know only that he had the reputation of being a miracle-worker, that he himself referred to his power of exorcism and that he was finally crucified under Pilate. The preaching about him has almost entirely supplanted his own preaching, as can be seen most clearly of all in the completely unhistorical Gospel of John.

The question will naturally arise: how could such a state of affairs come about? Now, I have already shown that further Easter stories came to be attached to the announcements of the Resurrection enumerated in I Cor. 15 and that ever more miracles came to be ascribed to him of whom it was told that he healed Peter's mother-in-law and many who were possessed with devils. Among the sayings we must distinguish various elements. First, there is secular material, previously circulating in the manner of proverbs, but now transferred to Jesus. Then the community, appealing in its internal disagreement to the Master or seeking to make his individuality more vivid, created in the so-called conflict discourses or apophthegms ideal scenes for his words and deeds. Finally—and most important of all—we have to remember the part played by the prophets in early Christianity. As we can see clearly in the Revelation of John, they clothed their own epigrammatic words in the form of 'I' sayings of Jesus, speaking as Spirit-filled men with the authority and in the name of the exalted Christ. When these words were handed on, the distinction between the exalted and the earthly Lord very quickly disappeared, more especially as primitive Christianity was not particularly interested in the latter. Thus it came about that countless 'I' sayings of the Christ who revealed himself through the mouth of prophets gained entry into the Synoptic tradition as sayings of Jesus.

These three basic axioms are alone vital to our understanding at this stage. (1) The framework in which the individual units of the Gospel tradition are set may guarantee us a connected narrative and build up, together with the logical order, a chronological order extending over much of the material and manifesting an historical interest detectable in few other pieces of tradition; but even then, it is not this historical interest but concern with the task of proclamation which has been responsible for passing on the relatively few genuine words of Jesus and combining them with the kerygmatic resources of the community—that is, for bringing our Gospels into existence. (2) The very reason why the historical facts of the life of Jesus as good as perished from the primitive Christian message was the community's awareness that its mission was one of proclamation. (3) Apart from a few fragments of the preaching and activity of Jesus which are only accessible to us through the proclamation of the community, and even then have to be separated out under very great difficulties, the Gospels are, both in form and content, documents of primitive Christian preaching; documents, therefore, of faith in the Risen Lord and therefore also of Church dogma. Here and there some material may in practice go back to an earlier stage, but in principle our Christian history begins with the Easter faith of the disciples. What lies behind that is only accessible now by theoretical reconstruction—and this applies above all to the Jesus of history himself.

Because these are the facts, it has been possible for two hundred years to paint his portrait in ever new colours and contours; because these are the facts, there is in our own time on this point nothing but a chaos of contradictory opinions and reconstructions and there will probably never be any stronger consensus on the problem. Certain definite cardinal emphases of the preaching of Jesus are generally acknowledged. But because there is disagreement as to whether other not unimportant emphases can be integrated into these or not, there is inevitably also a failure so to arrange the balance of these cardinal pieces as to make even a tolerably unambiguous and convincing theological whole, let alone to draw a picture of Jesus or to portray his biographical development. The representations of the New Testament scholars are dependent on their premises and the logic of their methodology. The Gospel which the Enlightenment attempted to grasp by laying hands on the Jesus of history has shown itself to be a *Fata Morgana*. We cannot base our faith on him whom we are accustomed to call the Jesus of history. That does not mean that we could, even if we wished, abstain from the attempt to gain greater clarity and wider consensus. Neither as historians nor as theologians could we take this course. There are no grounds for lapsing into a defeatist scepticism; there are at least some things about which we can have the maximum possible certainty and which free us from the necessity of judging the faith of the community to be arbitrary and meaningless. But this kind of knowledge merely entitles us to prevent the Christian message from dissolving into myth. It cannot be a substitute for the Gospel, inasmuch as these remnants of the history of Jesus are not able to give us the assurance that the fragments of his message still concern us today and do in fact bear witness to God's present action in our regard. It is only the faith which is gained through Christian preaching which is able to derive the certainty of the God who acts even from those fragments which must otherwise have remained a piece—and a highly problematic piece—of the history of ideas.

All this means that the Enlightenment can no more find the real Gospel along its chosen road than can orthodoxy, which mistakes the tradition of the Church for the Gospel. Both are bound to fail. For whether the Word of God is identified with the canon or, in a supreme effort at simplification, sought only in the Jesus of history, in both cases the thought is present that it is possible to present the Gospel objectively; and in both cases the attempt is made to guarantee faith by reference to an objectively measurable quantity. But neither miracle nor the canon nor the Jesus of history is able to give security to our faith. For our faith there can be no objectivity in this sense. That is the finding which New Testament scholarship has made plain in its own fashion. But this finding is only the obverse of that acknowledgment which Luther's exposition of the third article of belief expresses (in agreement with the real heart of the New Testament message); it is only through the Holy Spirit that we are enabled to come to Christ and believe in him as Lord. And that in turn means to hear and to decide to obey the Word as preached, as only the individual can hear and decide, and as he must always be hearing and deciding afresh.

III

MINISTRY AND COMMUNITY IN THE NEW TESTAMENT

As soon as we begin to investigate our subject,[1] we encounter a contradiction. We make the remarkable discovery that the New Testament has no technical definition of what we are accustomed to call ecclesiastical office, although it speaks without inhibition of the office and the functions of the secular power and of the Old Testament priesthood, and indeed refers by name to a multiplicity of ecclesiastical offices and functions. From time to time the word 'Amt' ('ministry') appears in Luther's translation of the Bible: when it does, we find that the word in the original is usually διακονία. This is symptomatic. For the New Testament seems of set purpose to have avoided the technical conception of office which could have been expressed by such words as λειτουργία, τιμή and ἀρχή; the use of these would have implied the presupposition and recognition of an authoritarian relationship which has no place in the ordering of the Church and which indeed is the precise target of the polemic found in such passages as Matt. 20.25f.; 23.11; I Cor. 3.5 and I Peter 5.3 against claims to domination and to positions of power. Starting from here, it is possible to reach a proper appreciation of a fact which has almost always remained opaque to the exegetes, although it has to be counted among the most significant phenomena of the New Testament proclamation. While there is no real equivalent in the New Testament for our

[1] This paper, previously unpublished, which I gave for the first time on 13 October 1949, in Herborn before the old students of Marburg, makes no attempt at a full discussion, which would only have been possible within the framework of a monograph. It will be obvious from much that I say that I am in fundamental disagreement with the presupposition and the conclusions of H. Schlier as expressed in his essay 'Über das Hauptanliegen des 1. Briefes an die Korinther', *EvTh* 9, 1948(49, pp. 462ff. It will be equally obvious that my views have much in common with the presentation of the problem by E. Schweizer, *Das Leben des Herrn in der Gemeinde und ihren Diensten* (ATANT 8), 1946, and by F. Grau's Tübingen dissertation *Der neutestamentliche Begriff Charisma, seine Geschichte und seine Theologie*, 1946. But my own approach has been along the road of exegesis, before I became acquainted with the available literature on the subject.

present-day conception of 'office', there *is* a concept in Pauline
and sub-Pauline theology which describes in a theologically exact
and comprehensive way the essence and scope of every ecclesiastical ministry and function—namely, the concept charisma. The
importance of this concept for the understanding, not merely of
the Pauline doctrine of the Church, but of the Apostle's whole
theology can be seen from the fact (which we can establish with
the maximum degree of historical certainty) that it was Paul who
was the first to use it in this technical sense and who indeed introduced it into the vocabulary of theology.[1] This in itself would lead
us to expect that the use of this concept heralds the emergence of
a critical posture over against other early Christian views about
the relation between the ministerial office and the community, a
posture which could only express itself by means of a new terminology. If this is really the case, we shall be concerned not merely
with an historical situation but with a theological question when
we take up the Pauline concept of charisma and attempt from this
point of departure to arrive at the necessity of the Pauline intervention.

'The charisma of God is eternal life in Christ Jesus our Lord',
says Rom. 6.23. Other charismata only exist because of the existence of this one charisma to which they are all related, and they
only exist where the gift of eternal life is manifested in the eschatologically inaugurated dominion of Christ. 'God's gift of grace' is
thus a misleading translation of the Greek word, because it does

---

[1] According to W. Bauer, *Greek-English Lexicon of the New Testament*, ET by Arndt
and Gingrich, 1957, the concept occurs, though very infrequently, in secular circles
where there has been no Christian influence; this suggests that it did in fact exist in
pre-Christian times. But its pre-Christian usage has not been proven with certainty.
The best quotation for our purpose, Philo, *De leg. alleg.* III 78, certainly has the word
twice, but has a question-mark against it (L. Cohn, *Neue Jahrbücher für klassische
Altertumswissenschaften,* 1898, p. 539, 1: J. Heinemann, *Schriften der judisch-hellenistischen
Literatur in deutscher Übersetzung* vol. III: Die Werke Philos von Alexandria, 3 Teil,
1919, p. 110, 3).
The second example is not well attested (as is also the case with Eccl. 7.33 and
38.30) and this creates a prejudice against the first, especially as the concept is consistently expressed in the following sentences by *charis*; this perhaps shows what the
original meaning was. In any case, apart from the Pauline tradition, the word
signifies 'gift' or 'token of favour' in a non-technical sense. F. Grau has rightly
reminded us (p. 19) of the lack of Hebraic equivalents. Even the Apostolic Fathers
use the concept infrequently and, apart from *Did.* 1.5, probably only under Pauline
influence. If we take all this into account, we can hardly avoid coming to the conclusion that it was the Apostle who first gave a technical meaning to the word, which
had probably been coined before his time but certainly very little used. It ought to be
emphasized that we are not in a position to make the same judgment about any other
Pauline concept.

not indicate that the gift is inseparable from the gracious power which bestows it, and that it is indeed the manifestation and concretion of this power, so that eternal life is not one gift among many but *the* sole and unique gift of the End. There are variations of expression in Rom. 5.15 (χάρις, δωρεά, δώρημα) but the thing signified is still the life which has appeared with the coming of Christ and has laid hold on men. The same is true of I Cor. 12.6, 11 where the various charismata are described as ἐνεργήματα from which the φανέρωσις τοῦ πνεύματος of v. 7 follows. The Spirit is our present participation in eternal life, but we can possess him and participate in his gift only as he possesses us. Eternal life does not encourage sleeping partners or uninvested capital. We can only have *charis* (which in Paul is normally to be understood as power) to the extent to which it seizes hold of us and to which the lordship of Christ acting through it brings us into the captivity of his service. Thus in I Cor. 12.4ff., διακονίαι are interchangeable with the charismata and finally, in Rom. 11.29 as in I Cor. 7.7, 17ff., charismata and κλῆσις τοῦ θεοῦ are connected or interchangeable. All this adds up to the same thing: the manifestation of grace, of the Spirit, of eternal life, of the divine calling—this all happens eschatologically in Christ. Christ is the embodiment of life, of grace, of the Spirit and, embodying these, is our Lord. For Paul, to have a charisma means to participate for that very reason in life, in grace, in the Spirit, because a charisma is the specific part which the individual has in the lordship and glory of Christ; and this specific part which the individual has in the Lord shows itself in a specific service and a specific vocation. For there is no divine gift which does not bring with it a task, there is no grace which does not move to action. Service is not merely the consequence but the outward form and the realization of grace. Eternal life quickens, and announces its presence within earthly reality by begetting new obedience. First of all, the lordship of Christ brings me into subjection and then, through my act of submission, there shines the glory of him whose purpose is to bring all the world into subjection and who in me has taken possession of one single fragment of this world which is his by right.

We do well to recall immediately that both Judaism and Hellenism are familiar, if not with the technical designation charisma, at least with the content of the concept, although each places its own peculiar inflection upon it. Paul himself is well aware of this. Otherwise he could not speak in I Cor. 12.1, and 14.1—and probably also in 2.13—of charismas as πνευματικά, thereby taking up and using a technical term of Hellenism. The rarity of this usage is admittedly significant and corresponds to a second fact, namely that Paul only employs it when dealing with the enthusiasts at Corinth. Here he is adopting their own terminology, which comprehends under πνευματικά all the powers of miracle and ecstasy—i.e. all the potentialities of the θεῖος ἄνθρωπος—which they so passionately seek after, of which they are so inordinately proud and the true meaning of which for the community must therefore be properly evaluated in I Cor. 12–14. We must not, however, fail to observe that Paul usually displaces, or rather forcibly removes, the term πνευματικά and substitutes for it the idea of charisma; because he takes such pains to do this, it is clearly meant to be the starting-point of a theological critique. This critique becomes explicit in I Cor. 12.2. Even idols display power by which their slaves are driven and the influence of which sends them into transports. But the idols are dumb. They can produce a state of possession, but they lack the Word which tells how God has loved the world and how he justifies the ungodly. Therefore these idols cannot call forth the response 'Jesus is Lord' which is uttered by the slave of the Christ when the Spirit lays hold of him. They do not lay the foundation for personal and specific responsibility in which the power of grace becomes visible. Rather, there is manifested in the heathen counterparts of the charismata a demonic spirit which causes them to remain unfruitful and does not issue in service. In them the numinous and the praeternatural irrupt into the world as mere marvels and produce chaos in which there is a babel of conflicting voices. Paul does not deny the possibilities of miracle and ecstasy. By his use of the term πνευματικά in I Cor. 12ff. he indicates that he sets a certain value on these potentialities. But as these chapters show, he does it by putting them to work in the service of the Christ and of his community; in other words, he places them in the category of charisma. For this is what distinguishes charismata from heathen πνευματικά: they are validated not by the *fascinosum* of the praeternatural but by the edification of the community. Matt. 24.24, Mark 13.22 and II Thess. 2.9 tell us that Antichrist also can produce signs, wonders and powers. Even existing charismata can be misused, as in Corinth. According to II Cor. 11.13 there can even be false apostles. The spirits must be tested. This last is a terrifying pronouncement and exegetes try over and over again to evade it in their treatment of I Cor. 14. How is it possible to confine and test in an appropriate way the Spirit which carries us away? But this chapter shows that this is exactly what Paul has done in the context of ecclesiastical order and ecclesiastical authority. For him the test of a genuine charisma lies not in the fact that something supernatural occurs but in the use which is made of it. No spiritual endowment has value, rights or privileges on its own account. It is validated only by the service it renders. More significantly still, in this passage the Apostle, in the face of the views of the Enthusiasts, falls back on proverbs from popular philosophy and even, as it seems at first sight, makes utility the criterion of heavenly energies and revelations in a very prosaic fashion; although he equates 'useful' with that which edifies the community! This is Paul's way of putting an end to the confusion between Church and Mystery-cult and of bringing the Enthusiasts back down to earth out of their fantasy-heaven. Again, for Paul *Pneuma* is the power of the Transcendent and therefore the community which received this *Pneuma* is, according to I Cor. 2.9ff., the place of the presence of the heavenly reality in our world, of which it can be said: 'The things which no eye has seen, nor any ear heard, the things which have entered no man's heart, all these has God prepared for them that love him!' For this reason the Apostle does not scruple to set forth the powers of miracle and ecstasy, even including speaking with tongues, as being characteristic marks of this community. He can hardly go further in his approach to his opponents at Corinth and to the world of Hellenistic mystery religion which lies beyond them. But this is precisely the point at which he diverges most sharply from his environment, and, to those who see their Christianity in terms of this environment, his theology must appear a radically critical theology. Its critical power lies in the Gospel itself which shatters the autonomy and the self-justification of the pious, even of the spiritually gifted. Heaven comes to earth when grace creates obedience and the acceptance of responsibility towards God and is understood as purely the foundation of service.

Thus in Rom. 1.11 the *mutua fratrum consolatio* is seen as the effect of the various charismata, and in I Cor. 12.25ff. the solidarity of the charismata and of those who have been endowed with them is a manifestation of the unity of the body of Christ, this unity being nothing else but the lordship of the Christ in and over all his members. In our contemporary situation, which is not yet completely free from the influence of Idealism, it is necessary to emphasize what weight is put in this connexion on the element of corporeality. *Pneuma* is for Paul the very antithesis of spirituality and inwardness—it is the power of the Resurrection because it is the power of the Risen One. Therefore the truly spiritual service of God consists self-evidently, according to Rom. 12.1ff., in the offering of our bodies; and the baptismal instruction in Rom. 6.12ff. teaches that this bodily obedience is the sign that our existence as Christians springs from the resurrection of Christ and moves towards our own resurrection. The concept 'Body of Christ' may not therefore be interpreted as an edifying metaphor or as a daring idea. It is for the Apostle in its very corporeality the reality of the community inasmuch as the community itself, as the place of the Risen Lord's dominion, represents the new world. A mere communion of souls would not bear visible witness to the fact that Christ is the Cosmocrator. But where this fact is not made visible—and Paul knows nothing of the later conception of the *ecclesia invisibilis*—the Spirit of Christ is not at work, for this Spirit invariably claims us for the Lord as we are in our corporeality, makes us ready and willing for service in our body and thus draws us in to the Body of Christ as its members. In our bodies the Cosmocrator is taking possession of that world which hitherto has not acknowledged his lordship, and the Body of Christ is the real concretion before the Parousia of the universal sovereignty of Christ. Thus in Eph. 4.7ff. the various charismata can be designated as the gifts of the victorious Christ, who has passed through heaven and hell that he might fill all things with his fullness. This he accomplishes after his Ascension by means of these very charismata which he pours out and which leave no sphere of existence without his power and his claim and in which he himself declares his omnipotence and his ubiquity.

But such statements, for which 'bold' would be a mild word, need further explication and support if they are not to appear merely fantastic. We must remember that in I Cor. 1.5ff., Eph. 1.3f. and I Peter 4.10 the fullness of enrichment and blessing is said to be a characteristic of God's revelation; in Eph. 2.7 it is the superabundant riches of his grace, which make the community the place of περισσεία and πληροφορία; cf. also I Cor. 14.12; II Cor. 8.7 and 9.8; Eph. 1.8; Col. 2.2 and 4.12; I Thess. 1.5. Here we cannot particularize the different charismata. But we can try, even if rather unsatisfactorily, to indicate the multiplicity of the gifts named and to classify them in summary fashion. Among the charismata belonging to the ministry of kerygma, we might include those of inspiration and ecstasy, besides the functions of the apostles, prophets, evangelists, teachers and admonishers. To those of the ministry of *diakonia*, comprising deacons and deaconesses, those who give alms and tend the sick in Rom. 12.8 and the widows of I Tim. 5.9ff., we might add the gifts of miraculous healing and of exorcism. The cybernetic charismata extend from the 'first-fruits' mentioned in Rom. 16.5 and I Cor. 16.15 to 'those who are over you' in I Thess. 5.12, who may well correspond to the pastors of Eph. 4.11 and the 'bishops' of Phil. 1.1. II Cor. 4.7ff. and Col. 1.24 speak with special emphasis of charismatic suffering. But in general it is important to notice that it is not only the outstanding services in the community which count as charismatic. The noteworthy juxtaposition, among the functions we have just enumerated, of apostolate and inconspicuous act of charity, of miraculous powers and what we should today inelegantly describe as 'technical' service, suggests to us that the circle will be widened to include gifts other than those already mentioned. This becomes quite clear in I Cor. 7.17. It is true that the concept of charisma is not employed here. But the formula 'as the Lord has distributed to each man, as the Lord has called each man' must bear the same meaning. This is demonstrated beyond doubt by the characteristic 'he dealt out to us' used of the catalogue of gifts in Rom 12.3ff., by the use of charisma and κλῆσις as parallel terms and finally by the express use of the concept in I Cor. 7.7. Therefore whatever is mentioned in the same context—the condition of circumcised or uncircumcised, of slave or free man—must also be counted as a charisma. This conclusion becomes even more inescapable when marriage and virginity are introduced as charismata in v. 7. The objection that marriage was only included out of an exaggerated sense of rhetoric carries no real weight, although it may be literally true. Exactly the same rhetoric is to be found in the parallel antithesis; the same pattern occurs in Gal. 3.28 with the addition of 'male and female' and is further widened in Col. 3.11. In all these passages we are dealing unmistakably with a familiar theme of the Pauline tradition in which the differences and oppositions between various conditions of humanity are contrasted with the unity of the body of Christ which overlaps and combines them. This theme is developed on a broad front in I Cor. 12.13ff. where it occurs in the context of a renewed discussion of the problem of the various charismata. This rhetorical passage, which many exegetes find such a stumbling-block, is designed to express —as so often in Paul's writings—a paradoxical state of affairs. We may not write it off as pious hyperbole; it requires strict interpretation according to its context. According to I Cor. 12.4ff. the different διαιρέσεις, from which the multiplicity of charismata results, are constitutive of the body of Christ, of which v. 14 says: 'The body consists not of one member, but of many.' Conversely, this multiplicity does not cause the body to disintegrate but makes its true unity possible. For while like entities can only cancel each other out and render each other superfluous, unlike entities can perform mutual service and in this service of *agape* can become one. In so far as the Church understands itself as the dynamic unity of charismata and of those endowed with them, she cannot find her order in uniformity and rationalization. Neither must she give so much prominence to individuals among her members that others are overshadowed and condemned to passivity: otherwise she would be transgressing against her God-given order, against the revelation of grace and of the Spirit who sunders the new world from the old, against the omnipotence and the ubiquity of Christ. The unity of the body of Christ which, according to I Cor. 12.13, Gal. 3.28, Col. 3.11, comes into existence through baptism, the identity with himself of the Christ who reigns in and over all his members, this unity and identity is only potential and actual in the multiplicity of charismata; it cannot be objectified or manipulated, it exists only *in actu*—in the act of *agape*, of service. Within this unity are joined, with a necessity which confounds the world's logic, the extreme opposites exemplified by the antitheses we have just been considering.

We have now finished our détour and are back again at our starting-point, namely, that the rhetorical nature of these antitheses does not deprive them of their validity but makes us more attentive to their meaning. We must take their language seriously even when they speak of marriage, or of male and female existence, in terms of charisma. To sum up, Paul bases the prescriptions of the so-called 'household code' firmly on the idea of charisma and in so doing mirrors the scope and the riches of him who fills all in all, that is, who reveals himself as the Cosmocrator in and over the multiplicity of these charismata which penetrate so deeply into the secularity of the world. But still more remains to be said. The historical and theological phenomenon we have been describing cannot be clearly understood until all its implications have been grasped. Paul has based not only the household code but all his catechetical matter on the concept of charisma. For this reason, even his utterances in Rom. 14 on the right attitude to food and drink, to the eating of meat, to vegetarianism and to festivals, are anchored in the same concept. Such a statement may cause us some apprehension and make us ask where this line of thought is leading us. Do we not see the warning figure of R. Rothe looming up in front of us, even if we do not consider him absolutely justified in his forebodings? If what we have just maintained is true, are there any limits to the sphere of the charismatic?

I have already indicated these limits by saying that the criterion of a genuine charisma lies not in the mere fact of its existence but in the use to which it is put. For instance, the conditions of being male or female, of being sexually committed or virgin, of being involved in family life and social relationships, of adopting this or that religious attitude towards eating and drinking, of standing under or outside the Torah—none of these in themselves are charismatic. But they can become so; and indeed each of these modes of relation does become so when it is overshadowed by the μόνον ἐν κυρίῳ I Cor. 7.39; when within it, according to Rom. 14.4ff., each man stands or falls to the Lord, for the Lord's sake keeps or breaks prescribed customs, eats or fasts, lives or dies. Once again we must pay careful attention to the scope of these pronouncements which are here deliberately argued with the aid of mutually exclusive opposites. The intention is to embrace the total reality of our life, and this is clearly a polemic against an

Enthusiasm which contents itself with segments of this reality or with some illusionary inwardness; which tries to regiment the promises of God, which judges faith by arbitrarily chosen norms and criteria and which is out to dragoon Christian brotherhood into uniformity; and which ends up by being unable to discern the shape of the charismatic gift against the background of the various observable phenomena. But the true measure of this gift is the way in which, in and for the Lord, an existing set of circumstances is transformed; that is, it is the obedience of the Christian man. But again, because the ἐν κυρίῳ defines the limits of the charismatic sphere, it must also (Rom. 14.22f.) be the voice of the doubtful and accusing conscience. My previous condition of life becomes charisma only when I recognize that the Lord has given it to me and that I am to accept this gift as his calling and command to me. Now everything can become for me charisma. It would be not only foolish but a slight to the honour of Christ, who wills to fill all things, if I were to attempt to take the realms of the natural, the sexual, the private, the social out of his sphere of power. We are not speaking here of a 'transfiguration of the universe': we are simply saying that the Church can no longer be regarded as some sacred temple precinct. The field of the Church's operation must be the world in its totality, for nothing less can be the field of Christ the Cosmocrator. The secular is no longer abandoned to demons and demonic energies. Grace pushes home its attack to the very heart of the world; it liberates it from the demons. Grace alone can do this. This is why Rom. 14.14 can read: 'I am absolutely convinced, as a Christian, that nothing is impure in itself.' A thing can only be purely secular to a man who thinks of it in this way. As nothing is charisma in itself, so nothing is secular in itself. For, in the time of the Eschaton, this sphere of the 'in itself', this demilitarized zone, this 'indifference' exists no longer. The *regnum Christi* and the *regnum Satanae* stand face to face and are embodied on earth in obedient or disobedient men. All things, which we do not ourselves defile, are God's gift. All things stand within the charismatic possibility and are holy to the extent to which the holy ones of God make use of them.

We have still one more step to take. Up to this point we have been saying: 'The whole of life, including death, stands under the promise of the gift of charisma, in so far as it is Christians who are living this life and dying this death.' We must now add: 'As Christians themselves stand beneath the shadow of the ἐν κυρίῳ and are members of the body of Christ, are they all, in so far as they are true to their condition, endowed with charisma?' To put the question is to answer 'yes' to it. This conclusion is implicit in our definition of charisma as the concretion and individuation of grace or of the Spirit, because every Christian is a partaker of grace and of the Spirit; it is implicit also in our account of the body of Christ which we described as being composed purely of charismata and of those endowed with them. There is no passive membership in the body of Christ. Every Christian stands equipped and ready for service in the armour of Eph. 6.10ff. Finally, this conclusion provides an explanation of the strange transition in Rom. 12.9ff. from detailed instructions about functions exercised in the community to what is apparently a catalogue of private virtues. Such a transition would be hopelessly un-Pauline. But every Christian finds himself at all times face to face with Jesus Christ as Cosmocrator and Universal Judge and thus in the presence of that tribunal from which, according to I Cor. 4.9, the world and angels and men look down upon him. He is exposed thus to the public gaze of the Last Times, he is planted there to be in his own person the banner of the ultimate Victor, the earthly proxy of his Lord. This is true not only of apostles, prophets or even of those who speak with tongues, but of those who give hospitality to the saints, whose care it is to practise honesty towards all men, who do not pay back evil for evil, who rejoice with them that rejoice and weep with them that weep. Rom. 12–15 is speaking, as we have already seen of ch. 14, exclusively of charismata and those conditions which are the raw material of charismata. Therefore this whole section ends with a doxology for that Church which is able to praise God's mercy among the Gentiles. The revelation of the charismata is the prerogative of the Church composed of Jews and Gentiles—the true Israel, over against the Israel which has shown itself to be hardened; it is also the continuation of the statement in Eph. 3.6, that the Gentile Christians have been made fellow-heirs and partakers of the promise. Charisma is no longer the distinguishing mark of elect individuals but that which is the common endowment of all who call upon the name of the Lord, or, to use the phraseology of the primitive

Christian tradition as we have it in Acts 2.17ff., a demonstration of
the fact that the Spirit of God has been poured out on all flesh. It
is for this reason that the life of the community as a whole as well
as that of the individual Christian is embraced in the acclamation
of I Cor. 14.25, in which the heathen participant in Christian
worship acknowledges in fear and trembling the eschatological
presence of God and bears witness: 'ὄντως ὁ θεὸς ἐν ὑμῖν.' In the
light of this acclamation we can, in conclusion, cast our glance
back at the passage in Eph. 4.7ff. with which this section opened.
In it the apparently quite fantastic statements about the omnipotence and ubiquity of Christ in all things are confirmed by the
Apostle himself and, as it were, interpreted in advance. Because
and in so far as the body of Christ, the sphere of the eschatologically realized lordship of Christ on earth, is God's new world and
creation; because and in so far as Christ in and with his gift calls
each of his members to the *nova oboedientia*, quickens him and
moves him to service and suffering, clad in the spiritual armour of
Eph. 6.10ff.; because and in so far as, in his gifts and in the ministries which they express and indeed create, he himself is present,
proclaiming his title to the lordship of the world, consecrating
the secular, ridding the earth of demons; therefore and to this
extent can it be proclaimed in truth that he fills all things with the
power of his resurrection. The presupposition of this chain of
reasoning is the principle which we have already seen in his
doctrine of the Lord's Supper to be normative for Paul: that the
Giver is not to be separated from his gift but is really present in it.
Every ministry within the community, because and in so far as it
is grace received, held fast and used, points to him, who is the first
and proper apostle, prophet, bishop, deacon, teacher, pastor,
evangelist and miracle-worker; who loves, not returning evil for
evil, comforts, warns, judges, forgives and is truly humble. All
charismata are embodied in him and together compose his body;
conversely, his image is mirrored in each of his members (II Cor.
3.18), every Christian is conformed to the image of the Son (Rom.
9.29f.) and thus regains that glory of God's image which was lost
in the Fall (Rom. 3.23). As with Paul's doctrines of the Spirit and
of the Church, his doctrine of the charismata can only be understood in the light of its inseparable connexion with Christology.
The Apostle was certainly not the first to know and to speak of the

powers of the new age and of the manifold gifts of the Spirit. But because his predecessors had not followed to its conclusion the true theological relation of these powers and gifts to Christology, they had fallen into those attitudes and practices of Enthusiasm which were now rife in Corinth. The gift, isolated from the Giver, loses the character of a claim made by the Lord, leads to the self-appointed leadership of those who are fundamentally undisciplined themselves, and makes the community into an arena for competing religious 'gifts', a chaos which stands over against the peace of Christ as the effective presence of the old world.

It is impossible for reasons of space to develop any further this theme of the strong and indeed decisive penetration of every area of Pauline theology by the doctrine of charisma and of the clarity with which the Apostle's basic theological conception emerges from it. But we must at least note that the various statements of the charisma doctrine are only rendered theologically possible and necessary in the light of the central Pauline doctrine of justification by faith and that, conversely, they themselves demonstrate the immense scope of this central doctrine. Paul's teaching on the subject of the charismata constitutes the proof, first, that he made no basic distinction between justification and sanctification and did not understand justification in a merely declaratory sense; further, that he binds justification by faith tightly to baptism, so that it is not permissible to drive a wedge into his gospel, separating the juridical from the sacramental approach; and finally, that he considers faith to be actually constituted by the new obedience. The doctrine of charisma is for him the concrete expression of the doctrine of the new obedience, just because it is at the same time the doctrine of the *justificatio impii*. God gives life to the dead and, through the invasion of grace, sets up his kingdom where before demons and demonic energies held sway; thus, the various lists of charismatic gifts are enumerated as counterblasts to the catalogues of vices. God creates among the rebels that *pax Christi*, which is at once the subjection, the reconciliation and the new creation of the cosmos. Godless men become obedient and are endowed with charismatic gifts; this is the eschatological miracle, the decisive action of God in his divine majesty, the triumph of grace over the world of wrath. Paul's doctrine of the charismata is to be understood as the projection into ecclesiology of the doctrine of justification by faith and as such makes it unmistakably clear that a purely individualistic interpretation of justification cannot legitimately be constructed from the Apostle's own teaching.

The whole question of order within the Christian community is also treated from this standpoint. Once again I must be careful not to be led away into various ramifications and questions of detail; to avoid this, I shall limit myself to bringing out one or two fundamental facts. We ought to have been struck already by the frequency with which the watchword 'To each his own' occurs in connexion with the charisma doctrine. We have, for instance, the stereotyped repetition in Rom. 12.3; I Cor. 3.5; 11.18; 12.7; Eph. 4.7 of the fact that God gives to every man. I Cor. 7.7 proclaims the principle: 'Everyone has his charisma from God.' Ecclesiastical egalitarianism is thus ruled out of court. God does not repeat himself when he acts, and there can be no mass production of grace. There is differentiation in the divine generosity, whether in the order of creation or of redemption. Equality is not for Paul a principle of Church order. He recognizes in I Cor. 12.28 a whole series of charismata, ranging from the apostle to the widow who instructs the young married women and brings up the orphans. Within the ranks of the community there are to be found both strong and weak, aristocrat and proletarian, wise and foolish, cultured and uncultured. No one, according to I Cor. 12.21, may say to his brother 'I have no need of you.' Over them all stands the sign $\kappa\alpha\theta\grave{\omega}\varsigma$ $\beta o\acute{\nu}\lambda\epsilon\tau\alpha\iota$ or $\mathring{\eta}\theta\acute{\epsilon}\lambda\eta\sigma\epsilon\nu$ (I Cor. 12.11, 18); this expresses the sovereignty of the divine grace and omnipotence, which is both liberal and liberating, which puts an end to worry and envy by giving individually to every man. No one goes away empty, but no one has too much. But as gift and task, grace and ministry coincide, so do freedom and order. Therefore my charisma is always at the same time my $\mu\acute{\epsilon}\tau\rho o\nu$ $\pi\acute{\iota}\sigma\tau\epsilon\omega\varsigma$, the measure I have received (Rom. 12.3). And therefore also not only the prophet but every Christian must orientate his discipleship by the $\mathring{\alpha}\nu\alpha\lambda o\gamma\acute{\iota}\alpha$ $\pi\acute{\iota}\sigma\tau\epsilon\omega\varsigma$ of Rom. 12.6. '*All* is yours,' says I Cor. 3.21 emphatically. But at the same time the Apostle turns with violence on the Corinthians who put an arbitrary interpretation of their own on this watchword. They have forgotten that they and their bodies belong not to themselves but to the Lord. So the converse of I Cor. 3.21 is expressed in 7.24: 'Let each man remain before

God in the condition in which he received his call,' that is, as we saw earlier, in his charisma. Grace liberates me for the new obedience within the specific range of possibilities which has been opened up to me. It does not entitle us to make a grab for whatever may take our eye. As prophecy is tied to faith, so the giver of alms is to devote himself in all simplicity to his giving, the man who bears rule in the Church is to act with objectivity and attention to detail, he who tends the sick is to surrender himself wholeheartedly to his particular ministry. We might well adopt Barth's exegis of this passage and say that my charisma is always the only ethical possibility which is open to me. It is a matter of σωφρονεῖν, of not exceeding the limits of the given, of the sober matter-of-factness which marks the steward. I cannot choose my own calling nor can I reject it in favour of another. If all this is true, it involves the collapse of the ideal or model of the pastor and theologian who tries to be an expert in every field.

The second watchword coined by Paul in this context is 'For one another' (I Cor. 12.23). The pagan can use his talent as equipment in the general struggle for existence. The Christian is compelled, as a steward of the manifold grace of God (I Peter 4.10), to serve his neighbour in the mode and according to the measure of the charisma he has received. His particular gift frees him from men, from the things they worry about and the tyranny they exercise, and binds him solely to the Lord. But it also frees him from his own self, the tyranny it exercises and the worries it engenders, so that he can become in love the servant of all. I Cor. 8.9 impresses upon him that he has power over everything except his brother's conscience, foolish and misguided as that conscience may be. If we do wound our brother's conscience, v. 12 tells us that we are sinning against Christ himself. It is only in the objective exercise of ministering love, of which not only wide knowledge but also discrimination and tact are essential components, that charismatic gifts can be safeguarded against abuse. This might throw some light today on many aspects of the problem of the confessional Church, especially as Paul is conducting his argument in the Corinthian passage with an eye on the confessional problem of his time.

The third watchword designed to stifle self-will is to be found in Rom. 12.10, Phil. 2.3, I Peter 5.5 and with special force in

Eph. 5.21. It runs: 'Submit yourselves to each other in the fear of Christ.' The fear of Christ is no empty rhetorical phrase here. The word ὑποτάσσεσθαι signifies that particular shade of obedience which is due from a subordinate τάγμα. My brother Christian has also received his endowment, his liberty, his charge and is thus in his station the representative of the ascended Lord. The virtue of ταπεινοφροσύνη must be exercised in face of the *praesentia Christi* even when—indeed, precisely when—I encounter this presence embodied in the person of my brother who has also his charisma. This means concretely that authority and charisma go together in the community and, as charisma is only manifested as genuine in the act of ministry, so only he who ministers can have authority and that only in the actual exercise of his ministry.

We have now reached the point at which we must speak explicitly of the relation between community and office in the Church. This relationship also is treated by Paul exclusively on the basis of the charisma concept. What such treatment implies is best explained by means of a negation: a situation in which all Christians are regarded as endowed with charisma is a situation which does not admit the possibility of sacred space, sacred time, the right of representative action in the cultus, of sacred persons in the sense of both Judaism and the pagan religions—in fact, the whole possibility of objects or persons thought of as specially privileged in the realm of the holy by reason of their connection with the *temenos*. There is no longer any suggestion of the sacred office of the sanctuary, from which Ignatius (Eph. 5.1f.) derives the episcopal office and the essence of the Church. Again the question may be raised: 'Does not all this lead to the profanation of what is holy?' The answer is, that the exact opposite is true. The fenced-off boundaries of 'religion' are broken through when grace invades the world and its everyday life. It is not mistrust of the cultic element as such which leads Paul to avoid as a general rule the terminology of Old Testament or heathen sacrifices. On the contrary, in Rom. 12.1f. he deliberately resorts to cultic language of this kind in order to describe the sanctification of everyday life as the true sacrifice of Christendom. Thus sacramental worship stands at the very heart of the life of the community and of the Christian assembly. The New Testament speaks without any inhibitions of the worship of heaven; similarly, the meeting of the congregation appears as the earthly counterpart of this worship. Neither may we ignore in this context the significance of liturgy within the framework of the New Testament preaching. This significance rests upon the fact that for primitive Christianity the liturgy was the means whereby the frontier between the spheres of power of the former age and of the new could be constantly marked out afresh—a frontier which in everyday life was continually on the point of becoming blurred. Liturgy is the most ancient form of confession; as such, it is therefore for Paul the criterion of the proclamation of the Gospel and, if I am not mistaken, for the same reason it very early became the most important starting-point for the formation of dogma. If this is true, it is easy to see how the creation, development and handing-on of the liturgy took on in a special way the character of a charismatic work. More important still, it is the Christian assembly, the culmination of which is the celebration of the Sacrament, which manifests as such the body of Christ; the individual endowed with charisma only reflects the *praesentia Christi* in everyday life in so far as he is orientated towards the assembly. Indeed, Christians are only really the holy ones of God by reason of their adherence to it. Does this not suggest the very thing which we have already refuted in the case of the sacred time and the sacred spot? Not at all. For the Christian assembly is the place where the *Kyrios* becomes manifest in Word and Sacrament and where the eschatological event of the turn of the ages is perpetually proclaimed anew and firmly upheld in its character as an event calling for decision; as it happened once and for all in the Cross and Resurrection of Christ, so it is activated by baptism in the body of the individual. It is precisely *not* time and place, even less representative actions and duly authorized persons, which constitute the essence of this 'cultic' happening (even if indeed we are prepared to apply such an adjective to Christian worship); it is, as we have said, the self-manifestation and the presence of the *Kyrios* who takes up yet again his lordship over his own and in so doing exhibits his community as the new world. It is therefore possible to quarrel over the use of the concept 'cultic', which is certainly suspect because of the sense in which it is generally accepted. The eschatological note is the dominant in the movement we are considering here; and it is an essential characteristic of this unique eschatological happening, at least in the framework of the Pauline community, that it does not depend on any institutional validity, that no part is yet played in it by persons with special prerogatives and that, as can be seen from I Cor. 14.2ff., it does not even take place within the framework of a fixed rite. We might say, if we wished, that the gathered community orientated towards Word and Sacrament is the sole and sufficient external guarantee.

In such a context, then, all the baptized are 'office-bearers'; they have each his charisma and therefore each his special responsibility, and it is precisely on the grounds of this responsibility that they are challenged in I Cor. 14. Nowhere is this truth more clearly expressed than in I Peter 2.5–10. As stewards of the manifold grace of God, that is, as charismatically endowed persons who are under an obligation to serve each other to the measure of their gift, all Christians are living stones in God's building and representatives of him who is *the* Living Stone. As a spiritual priesthood they offer the sacrifice which is well-pleasing to God—the building-up of the community. The concrete expression of this is their proclamation of the mighty acts of him who has called us out of darkness into his own marvellous light. These last words refer unambiguously to baptism and reflect in their terminology the baptismal confession. The universal priesthood of all believers is therefore deduced here from the fact of baptism—an absolutely self-evident procedure if charisma is to be understood as the individuation of grace, our personal participation in the *Pneuma* and the concretion of our Christian calling. But when the universal priesthood of all believers is spoken of today, there is not the same self-evident unambiguity. For modern Protestantism has hitherto understood this universal priesthood merely as the private relationship of the individual Christian to his God and has seen private prayer as the fulfilment of its chief function. It will therefore help us if we remember that τὰς ἀρετὰς ἐξαγγέλλειν is a technical phrase belonging to the confession of praise with which he who has been healed or delivered, or has had his sin forgiven, dutifully and publicly acknowledges that he has personally experienced the gracious power of the Godhead manifest. A procedure laid down by holy law thus constitutes the answer of man to the manifestation of the divine and this procedure is, in the strictest sense, *officium*. This means that the passage in I Peter is speaking deliberately of real official action. Whenever we proclaim the mighty acts of the Christ, we find ourselves in concrete opposition to the world and engaged in an official mission into the bargain. We are carrying out the *ministerium verbi divini*, the διακονία τῆς καταλλαγῆς of II Cor. 5.18. We are carrying it out *jure divino*; for it is committed and commanded to every Christian, if he is not going to cease to be a Christian. We must not ignore the fact that such a statement is in direct contradiction to the modern Lutheran understanding of ecclesiastical office; neither can it easily be reconciled with the language used in many pronouncements of the Reformation. Conversely, we must be under no illusions; it is the necessary conclusion to be drawn from all the evidence that has so far been adduced. According to I Cor. 12.20 no individual possessor of a charisma has any special prerogative over against the Body of Christ. There is not even a prerogative of official proclamation, vested in some specially commissioned individual or other. For the Pauline community, the diversity of charismatic functions is normative even for the ministry of preaching; all in their different modes, according to their different grades and within mutually recognized limits, are bearers of the Word of God and contribute to the edification of the community. Even the apostle is, as Paul is always emphasizing, only one charismatic among many, though he may be the most important. I Cor. 14 teaches that everybody may not begin operations just when he feels like it and that the Holy Spirit does not pass lightly over matters of organization and of external order. But, according to the divine law, no Christian can exempt himself or be exempted by others from service in word and deed as an office-bearer of Christ and his body. Ever since his baptism, grace has been equipping him for this very thing.

But if all those endowed with charisma are *ipso facto* officebearers, this seems to be as good as saying that really none of them are. Surely all trace of order is bound to disappear in a community run on these lines? The historian will immediately suggest as a part answer to this question first, that the Pauline community knows as ministries certain functions which we should describe as fixed offices within the community, for example, the bishops and deacons of Phil. 1.1 (who may well have been treasurers), the deaconess Phoebe in Rom. 16.1f. and the functions enumerated in

Rom. 12.6–8; and secondly, that the series of charismata show distinct marks of a grading process. Certainly a universal obligation to service does not imply the equality of all. But these suggestions must be developed theologically and with careful attention to the peculiar dialectic which governs all Paul's thought and which is expressed in a particularly instructive form in his attitude to the possessors of the various charismata. His letters are constantly seeking to establish a basis for authority; for the authority of the first converts, or of Phoebe, of his delegates and fellow-workers; for the authority of masters over slaves, of husband over wife, and—at great length—for the authority of his own apostolate. He takes seriously the admonition that each Christian owes to his brother ταπεινοφροσύνη and φόβος Χριστοῦ and he draws from it concrete implications for the situation in his own time. Nevertheless it does not occur to him to leave Peter's position at Antioch unchallenged and, according to Gal. 2, he adopts as critical an attitude towards the authorities of the Jerusalem church as he does in I Cor. 14 towards those who speak with tongues at Corinth. In the face of claims which are being put forward in the name of the Spirit and of those who are endowed with charismata, he recalls the community to its senses with the words 'Do not become the slaves of men' (I Cor. 7.23). He refuses the right of speaking in the congregation to prophetesses, as he does to those who speak with tongues, unless there is someone present who can interpret. Even then he limits the number and length of the speeches. Thus he does not hesitate to set limits to the *Pneuma* which indwells the community and its worship and to do it in the declaratory style characteristic of juridical pronouncements. It is precisely in this manner that he treats the question of the celebration of the Eucharist in I Cor. 11 and the case of incest in I Cor. 5; and he orders the observance of other injunctions and traditional customs which the community might well have looked upon as in some measure attacks on their freedom, such as the matter of the veil in I Cor. 11. Since R. Sohm, it has been hotly debated how the individual pronouncements and the praise of the charismata can be brought under the same denominator. We are enabled to answer this question on the premise we have already laid down, namely, that it is not the mere possession of a charisma but the mode in which it is exercised which is decisive for Paul; whereas his interpreters have always presupposed that it is the Hellenistic concept of πνευματικά which lies at the root of his discussions. The Apostle's theory of order is not a static one, resting on offices, institutions, ranks and dignities; in his view, authority resides only within the concrete act of ministry as it occurs, because it is only within this concrete act that the *Kyrios* announces his lordship and his presence. Thus he is not driven to distinguish between spiritual and technical ministries as we, misinterpreting the historical situation in the New Testament, sometimes do today. To obey the Lord is to be ἐν πνεύματι, even as church treasurer at Philippi. Admittedly Paul distinguishes between *pneuma* and *pneuma*, himself tests the spirits, as he requires every Christian to do, and thus gives proof of the Spirit and of power. He does this in I Cor. 14.33 on the remarkably common-sense basis that God is not a God of confusion; and just as remarkable, and indeed thoroughly rationalistic, are the criteria he adopts for charismata and their possessors— the συμφέρον, the πρέπον, the appeal to φύσις, the typically Greek ideal of σωφρονεῖν. But it must be remembered that Paul has set himself to bring the enthusiasts back from the heavenly places of their own imagination down to earth, to the *theologia crucis et viatorum*, to the *agape* which is always ready and eager to minister. In the execution of this task he is not too proud to ally himself with popular philosophy and in this respect the Pastoral Epistles are vehicles of good Pauline tradition. For the popular philosophy of the time preached sober practicality—and practicality is the presupposition of right ministry and of that *agape* which is the costlier way because it sets bounds to the ego. This is what Sohm did not grasp when he formulated his famous thesis that Christian obedience springs from the compulsion of love rather than of law. *Agape* for Paul is not the virtue which moves the individual with a charismatic gift to make certain concessions to the brotherhood. It is much more a very critical attitude over against all charismata, because they are always liable to over-estimate or to abuse their endowment and to confuse their own authority with that of the Lord over his gifts and his servants. But only when this divine authority is set over these gifts and these servants and acknowledged by them have they themselves authority. For only then is this authority understood as belonging properly to the Giver and Lord alone and as given in trust to the servant by him.

This whole theological dialectic is expressed most starkly and characteristically by Paul in his doctrine of the charismatic as the man who is being tempted and will be again and again subject to temptation. Grace brings life by creating for itself bearers of its ministry and of its sovereign power. But at the same time it causes its servants to be consumed in its service. Over them hangs that sentence of death of which Paul, using himself as an example, speaks in II Cor. 1.9 just as in Gal. 6.17 he claims to bear the stigmata of the Crucified and in II Cor. 4.17ff. to carry in his body the νέκρωσις τοῦ Ἰησοῦ. As I do not wish to repeat what I have already written elsewhere,[1] I shall say very little here about his large-scale defence of his apostolate in II Cor. 10.13. But it does leave no doubt that the Apostle is exposed, and that in a special way, to those temptations which are necessarily connected with the preaching of the Gospel and are therefore to be regarded as eschatological; nor that, conversely, his suffering, just because it necessarily arises out of the preaching of the Gospel, has exemplary significance for the service of Christ in general. For every kind of service to Christ is governed by the law formulated by Paul in II Cor. 12.9, namely, that God's power manifests itself only in the experience of temptation and in those who undergo it. There is a variant on this law in 13.4 to the effect that the life from which springs the power of the Risen Lord is only to be had in the shadow of the Crucified Lord, and this is the reason why II Cor. 1.4ff. says that only the bearer of the παθήματα τοῦ Χριστοῦ is really able to convey the comfort and the salvation of the Christ. This nexus of problems goes too deep and is too complicated to be treated properly except in a separate monograph. I was only concerned here to show how far Paul was from subjecting Church order to judgment by any criterion of objective or ascertainable validity. While he set his doctrine of charisma in opposition to the theory of an institutionally guaranteed ecclesiastical office, he had also, and primarily, to cope with the dangers of Enthusiasm, which was already associated in his own communities with a misunderstanding of the meaning of charisma. To this end he spent his whole life combating the self-will of the charismatics, keeping their activities within bounds by appealing to reason, to decency, to *agape*, to the Cross of Christ; and, through it all, proclaiming

[1] Cf. my essay 'Die Legitimität des Apostels', *ZNW* 41, 1942, pp. 33–71.

that it is just these charismatic gifts which must be subordinated to the freedom and the yoke of the Lord as the ground and energy of a properly ordered Church. In so doing he removed the Church's growth, its preservation and its order from the realm in which men are able of their own sufficiency to establish and guarantee things and saw all the Church's hope to be comprised in this, that 'the One who started the good work in you will bring it to completion' (Phil. 1.6). Here again the Pauline doctrine of justification with its polemic against all the good and pious works of men is once again forcibly expressed. This doctrine does not apply only to the salvation of the individual but, as Paul understands it, defines and limits the very being of the Church, the law of its living and its dying and the truth and promise of its action, as carried out in all its offices and functions. It is therefore not to be wondered at if this view of the relation between office and community was only kept alive even in primitive Christianity so long as the dominant theme of the Apostle's doctrine of justification was shared and preserved.

It would not be practical for us to extend this investigation of the relation between office and community over the whole of the New Testament. But it is nevertheless useful to sketch in bold outline, and as a kind of foil to the Pauline outlook, that antithesis of it which has gained a foothold in the New Testament itself, especially in the Pastorals and in Luke's writings. The Church order of the Pastorals has sometimes been seen as an expression of the fact that Christians were settling down in the world. This may be true to some extent; the dwindling of the element of primitive Christian eschatology is certainly evidence for it. But more important still is the fact that the community of which the Pastorals are the mouthpiece is being heavily pressed back on to the defensive and its order represents something in the nature of a stockade erected against its assailants in a last despairing effort for survival. This order is chiefly designed simply to mark the frontiers which separate the Church and the world. For the Church is no longer seen here in the context of the Pauline missionary situation; it is no longer the world-wide body of Christ, the dominion of that grace which has invaded the world in its total being. Rather it is the house of God, *familia Dei*, and as such exposed to attack from outside and in need of protection. It is by no means certain that the Church was yet aware of the increasing threat from the Roman Empire. On the contrary, the natural conclusion to be drawn from II Tim. 1.15ff. is that the Pauline character of the communities in the province of Asia was being surrendered in favour of other ecclesiastical connexions, some of them deliberately partisan in origin. In particular, Gnosticism was causing the community a good deal of concern and thus compelling it to wage war on a double front. The fight to preserve the Pauline tradition was being carried on by calling in popular philosophy as an ally against the Enthusiasts, just as the Apostle himself had done, and by exploiting to the limit its motifs and slogans. Resistance was based on a single strong point; the community rallied round the apostolic delegate and the presbytery associated with him. The sudden prominence of these courts of appeal is very remarkable. For we may assert without hesitation that the Pauline community had had no presbytery during the Apostle's lifetime. Otherwise the silence on the subject in every Pauline epistle is quite incomprehensible. It seems quite out of the question that, had it been available, the Apostle would not have had recourse to such a court in his fight against the Gnostics and in defence of his own authority. An accessible and accepted leadership would have been of inestimable value when it came to protecting Church order against threats or to the necessity of re-establishing it, once it had been destroyed. Such a leadership could be made responsible in matters of dispute and, as is done in the Pastorals, could be set up at any time as the executive organ of the apostolic will by appeal to ordination and vows. If we cannot trace the slightest effort to do this, we can only draw one conclusion. The building-up of the presbytery as a closed circle of government in the community probably originated in Jerusalem; in any case, testimony to its existence there is borne by Gal. 2 in its allusion to 'those authorities' and, irrefutably, by Acts. When the community of the Pastorals acknowledges in its time of crisis the need of a firmly established church government and for this reason sets up presbyteries everywhere within its jurisdiction (Titus 1.5), it is providing evidence on the one hand, that in its eyes this court of appeal has only recently come into existence, and, on the other, that as a community it now lies within the sphere of Jewish Christian influence. We can make this assertion with all the more certainty because the ordination mentioned in I Tim. 4.14; 5.22

and II Tim. 1.6 can only have found its way into the Pauline community from the Jewish Christian tradition. Thus, it must have the same meaning as it has in Judaism: it is the bestowal of the Spirit and it empowers those who receive it to administer the *depositum fidei* of I Tim. 6.20, which we are to understand, more exactly defined, as the tradition of Pauline teaching. But the significance of this is that an office which stands over against the rest of the community is now the real bearer of the Spirit; and the primitive Christian view, that every Christian receives the Spirit in his baptism, recedes into the background and indeed, for all practical purposes, disappears. It is equally clear that this state of affairs cannot be reconciled with the Pauline doctrine of the charismata. The Jewish heritage expels the Pauline, in at least one central area of the Christian proclamation. The word charisma now appears only in I Tim. 4.14 and II Tim. 1.6; it is very revealing that these passages both refer to ordination. It is clear that what is meant is the commission given at ordination and the authorization to administer the *depositum fidei*. We can now speak inelegantly, but with absolute accuracy, of the Spirit as the ministerial Spirit.

The situation we have been sketching becomes even clearer in outline when we turn our attention to the remarkable standing given in our epistles to the apostolic delegates. They are not only the ostensible addressees of the letters but it is also they who are made answerable for the whole ordering of the community, for the fight against the heretics and especially for the building-up of the presbytery. As the letters were not in fact written by Paul and therefore not really addressed to Timothy and Titus, this must have been something which was considered of cardinal importance at the actual time of writing. Arguing from II Timothy, which is ostensibly Paul's last will and testament but is in fact a picture of the ideal bishop, we may assert that the apostolic delegate is regarded in the Pastorals as the connecting link between apostle and monarchical bishop and as the prototype of the latter. Thus it is in reality the monarchical bishop who, under the guise of the apostolic delegate, is being addressed and reminded of his duties. His work is to continue the apostolic office in the sub-apostolic age. In other words, he stands in the apostolic succession in precisely the same way as the Jewish rabbi standing in the succession from Moses and Joshua receives the traditional corpus of instruction and the accepted exposition of the law and administers them *jure divino*—that is, in virtue of the Spirit imparted to him through ordination. This is the genesis of that conception of ministerial office which is to determine the cause of events hereafter. The distinction between clerics and laymen is now in being, in practice if not in theory. It is now tacitly accepted that the authority of the institutional ministry is guaranteed by a principle of tradition and legitimate succession which has become the basis of all Church order; and this ministry has surrounded itself with various executive organs in the shape of the presbyterate, the diaconate and the order of widows. The extraordinary interest of this development lies in the fact that it has actually taken place in the Pauline mission-field itself. For this shows that the Pauline conception of a Church order based on charisma disappeared in the very church the Apostle himself created; and that this happened because it seemed to that church to be an ideal incapable of being realized. The answer to the question 'How did this come about?' is obvious—the weight of the gnostic attack threatened to overwhelm the Christian community. The Gnostics, too, appealed to their baptism, to the Spirit speaking within them and working through them, to their Christian insight. It was now a matter of finding a defence against Enthusiasm. The method chosen was, first, to entrust teaching and administration to reliable hands and to create a settled ministry against which alien pretensions would beat in vain; then to tie this ministry to a solemn ordination vow (and thus to rule out unsuitable elements) and to surround it with auxiliaries bound by similar obligations, thus guaranteeing the care of the whole community down to the most insignificant member; and finally to insert the ministry into a fabricated chain of tradition and to render its position impregnable by a doctrine of legitimate succession. The community's inheritance from Judaism, obviously mediated by the refugee Jewish Christian community from Palestine, forms the stockade behind which the church Paul founded maintains its life in the face of the assaults of Enthusiasm. But popular philosophy provides the motifs and the slogans by the help of which sorties can be undertaken and individual combats fought out. We cannot overlook the fact that need and necessity were the godparents of this transformation and we shall therefore be guarded in our criticism of its rightness. The theological problem involved is not contained in the actual structural alteration of the relationship between community and office. To take this line would be wrongly to evaluate the *theological* significance of the historical situation and to prefer illusion to reality. It would also be to forget the fundamental Pauline decision to see relevance not so much in the 'that' as in the 'how' of a thing. From this point of view the change of structure can be fully justified. What makes the whole process so questionable theologically (from a Pauline standpoint, at any rate), and indeed marks the transition to early Catholicism, is that the change is associated with, and founded on, not need and historical necessity but a theoretical principle of tradition and legitimate succession; so that, in effect, the Spirit is made to appear as the organ and the rationale of a theory.

The same development is visible in Acts; and here the prevailing attitudes stand out even more clearly. The charisma concept has now completely disappeared. Paul himself is shown as setting up bishops and presbyteries in his communities everywhere, even at this early stage. The farewell speech in 20.17ff. confirms that this measure is part of the campaign against the Enthusiasts. It is precisely this principle of tradition and legitimate succession which runs like a red thread through the fabric of the whole first section of Acts, and indeed is already shown as definitive for the idea of the apostolate as such. 1.22 can still speak of the μάρτυς τῆς ἀναστάσεως, but this is something left over from what is probably a pre-Pauline tradition. Luke himself is no longer satisfied with such a view. For him the apostle is one who has been a companion of the historical Jesus from the first moment of his public ministry (1.21; 10.39). The point of this alteration is to present the apostle as the guarantor of the Gospel tradition as later he is to appear as the guarantor and criterion of the canonical tradition. For from this time on it becomes necessary for the Christian teacher, whether dealing with those inside the Church or those outside, to have a guarantor for the dependability of his own particular tradition. Correspondingly, the apostolic witness becomes witness to facts and, in contrast to the Pastorals, the original apostolate plays a prominent part. It is represented by Peter and, as the closed circle of the Twelve, it constitutes the foundation of the Church. Within the Church, only that which is based on this foundation can prosper. Thus, when the Hellenists evangelize Judaea and Samaria on their own initiative, Peter must afterwards inspect these gains, bestow upon them the apostolic blessing and thereby incorporate them into the society of the apostolic Church (chs. 8–10). When Philip baptizes in Samaria, he cannot impart the Spirit because he has not been commissioned to do so. According to 8.14ff. the subsequent laying-on of hands by Peter supplies what was lacking; for only the continuity of the apostolic Church can certainly impart the Spirit. In ch. 11 the Apostles come to an agreement over the mission to the Gentiles, which, in spite of the work of the Seven and all the activity in Antioch, has to be seen as inaugurated by the conversion of Cornelius through the Prince of the Apostles. Two long chapters, containing one miracle after another, demonstrate in a way which no reader could ignore, the importance of this procedure. In ch. 15 the Apostles similarly come to an agreement regarding the work of Paul, who stands in the dock before them and has almost nothing to say for himself. Indeed, he has no need to say anything because Peter and James themselves appropriate the Pauline gospel. It is by pointing out that the issue has long been settled in practice by the conversion of Cornelius that they take the wind out of the objectors' sails. The treatment of Paul himself in this account is, to say the least, bold. He receives his commission at the hands of Ananias (9.6) who also imparts to him the Spirit (9.17). Barnabas presents him to the Apostles who, on their part, confirm him in his ministry. He is sent out as a delegate of the community at Antioch to whom, as in duty bound, he reports at the conclusion of his first missionary journey. According to 11.32f. Barnabas, who himself functions as a delegate of the Jerusalem church, recalls him to Antioch. Apart from the tradition of 14.4, 14 Paul is consistently denied the title of apostle. His activity is described, even by himself, in the same terms as that of the Seven; it is 'preaching the Gospel' (13.32; 14.7, 15; 16.10; 17.18). As distinct from the Twelve, he is portrayed throughout Acts as an evangelist, a hander-on of the apostolic tradition in the sphere of the Gentile mission. In exactly the same way, the Seven receive their office from the Twelve by laying-on of hands (6.6); Apollos receives Christian instruction through Paul's fellow-workers, Aquila and

Priscilla, although he possesses the Spirit and is already exercising a powerful preaching ministry; and, finally, Paul receives into the Christian community the disciples of John at Ephesus who have not yet heard of the Holy Spirit, although a Christian community is in existence there and although any adherent of a Hellenistic mystery-religion, even, knows about the power of *pneuma*. We cannot doubt that it is not a question here of drawing from more or less accurate historical sources but of theological construction all along the line; even though we must remember that Luke is only carrying further conceptions and traditions which are already in circulation and is therefore not deliberately falsifying history. The obvious answer to the question 'What interests could be served in this way?' is that the only possible interested party is a church which is under the necessity (in the context of its conflict with heresy) of demonstrating the legitimacy of its own position; and which does so by maintaining that this position is based on continuity with the original apostolate. Outside the boundaries of this church, which has become a sacred area within the world and which bases itself on the sacred office and the sacred tradition of the original apostolate, there is no salvation and no possession of the Spirit. So far as we can see, then, it was Luke who was the first to propagate the theories of tradition and legitimate succession which mark the advent of early Catholicism. No doubt this was not his deliberately willed end but the means by which he felt he could best defend the Church against the dangers which threatened it. The historian is bound to concede that the theory we are discussing proved itself to be a most effective way of combatting Enthusiasm and did in fact save infant Christendom from being smothered by the sectaries. The canonization of Acts was to this extent an understandable and well-merited gesture of thanksgiving on the part of the Church.

Yet the theologian finds himself face to face with very pressing questions. One underlying problem is this: how could a situation arise in which such an interpretation of history became possible? For certainly it did not materialize out of nothing. As in the matter of the origins of ordination and of the presbyteries in the Pastorals, I should myself look in the direction of Jewish Christianity for the answer. The roots of the early Catholic theory may well be sought in the apocalyptic concept of the new Israel, whose twelve tribes were to be judged by the twelve Apostles with the full authority of the Spirit and according to sacred law, and whose centre was Jerusalem. The apocalyptic dream of primitive Jewish Christianity was shattered by the rising Gentile Church, not least by Paul; but its ideas may well be thought to have continued their march via the Jewish Christian Diaspora in Hellenistic territory and to appear before us in a new guise in the early Catholic conception of the Church as an institution purveying salvation. Apocalyptic was replaced by the theology of history which is visible at times in the speeches in Acts. Its sign manual is the thesis of the continuity of salvation history—a continuity which can be verified by reference to the Scriptures and which only those who have been blinded can fail to discern. In this setting, the Cross of Jesus is no longer a scandal but only a misunderstanding on the part of the Jews which the intervention of God at Easter palpably and manifestly corrects. But the Church itself is the willed and intended end-product of this history as thus edifyingly interpreted. She is the teacher of the ignorant Jews and Gentiles. She enlightens the latter, as in the Areopagus speech, to the extent of giving them proofs of God's action amongst them: her word is confirmed by numerous miracles, she convinces the unbelieving, condemns false teachers (as instanced in Peter's dealings with Simon Magus) and punishes sinners (as portrayed in the story of Ananias and Sapphira). If Paul could say in Gal. 4.26 of the heavenly Jerusalem that it is the mother of the faithful, this thought is now transferred to the empirical Church as the guardian of the sacred tradition and as the area of revelation within which God manifests himself as the God who works miracles.

Fabrication is interwoven with proclamation. A *theologia gloriae* is now in process of replacing the *theologia crucis*. The fictional character of this reconstructed history is indicated by the tensions between tradition and composition in Acts; but also at an earlier stage by Paul's passionate protest at the beginning of Galatians that he has not received his ministry either from or through men. Thus his conception of the essence and order of the Church cannot possibly be harmonized with that which comes to prevail in early Catholicism. It is in the starkest contradiction to it. The clearest proof of this lies in the fact that the Pauline concept of charisma was not understood by posterity. It may have been retained, but it was given a non-Pauline function to fulfil. It served to characterize those members of the community who stood out from the rest by reason of a particular endowment of some extraordinary kind. In other words, charisma becomes identified once again with the πνευματικόν of the Hellenistic world to which Paul had directly opposed it. On this point as elsewhere the Pauline theology was forgotten and replaced. The New Testament itself already demonstrates this. As a historical document, it reflects the historical contradiction, crises and transformations which determine the whole of Church history, and thus brings us face to face with the problem of the unity of Scripture and of the message which lies at its heart.

But the problem which should concern us most closely is this: why even Protestantism itself, as far as I can see, has never made a serious attempt to create a Church order which reflected the Pauline doctrine of charisma, but has left this to the sects. If we do ask the question, the answer seems to have been given already by the early Catholic Church—such an attempt would inevitably open the doors wide to fanaticism. For it can scarcely be denied that the Pauline communities—those which did not entrust themselves, more or less voluntarily, to other leadership—were, within one generation, swallowed up by Enthusiasm. Is it therefore an illusion that all responsibility and every kind of ministry in the community should be grounded on baptism, and is it possible to proclaim and practise the common priesthood of all believers without falling a prey to religious individualism and leaving the Church as a whole to disintegrate? Even if we thought this, we could still not ignore the fact that Paul exposes the artificial nature of that conception of Church and ministry which was to replace his own, and drives us to a critique of the ideology involved. But is his significance in the last resort dependent on this critical function of his theology? Are we driven to the conclusion that Paul, who spent his life fighting the Enthusiasts, was not capable of establishing Church tradition but only of causing its disintegration, because he asked too much of the Christian and of the fellowship of the Church and for this reason was himself one of the principal factors which led to the triumph of Enthusiasm?

The historian cannot, as such, give the answer to this question. All history leaves us with unsolved problems and distressing perplexities—even the history which was set down in the pages of the New Testament. That direct answer to our needs which we are always seeking is not to be found there in the form of some simple prescription. Such can only be found there if we read back our own solutions into the past; and this has indeed happened in all ages. The direct legacy of all past time to us can only be the questions and the needs of bygone ages and the various ways in which men have attempted to deal with them. But perhaps the past sharpens not only our insight but also our conscience and tells us that no age is exempt from the necessity of beginning all over again, of testing, critically and yet humbly, the spirits of the ages that have gone before, because we, too, are called to decision. Perhaps, as we learn this, we are brought to acknowledge that the Church can only exist as the community of Christ in so far as grace repeatedly lays hold on us and re-creates us as instruments of his service; and that we must leave him to care for the continuity of the Church, who alone is able to ensure the continuance of grace.

IV

THE CANON OF THE NEW TESTAMENT AND THE UNITY OF THE CHURCH[1]

DOES the canon of the New Testament constitute the foundation of the unity of the Church? In view of the many different versions of the Christian proclamation to be found in the New Testament, the historian must return a negative answer to this question. Within the framework of a short lecture, the evidence for this statement can only be adduced in outline and limited to uncomplicated facts and a few examples.

1. A theological problem is already implicit in the fact that the canon presents us with four Gospels instead of one and that even the first three reveal important divergences in order, selection and presentation. Naturally, the differences in the traditions drawn upon at various points and the individual characteristics of the Evangelists contribute to this state of affairs. But only a far too superficial approach which understands the Gospels primarily as factual reports and ultimately refuses to reckon with them as proclamation can be satisfied with this solution. We can postulate with certainty that none of the Evangelists himself knew the historical Jesus. To express the situation paradoxically, for all of them the exalted Lord of faith preceded the Incarnate One in the order of knowledge and determined the aspect under which he was seen by each of them from his own particular angle of vision. In addition, all of them belong to the Hellenistic Christian community. Matthew and Luke both presuppose Mark and a source usually known as the Logia; all three presuppose an already formulated narrative of the Passion and Easter. John avails himself of what is certainly a version of the Synoptic tradition, even if it is one that has run wild. There is a time-lag between the Gospels,

---

[1] A lecture delivered on 20 June 1951, at the Oecumenical Symposium of the Göttingen Theological Faculty. First published in *EvTh* 11, 1951–52, pp. 13–21, under the title 'Begründet der neutestamentliche Kanon die Einheit der Kirche?'.

but not such as to make important differences inevitable on that ground alone. However, they do in fact take divergent roads. The pattern is as follows: Mark, by means of his many miracle stories, depicts the secret epiphany of him who receives his full glory at Easter, Matthew points to the bringer of the Messianic Torah, John to the ever-present Christ, while Luke, historicizing and portraying salvation history as a process of development, composes the first 'Life of Jesus'. To give another example: no Hellenistic Christian ever doubted that the predicate 'Son of God' in the metaphysical sense was rightly to be ascribed to Jesus. It is true that, in his Baptism narrative, Mark reveals the continued existence within the community of an older view standing for an Adoptionist Christology and seeing in the Baptism the consecration of the Messiah (cf. Rom. 1.4; Acts 2.36; Heb. 1.5). But in his own work all traces of this view have been obliterated and Jesus is delineated without any reserve in the colours of the Hellenistic *theios anthropos*. Both the other Synoptists already speak of the divine conception of Jesus, Matthew representing the Messiah as the second Moses and the Saviour of the eschatological People of God, Luke harking back to classical mythology and representing the divine Child as the World-Redeemer, as in the Fourth Eclogue of Virgil. In the Fourth Gospel, the motif of a Virgin Birth is seen as incongruous in relation to him who, as the Logos, is from the beginning in the bosom of the Father and one with him, and, therefore, can alone be the Revealer. The confession (common to all the Evangelists) that Jesus is the Son of God is thus differently explicated with the help of conceptions assimilated from the contemporary environment. The proclamation of the Incarnate One is qualified in each of our Gospels by a particular theological interest.

Thus the Evangelists are in a position to exercise criticism on each other without any inhibitions. Already we find Matthew treating the source of his Baptism narrative in this way because he found its Christology intolerable. His successors did likewise. For instance, Matthew takes offence at the drastic manner in which the healing of the woman with the issue of blood is treated in Mark 5.27ff. The idea that the garment of the miracle-worker imparts divine power which is transmitted by touch and has healing properties is a popular Hellenistic conception. It occurs again in the accounts of Peter's healing shadow and Paul's miraculous handkerchief (Acts 5.15; 19.12) and in later ages is at the root of the cult of relics. Matthew corrects this crudely magical outlook by making the healing effective not through contact with the garment but simply through Jesus' word of power. In order to bring the mysterious majesty of Jesus into sharper relief he drastically reduces the broad sweep of Mark's miracle narratives in which the story teller's pleasure in his craft is all too evident and in which even motives of purely secular literary technique are operative. Luke doubtless omits deliberately the anathema pronounced on Peter by Jesus in Mark 8.33 because he finds it unbearable. He alone of the Evangelists has made the call of Peter the object of a special miracle story and at this, as at other points in his Gospel, sets the other Apostles in the shadow of the Prince of the Apostles who is for him the embodiment of the Church's *ministerium*. Obviously, too, dogmatic interests have determined the plan of the Fourth Gospel. For this reason a symbolic introduction precedes each of the two first sections (chs. 2 and 13). The wedding at Cana and the Cleansing of the Temple (which is quite arbitrarily transferred to the beginning of the Gospel) mark Jesus out as the salvation and judgment of the world; the foot-washing illustrates the fact that the disciples, hated by the world, yet stand in the divine *agape*. Thus the Evangelist has 'slanted' the familiar stuff of the tradition as contained in the Synoptists so that it can be used as material for his own proclamation and has thus robbed it of its autonomy. This is most evident with regard to the miracle stories and the Johannine critique of the traditional ecclesiastical approach is at its sharpest in this regard. This critique sees the miracles of Jesus as symbols which (4.48; 6.26; 20.29) he expressly removes from the sphere in which current Christian interpretation conceived them to move—that of 'evidence'. Examples of this kind can be multiplied almost indefinitely and can indeed be extended to include passages in which the same word takes on a different meaning through being used in a different context. From what has so far been said we may legitimately conclude that a comprehensive explanation of the variations in our Gospels, and particularly of the divergences in the selection of material from the tradition, may rightly be sought in the different theological outlooks of the Evangelists.

2. The existence of the canon has produced the assumption now

current in the Church (and to which Systematic Theology has often lent countenance) that the New Testament gives us a reasonably complete picture of the history and message of primitive Christianity. It is true that we undoubtedly know much more about them than we do about most of the comparable phenomena of the classical period, because the Church has preserved and transmitted her tradition with such care. But in spite of this we should not allow ourselves to forget the fragmentary character even of this knowledge. We are brought up against it with particular force when we make the attempt to reconstruct the authentic tradition about Jesus from the New Testament sources. While we can say with certainty that the great bulk of the tradition does not enable us to lay hold of the historical Jesus, equally we can say that even the most highly perfected procedures of historical science permit us to make on this point only very approximate estimates of probability. This can be seen clearly in the many extremely disparate versions of the life and message of Jesus and in A. Schweitzer's comprehensive account of *The Quest of the Historical Jesus*. Paradoxically enough, the necessary reconstruction is difficult for us (and indeed appears at times almost hopeless) not because there is too little material in the tradition, but because there is too much. The primitive Christian community did not distinguish, as we do, between the historic Jesus and the exalted Lord. Palestinian and Hellenistic Christian prophecy alike spoke in the name of the Exalted One, as we can see in the Apocalypse of John. In the development of the tradition, these sayings—couched for the most part in the first person—have become confused with the words of the historical Jesus and ascribed to him simply because primitive Christianity was concerned not, as we are, with the exact period of their origin, but with the Spirit of the Lord revealing himself in both groups alike. We cannot simply accept this situation without questioning, but must make critical distinctions within it. For inspiration does not annul the fact that, when the prophet speaks, he uses the thought-forms of his time and therefore also its theological conceptions. Thus the tradition concerning Jesus cannot be brought under a single denominator. The work of the Form-Critics has shown that the narrative material must be viewed in the same light as the sayings; the connecting links between the pericopae are almost entirely the Evangelists' own composition and serve as the skeletal structure for the individual fragments of the tradition. Thus, however much the canon by its very existence tempts us to regard all sections of the Gospel material as being on the same level, such a procedure does not do justice to the facts of the case. The final secret of the art of exegesis lies in seeing the differences and in drawing distinctions.

There is a second point to be noted, closely connected with this one. We are accustomed to think, and are encouraged in our opinion by the very existence of the New Testament canon, by the current ecclesiastical outlook and frequently by Systematic Theology, that we have in the New Testament a set of self-contained assertions so that the whole can be rightly conceived as a fixed number of *dicta probantia*. But this is to misunderstand the occasional nature of most New Testament utterances. We find that they are really concerned with answers to concrete questions, with the refutation of certain well-defined errors, with warnings and consolations addressed to concrete individuals; they presuppose certain premises and admit of different conclusions. The exegete is handicapped because, as a rule, he can only view the second party in a discussion or dissension through the eyes of the first and is thereby seduced into passing one-sided judgments and drawing premature conclusions. Once again, some examples may help to illustrate the point: was Peter unable to answer Paul's complaints against him in Antioch and did he therefore admit the justice of them, or did the two part in open conflict? What conclusions did Barnabas, his fellow-accused, draw from the quarrel? Luke is certainly still aware of the problem, but here as elsewhere he finds both a ground and a camouflage for essential theological differences of principle in personal differences of opinion. Why, after this conflict, does Antioch seem to have been off the map for Paul? How did it happen that most of the Pauline communities came under other leadership after only one generation? What of Apollos, to whom the Enthusiasts at Corinth seem to have been in the habit of appealing? How did they justify this appeal? Who were those whom, when the Epistle to the Philippians was written, were 'preaching Christ in envy' and using the fact of Paul's imprisonment against him? How questionable must his authority have been during his lifetime if anybody dared to do this! How did Peter come to be replaced by James in the original community at

Jerusalem—an event which seems to have occurred simultaneously with the end of Palestinian Enthusiasm and the rise of a Christian rabbinate? What were the doctrinal differences—reported in Acts 6—separating the Palestinians and the Hellenists? Only doctrinal differences account for the fact that the latter could not hold out in Jerusalem while the adherents of the Law remained relatively unchallenged for at least fifteen years. From what milieu does the enigmatic phenomenon of the Fourth Gospel arise, or for that matter the equally puzzling Epistle of James? This series of questions, which can be extended indefinitely, shows that the New Testament contains an inexhaustible wealth of unsolved (and, in part, probably insoluble) historical and theological problems. Only those speak to us out of its pages, who were capable of writing, were obliged to write and whose writings the Church of later days, for whatever reasons, thought it good to preserve. But they represent only a diminishing minority over against the many who passed on the message without leaving behind them a written deposit and therefore an abiding memorial. What entitles us to assume that the speech and the writings of this vast majority would not have differed from those of the New Testament authors? From time to time we catch some echo of their voice which suggests the contrary, and indeed the probability of this is already clear from the many-sidedness of the New Testament itself. This in turn means, however, that only fragments of the discussion within primitive Christianity have been preserved for us and that the variability of the primitive Christian kerygma must have been very much greater than a consideration of the state of affairs as revealed in the canon would lead us to suppose.

3. Yet this variability is already so wide even in the New Testament that we are compelled to admit the existence not merely of significant tensions, but, not infrequently, of irreconcilable theological contradictions. An approach to this judgment may be made through the evaluation of a point which has not usually been taken as seriously as it deserves. It is generally acknowledged that the Fourth Evangelist employs the literary device of introducing and underlining a master theme by means of a misunderstanding on the part of the disciples. In so doing, is he not raising a theological problem which demands the most thorough examination? Our conviction that primitive Christianity rightly interpreted its

Lord (or rather, the tradition about him) in every respect and also handed on this tradition without distortion is by no means a *priori* unassailable; indeed, in a number of cases it is demonstrably false. When Jesus in Mark 7.15 refuses to agree that man contracts defilement from external sources, he is abandoning the foundation principle on which the whole Jewish cultus was based. And when, in his turn, he finds the source of all impurity in man's own heart, the inescapable implication is that man as such is corrupt and can come to salvation only through forgiveness. A critical analysis of the rest of the chapter shows how this word of Jesus has been hedged in by glosses originating both in Palestinian and Hellenistic Christianity. We find that, on the one side, the saying is toned down by being made to serve the polemic against the rabbinate for overlaying the will of God with its own exceptions and casuistry. On the other side, however, the whole saying is given a moralizing twist: it is vice which essentially constitutes defilement. Neither gloss is incorrect in itself, but both take the edge off the radically new element in the attitude of Jesus. The real point of his saying here is precisely that it does *not* distinguish between a divine commandment and the injunctions of men. Such a distinction would not have been recognized by Judaism, because in Judaism a rabbinic decision is understood as the explication of a divine commandment and therefore possesses derivatively the authority of revelation. This word of Jesus strikes not merely at rabbinic exegesis and practice but at the very heart of the legislation governing ceremonial and ritual purity; on this occasion Jesus did not scruple to attack and abrogate what for Judaism had the force of, indeed, according to the literal sense of the Old Testament, actually *was*, a divine commandment. The Palestinian Church, however, remains blind to this new insight, because it maintains the distinction between divine commandment and human injunction. Hellenistic Christianity adulterates the word of Jesus equally, although in another way: it enumerates evil deeds from which we must and can keep ourselves, while Jesus declares our heart to be guilty and makes it responsible for the genesis of wickedness. Thus the exposure of our lost condition is turned into merely moralistic admonition and the Judge of all becomes simply the purveyor of a superior ethic. The same kind of thing happens in Mark 2. The saying of Jesus in v. 27 that the Sabbath is made for man is

immediately qualified in v. 28 by the added statement that the Son
of Man is Lord of the Sabbath. The community was prepared to
ascribe to its Master what it had not the courage to claim for itself.
This qualifying insertion shows that it shrank from exercising the
freedom given in Jesus and preferred to take renewed refuge in
a Christianized form of Judaism. Conversely, its polemic against
Pharisaism on grounds of hypocrisy (Matt. 23 is example enough)
only succeeds in deadening the impact of the actual attack made by
Jesus himself. The latter is in fact aimed at the self's struggle to attain
righteousness: thus, its target is every form of the religion of works
and therefore, in the last resort, every human being. The equation of
Pharisaism with hypocrisy produces a situation in which the
judgment of Jesus falls merely on moral defect; and a path leading
to a religion of works within Christianity is opened up, although
Jesus' attack on the true essence of Pharisaism has already put up
the sign 'No entry'. The caricature of the Pharisee as a hypocrite
has cost the Church itself very dear. Important as they are, these
examples are only the most outstanding among a wealth of others.
They are designed to show that the history of Christianity and of
its doctrinal tradition cannot be viewed and described purely in
terms of continuity with Jesus. It is also a history of discontinuity
between the Lord and the disciples. At the earliest stage in its life
to which we can have access, the primitive community is already
in part an apprehending, in part a misapprehending, community.
While it bears witness to the majesty of its Lord, at the same time
it obscures it. Even its faith was hidden in the earthen vessel of its
humanity and the correctness of its belief was as questionable as
orthodoxy always is.

But once all this is admitted, there can no longer be any grounds
for surprise when opposing doctrinal viewpoints are found in
violent collision in other parts of the New Testament. Luther was
quite right, in my opinion, when he judged the Pauline doctrine
of justification and that of the Epistle of James to be theologically
incompatible. The treatment of Paul's apostleship in Acts makes
assumptions which Gal. 1 passionately contests: and this not in
any polemical fashion, but as a matter of self-evident fact. It is
incomprehensible to me how anyone can reconcile the eschatology
of the Fourth Gospel with that of Revelation. It is obvious that
the phrases 'the faith once for all delivered to the saints' (Jude 3)

and 'the truth you already have' (II Peter 1.12) are designed to play off the objective nature of Church tradition against new revelations of truth which, according to the Gnostics, the Spirit is always giving. The writers concerned had probably no viable alternative. But what kind of tradition is it which can quite happily allow canonical authority to Jewish legends about the fight between Michael and Satan for the body of Moses and, with equal lack of embarrassment, describe Christians as becoming partakers of the divine nature by baptism (II Peter 1.4)? Surely such methods of argument sound the death-knell of the primitive Christian doctrine of the Spirit found in Paul and John and demonstrably going back to Jesus himself? For we have reached a stage when it is not enough for the Spirit to be effective in and through the process of tradition: the Spirit is now dissolved *into* tradition. The *ecclesia docens* has now acquired proprietary rights over the 'Spirit of Ministry'. Every unauthorized exegesis and interpretation of Scripture can now be prohibited; the *locus classicus* for this is II Peter 1.20. Ordination is now the expression of a principle of legitimacy and succession. In short, we have now crossed the border out of primitive Christianity and laid the foundations of early Catholicism. The time when it was possible to set up Scripture in its totality in opposition to Catholicism has gone beyond recall. Protestantism today can no longer employ the so-called Formal Principle without rendering itself unworthy of credence in the eyes of historical analysis. The canon of the New Testament does not divide Judaism from early Catholicism: it affords a foothold to the latter as well as to the former.

4. We now have three results: (*a*) the variability of the New Testament kerygma; (*b*) the extraordinary wealth of theological positions in primitive Christianity (a phenomenon going beyond the horizon of the New Testament); (*c*) the incompatibility between some of these positions which has already partly emerged in the above discussion. From these three premises we may now formulate the conclusion on which our thesis is based. It can only run thus: the New Testament canon does not, as such, constitute the foundation of the unity of the Church. On the contrary, as such (that is, in its accessibility to the historian) it provides the basis for the multiplicity of the confessions. The variability of the kerygma in the New Testament is an expression of the fact that

in primitive Christianity a wealth of different confessions were already in existence, constantly replacing each other, combining with each other and undergoing mutual delimitation. It is thus quite comprehensible that the confessions which exist today all appeal to the New Testament canon. Fundamentally, the exegete cannot dispute their methodological or their material right to do this. If the canon as such is binding in its totality, the various confessions may, with differing degrees of historical justification, claim as their own larger or smaller tracts of it, better or less known New Testament writers. Their claim is incontestable in principle and capable of demonstration in particular instances. The opposite is the case with the unity of the Church: taking the same point of departure, we find that it is fundamentally not susceptible of proof and that all confessional claims to finality are highly disputable. Must we then admit that Lessing's fable of the three rings in *Nathan the Wise* is our last word also? This would certainly be my view, if the task of exegesis stopped at historical confirmation. Wherever the attempt is made to build a case solely on 'It is written . . .', the scientific criticism of the New Testament must, I am profoundly convinced, lead in the last resort to an acknowledgment of Lessing's fable as a true picture of the situation. But we should then be missing the crucial point that the New Testament itself sets over against theological *statement* (even the statements contained in the canon) the theological *task* of 'discerning the spirits'. In other words, careful attention must be paid both to the unity of letter and spirit and to the distinction between them. The principle which Paul establishes in II Cor. 3 with regard to the Old Testament cannot be restricted to the Old Testament but is applicable in precisely the same way to the canon of the New Testament. Idealist thinkers have been accustomed to interpret the antithesis of letter and spirit in the Greek sense; that is, they have seen it as analogical with the antithesis of inward and outward, content and form. This analogy is certainly false. Paul, who is always stressing corporeality as the domain of the Spirit, can hardly be summoned as the star witness in an action on behalf of 'inwardness'. We must not so separate letter and spirit as to allot to them different regions of man's being. Paul clearly sees both as powers which span and move the universe, and thus such a separation would result in a dualistic cosmology quite foreign to the Apostle's thought. Further light is thrown on the problem when we remember that, in Pauline thought, spirit and flesh are not things in themselves but modes in which man exists as obedient or disobedient to God. The Pauline doctrine of the Law shows that the same is the case with the relationship of spirit and letter. It is, without any doubt, dialectical. Paul refused to be driven into antinomianism and maintained steadfastly that the law (understood as the revealed will of God) was just, holy and good. But he was careful to distinguish between the law or the will of God and that law as distorted by the pious man to aid him in his efforts to acquire a righteousness of his own. It is just this law distorted by us as a means to our own self-righteousness which Paul in II Cor. 3 calls 'the letter'. To the question 'Wherein does the abuse of God's revealed will actually lie?' we return the answer 'In the fact that men do not let God's claim upon them remain *his* claim, but imagine him to be a prisoner of his own ordinance and therefore begin to venerate the law as a self-existent reality rather than as a proclamation of the divine will: thus they allow it to usurp God's place.' Similarly creation becomes 'cosmos' and the human creature becomes 'flesh' when the relation of the immediately apprehensible to the Creator goes unheeded; and thus the gift is isolated from the Giver so that it becomes the instrument of human self-will. That all gifts of God *can* be misused we see in the example of Corinth when the Enthusiasts transform the Lord's Supper into the heavenly banquet and the medicine of immortality. They base their assurance and self-assertion on the divine gift, just as the legalist bases his on the law. Paul assailed both parties, teaching that the gift is a mode of the Giver's presence and not a substitute for him. We can never keep God in custody because he would then cease to be God and to be our Lord. We 'have' him only when, and as long as, he has us.

In terms of our present problem, this means that we cannot keep God imprisoned even within the canon of the New Testament. Because the Jews held this view of the Old Testament, Paul speaks of the Old Testament canon as 'the letter that killeth'. The same is true of the New Testament if it is approached in the same way. The canon is not the word of God *tout simple*. It can only become and be the Word of God so long as we do not seek to imprison God within it; for this would be to make it a substitute for the God who addresses us and makes claims upon us. The turn of phrase 'the truth you already have' in II Peter 1.12 shows that the Church has always tended to do this very thing. If we identify Church tradition with 'the Truth', we are seeing it apart from the Spirit who, according to John 16.13, is always newly present to lead us into all truth; and we are also seeing it apart from the God who manifests himself as present by speaking to us. Certainly, this does not mean that we are to ignore the tradition for the sake of the Spirit. To do so would be to deny that God has already taken the field in his revelation of himself and that the Spirit, according to the same Johannine passage, does not speak on his own account but, remembering the word of Jesus, speaks what he has heard. Faith stands always, according to Heb. 11, in the continuity of the divine action and only sectarianism seeks to detach itself from this history. But it is necessary to distinguish between the continuity of the divine action and that of human tradition, even though it be Church tradition. They are not identical. Thus the fathers, to whom the Jews in the Fourth Gospel appeal, may not be played off against the present Christ. They are only his witnesses, as are the cloud of witnesses in Heb. 11, in so far as they receive their testimony from God and the Messiah respectively, and thus stand within the continuity of the presence of God. We finish up with an inescapable dialectic. The Spirit does not contradict the 'It is written . . .' but manifests himself in the Scripture. But Scripture itself can at any moment become 'the letter' and indeed does so as soon as it ceases to submit to the authorization of the Spirit and sets itself up as immediate Authority, seeking to replace the Spirit. The tension between Spirit and Scripture is constitutive: in other words, the canon is not simply to be identified with the Gospel and is only the Word of God in so far as it is and becomes the Gospel. Only within these limits is it the foundation of the unity of the Church. For the Gospel is the sole foundation of the one Church at all times and in all places.

But the question 'What is the Gospel?' cannot be settled by the historian according to the results of his investigations but only by the believer who is led by the Spirit and listens obediently to the Scripture. The unity of the Church is never immediately accessible; it exists only for faith. Like the Gospel, the unity of the Church is discerned not by saints already enjoying the beatific vision but by

those struggling *in via*; it is discerned by them among the confessions and in spite of their multiplicity: it is discerned along with and over against the New Testament canon: and the one condition of this discernment is that they hear and believe the Gospel.

V

THE PAULINE DOCTRINE OF THE LORD'S SUPPER[1]

RECENT researches into the problem of the Lord's Supper in the New Testament are almost completely determined by the fact that they seek to discover the original form of the Supper, and as a result are betrayed into reconstructions of varying degrees of plausibility. In contrast, the attempt to interpret the individual texts analytically is more and more falling into the background. It therefore seems appropriate to point out that, although the New Testament writings present us with differing accounts and views of the Lord's Supper, it is just by their varying understandings of it that they do so much to conceal its original content. Thus the question about the individual concerns and approaches of the different witnesses to the tradition must be clearly answered before the next question about the common origin of the tradition can be raised in any meaningful way. To this observation (which can unfortunately no longer be taken for granted) we must add a second. The present state of study makes it essential that the Pauline teaching about the Lord's Supper be grasped with sufficient historical and factual precision to provide a sure base for further penetration both backwards and forwards in time.

I

The attempt to shed light on Paul's teaching on the Lord's Supper from its links with Hellenistic cult-meals has completely broken down, so far as the essential issues are concerned. In I Cor. 10.19ff. Paul himself acknowledges this connexion and uses it for paraenetic and polemical purposes. Yet the existing analogies are limited to details which neither provide concrete historical proof that the connexion is one of dependence, nor permit us to expose adequately and in its full depth the conception implied in the

[1] First published in *EvTh* 7, 1947-48, pp. 263-83, under the title 'Anliegen und Eigenart der paulinischen Abendmahlslehre'.

Apostle's writings. It would be a mistake, however, to conclude from this that the existence of Hellenistic influence can be denied altogether. On the contrary, almost the whole of Paul's interpretation of the primitive Christian eucharistic tradition bears the mark of the fact that he has adopted and adapted the gnostic myth of an Archetypal Man, who is also the Redeemer; the same applies to the Pauline Christology. Only on this basis can we explain historically Paul's distinctive combination of the Sacrament and the Church as the Body of Christ.

Recently K. Stürmer[1] questioned this connexion with regard to I Cor. 10.16ff. in a very unconvincing argument. Certainly no one denies that the expressions κοινωνία τοῦ αἵματος and τοῦ σώματος τοῦ Χριστοῦ correspond, and that they refer to the elements of the Lord's Supper, which provide a means of participation in the blood and body of Christ. The problem arises with the transition to v. 17 with its conception of the Body of Christ in which we are not merely participants, but which we ourselves *are*. Stürmer simply ignores this shift of emphasis; yet everything depends on precisely this point, because it indicates that from now onwards the Apostle is giving his own interpretation to the tradition he has received. This interpretation suggests that participation in the body of Jesus makes us into the Body of Christ. There are other indications which confirm this. In v. 16 we meet with what is unmistakably already formulated sacramental terminology. That is why the Jewish expression ποτήριον τῆς εὐλογίας is taken up and used, why the term εὐλογεῖν appears in place of the more usual Pauline εὐχαριστεῖν and why the phrase 'the breaking of bread' occurs. Probably the formulae κοινωνία τοῦ αἵματος and τοῦ σώματος τοῦ Χριστοῦ also belong to this pre-Pauline eucharistic terminology. Since the Corinthians also recognize and acknowledge it, they have to answer in the affirmative the question put to them in v. 16. This verse contains the premises common to the Apostle and his church, and therefore makes use of the traditional primitive Christian sacramental language. To the question, 'What do the eucharistic cup and the eucharistic bread convey?' pre-Pauline thought had given the answer, 'Participation in the blood or body of Christ.' It had formulated both parts of its anwer in strict correspondence with each other in order to give expression to the

---

[1] 'Das Abendmahl bei Paulus', *EvTh* 7, 1947-48, pp. 50ff.

decisive fact that through the Supper we participate in Christ himself. Paul for his part agrees with this conception, but in v. 17 gives it a new turn. He no longer asks questions nor does he assume the agreement of the Corinthians. He begins simply to make affirmations and with the same abrupt intrusion into the argument and the same introduction of a strikingly new 'slant' as we frequently find when he is appending his own views to the exposition of the common kerygma. Having established this, we can now be clear as to why the cup is mentioned first and the bread afterwards. There is certainly no variation in the practice of the Church intended here. 11.23ff. show what order and sequence were traditionally maintained in the Pauline Church. The inversion of the normal sequence in 10.16 can only be explained by the fact that Paul wishes to shift the emphasis. His line of argument would not support the saying about the cup at the end of v. 16 because v. 17 could only be derived from the saying about the bread. Therefore the inversion of the normal order proves the same point as the terminology of v. 16; while Paul *refers* to the early Christian tradition in v.16, he *interprets* it in v. 17. Since the theme of the blood of Christ has not for him the same significance as the other New Testament writers, and he consistently employs it only in liturgically determined texts, he does not use it here as a point of departure. The traditional eucharistic terminology will allow him to derive the theologoumenon of the Church as the Body of Christ from the saying about the bread only. It is precisely this theologoumenon which is constitutive of his own conception of the Lord's Supper. If it is the element of the bread which, according to the traditional primitive Christian understanding, conveys participation in the Body of Christ, then the Apostle modifies this tradition to the point where participation in Jesus and his body becomes identical with incorporation into the Church as the Body of Christ.

Stürmer makes this objection: 'Although baptism also brings a person into relation with the unity of the Body of Christ (I Cor. 12.13) no one thinks of making this unity the point of departure for expounding the nature of baptism. On the contrary, general agreement prevails that the unity of the Body of Christ into which we are baptized is, according to Paul's understanding of it, a consequence and effect, not a presupposition, of baptism.'[1] This is a

[1] *Op cit.,* p. 51 n. 8.

surprising assertion. To begin with, it lacks precision because, by introducing the moment of unity into his line of argument, Stürmer has dislocated the formulation of the question in his first and second sentences. Again, it would be safer to speak of general agreement only when one's theses are tenable, and Stürmer's are not. The fact is that Paul's doctrine of baptism, as well as his doctrine of the Lord's Supper, must be interpreted in the light of his dominant theme—the Body of Christ. After all, according to the Apostle, Christ is 'put on' in baptism. Behind this turn of phrase lies not only the well-known metaphor of the body as a garment, but, behind this again, the gnostic myth with its conception of the giant body of the Archetypal Man, the Redeemer, which is likewise put on as a garment. Thus in I Cor. 12.13 εἰς ἓν σῶμα βαπτισθῆναι can be substituted for Χριστὸν ἐνδύσασθαι. Both have sprung from the same roots, and their content is identical. Baptism, like the Lord's Supper, according to Paul, effects incorporation into the Body of Christ. For him that is an exact expression of what takes place in the Sacrament. And if we put on the Body of Christ or are baptized into it, this Body is therefore already there before our faith and baptism, just as Christ is present prior to our faith. Nor is the unity of this Body based on baptism. According to I Cor. 12.13 we are baptized into the unity of the Body. Unity therefore is not the result of our coming together, but the sign manual of Christ. Hence, unity does not grow out of the members of the Body as if it could be thought of quantitatively as the sum of them, but it is qualitatively the identity of Christ with himself in all his members. If unity were the consequence of baptism, it could hardly be a matter to be taken seriously before the Parousia. If this were the case, Church history would have to be understood as a process of development towards this unity; no single congregation could be addressed, as in Paul, as the Body of Christ, and the Church would in the last resort be nothing more than a sociological phenomenon.

It is obviously difficult for modern modes of thought to assimilate this material, however clear it may be from the exegetical angle. This is presumably why we are unwilling to let the questionable expression 'the mystical Body of Christ' go. We have ceased to have any understanding of what the expositors mean by 'mystical'. Certainly it cannot be denied that at this point Pauline terminology is derived from the tradition of the gnostic piety of the Mysteries. But that by no means implies that the Apostle continued to attach to the terms he employed the same meaning which they no doubt bore when used by the Gnostics. Such an assumption would prejudge a theological issue of the utmost consequence. For instance, if we follow Stürmer[1] we are led to the proposition: Paul has no conception of the 'mystical blood of Jesus' and therefore, since there is complete correspondence in his eucharistic texts between body and blood, he could not have expressed any conception of the mystical body. This correspondence is certainly present in v. 16, and its theological weight ought not to be disputed. We may presuppose that the early Christian tradition which Paul quotes here does attach equal importance to the two clauses under discussion. We may, however, question whether Paul himself held the same view. Our text seems to indicate the contrary, since the inversion of the sequence lays greater stress on the text about the bread and offers to the Apostle the opportunity to add v. 17, which for him is the decisive sentence. Why this differentiation should represent a 'most doubtful venture from the methodological point of view'[2] is not apparent. For methodology has surely not finished its work when it has established the juxtaposition in our text of the two sayings about the body and blood of Jesus; it must go on to enquire into the reasons for this combination and its significance for Paul himself; it must then substantiate the shift of thought which we have alleged to follow in v. 17 and draw the logical consequences from it. If, in doing this, we find that Paul has gone beyond the premises of the primitive Christian conception of the Lord's Supper quoted in v. 16; if we find that in v. 17 he is ventilating the same theological interest which also lies behind his doctrine of baptism—namely, the Christian community as the Body of Christ—then we shall have arrived by this route at the heart of his own theological conception. This means that, instead of having to be satisfied with what illumination can be thrown on the background of this conception by the comparative history of religion, we shall have to determine more exactly its specifically theological significance.

[1] *Op. cit.,* p. 51.
[2] *Op. cit.,* p. 51 n. 6.

2

The parallelism between the Pauline utterances on Baptism and those on the Lord's Supper can be traced a significant step further. In I Cor. 12.13 the baptismal event—incorporation into the Body of Christ—is ascribed to the operation of the one Spirit. The same idea recurs in a modified form at the end of the verse: καὶ πάντες ἓν πνεῦμα ἐποτίσθημεν. It is admittedly debatable whether this last phrase applies to Baptism or, as seems more likely, to the Lord's Supper. But even if we adopt the former interpretation, we cannot get away from the fact that Paul does actually apply the same expression to the Supper in 10.3f. For βρῶμα and πόμα πνευματικόν undoubtedly mean 'food and drink which convey πνεῦμα'. This is why it is immediately suggested that the rock which followed was spiritual, i.e. Christ himself, who is again identified with πνεῦμα in II Cor. 3.17. The gift takes on the character of the Giver and through the gift we become partakers of the Giver himself. And this is also the sense of those passages[1] which expressly characterize the πνεῦμα as the baptismal gift. The πνεῦμα is thus the sacramental gift without qualification just as we found that incorporation into the Body of Christ was the sacramental gift without qualification. Are these propositions self-contradictory? Not at all. Paul can include them both in one sentence in I Cor. 12.13: ἐν ἑνὶ πνεύματι . . . εἰς ἓν σῶμα ἐβαπτίσθημεν. The gift is at once instrument and effective power just because it is participation in the Giver himself. In giving himself to us as πνεῦμα the Christ incorporates us into his Body. And if the parallelism at this point between Baptism and the Lord's Supper must be conceded, this thought must also be seen as the keynote of I Cor. 10.3f. Strangely enough, Stürmer[2] maintains that 'Paul never describes the elements in the Lord's Supper as πνευματικὸν βρῶμα and πόμα but reserves this description for the miraculous food and drink given to the people of Israel in the wilderness.' Why Paul does not speak of food and drink 'which God has given to man for his salvation', although this is his real meaning and could have been easily expressed in Greek, Stürmer does not reveal. But exegetical questions are not settled by apodictic statements and specious

[1] E.g. I Cor. 6.11; 12.13; II Cor. 1.22.
[2] *Op. cit.*, p. 58 n. 34.

play on words. However certain it may be that the gift of the πνεῦμα has something to do with our salvation, it is even more certain that πνευματικόν does *not* mean 'given for salvation'. And it is not true that the reference in 10.3f. is to Israel alone as Stürmer thinks. Israel is undoubtedly the type of the Christian people of God, to whom a warning example is here being held up. The Christian experience of saving event is thus exemplified in Israel. The whole trend of the passage is designed to present not mere similarities between, but the identity of, the old and new saving events. For this reason Christ becomes the rock which accompanies the wanderings of the Israelites, Moses is depicted as the forerunner and type of the Messiah and the extraordinary expression 'be baptized into Moses' can appear as a construction analogical with 'be baptized into Christ'. For this reason, too, the saving events of the journey through sea and wilderness are applied to Baptism and the Lord's Supper, i.e. interpreted sacramentally. Only the establishment of the identity between past and present saving events gives force to the paraenesis which follows and enables the important conclusion to be drawn that even sacraments do not guarantee salvation. Once that is clear, we begin to sense that behind the expressions πνευματικόν βρῶμα and πόμα there lies a primitive Christian eucharistic theology which Paul has taken up and used in this passage.

In any event, the conclusions we have reached provide us for the purposes of our chapter with a sufficient answer to the hotly debated question whether, according to Paul, the Lord's Supper conveys participation in the dying or in the exalted Lord. They answer it unequivocally in the latter sense. Because the Lord is the *Pneuma* and because in the sacrament the exalted Lord conveys, along with his gift, participation in himself as the Giver, therefore the gift of the sacrament must also be *Pneuma*. And so we are incorporated into the Body of the exalted Lord by means of this gift operating as effective power. Through the Spirit of Christ, I become a member of the Body of Christ.

3

This conclusion must extend into the wider area of all those Pauline passages in which the Apostle speaks dialectically, now of 'Christ in us', now of 'we in Christ'. The meaning of these expres-

sions has already been made clear by what has been said. We are in
Christ as members of his Body. And we become members of his
Body because the Christ enters into us as *Pneuma*. Both movements
coincide in the sacramental act and, whenever they are mentioned,
a reference back to this sacramental act is implicit.

We have now arrived at a point from which we can begin to
deal with the key question which has so far remained unanswered.
What meaning can these utterances, so alien to the thought of
contemporary man, have for him? Paul is falling back on traditions which are familiar to us from the world of Hellenistic
Gnosis. There, too, the doctrine of man's transformation through
the power of *pneuma* is proclaimed. Moreover, this transformation
is depicted as a kind of natural process. For *pneuma* is seen in
Hellenistic thought as heavenly matter, very delicate in quality,
which has the capacity to penetrate man's being and, in so doing,
to endow him with a new nature. As the σάρξ, the earthly matter,
stands in a cosmic context and forms a universal unity, while yet
existing in many different manifestations and contained in many
different vessels, so correspondingly does the πνεῦμα, the substance
of the world of light in *its* sphere. It is not confined and isolated
within its individual vessels but stands, with each of its parts and
manifestations, in the living context of the Whole which consists
of the heavenly world and nature, i.e. in the unity of the divine.
This is why the myths can speak of the unity of the body of the
Archetypal Man who is also the Redeemer, a body which embraces
countless members. This unity is based on a common participation
in the same heavenly substance—the *pneuma*—and consists in the
identity with itself of the divine substance, which remains always
and everywhere the same. We have here admittedly only one side
of the picture. For one of the most important elements in the
Hellenistic world-view is this: while its thought moves invariably
in naturalistic and physical categories, even when seeking to
apprehend heavenly reality, yet in the last resort it is not really
interested in matter. Over the whole area of Hellenistic philosophy
substance is always the substratum of some energy. But the earthly
and the heavenly worlds are filled with forces which either combine or conflict. These forces are not immaterial. They carry within
themselves the drive towards corporeality and thus can only be
fully realized in bodily form. Divine forces are actualized in some

form of *pneuma*, just as earthly forces manifest themselves as σάρξ. Hellenism knows no energy without a material substratum, but this serves only as a basis, as a mode of subsistence, for the energy which operates through it. The opposition between heaven and earth is therefore seen as the opposition between two different categories of matter. But the differing substances are only the expression of opposing energies which are actualized in different substrata. Thus heaven and earth do not merely stand and stare at each other blankly without making contact, but engage in a never-ending conflict—that of σάρξ with πνεῦμα. Man is the object of this struggle between the powers. He came into being when earthly matter managed to seize for itself elements of the heavenly world and thus acquired life: similarly he finds redemption when the *pneuma* invades his earthly nature and recaptures him for the heavenly world. The state of being resulting from this event is called 'metamorphosis'. While it only comes to final fruition in death, which is liberation from earthly matter, it nevertheless has a proleptic fulfilment in the cultic act. Men saw no reason to doubt the reality of this cultic transformation, although they continued visibly to bear about with them their earthly nature. There was no need for doubt, for the experience of divine power bore its own witness within them and in its infusion they saw guaranteed an unbreakable link with the heavenly world. Conversely, this link with the heavenly world would not have seemed to the devotee to be truly established, had the divine power not already taken bodily possession of him in the cultic act and transformed him in the very core of his existence by what was conceived of as a process of nature. This alone held out to him the pledge of eternal salvation, i.e. of complete freedom from the σάρξ and perfect existence in the πνεῦμα after death.

Our justification for keeping such considerations as these in mind in connexion with Paul's doctrine of the Lord's Supper lies simply in the fact that the Corinthians themselves were obviously viewing the Christian sacraments in a similar light. It is only when we see Paul in conflict with a conception of the sacrament as φάρμακον ἀθανασίας that we begin to grasp his own position. His purpose in portraying Israel as the first recipient of the Christian sacraments in I Cor. 10.1–13 is this: to refute the opinion of the Corinthian enthusiasts that the sacramental *opus operatum* is a pledge of the impossibility of damnation now or in the future. On his side the Apostle stresses with unmistakable sharpness that the sacrament does *not* provide insurance against apostasy or against the divine rejection. A guarantee of salvation is just what it is *not*; on the contrary it is, as 10.5ff. makes clear, a call to obedience, the possibility of a decision for faith and against the temptation to disobedience. But if this interpretation is correct, it is equivalent to saying that, in this passage at least, Paul has made a radical break with the tradition of Hellenistic Gnosis and its religion of redemption, as this was being maintained in Corinth. In any event, the sacramental act in his teaching is no longer understood as a kind of natural process.

But how then can the Apostle continue to avail himself of the terminology of this Hellenistic religion of redemption and make use of gnostic mythology to expound his doctrine of Christ, of the Church and of the sacrament? His very doctrine of *Pneuma* itself is incomprehensible without some insight into its Hellenistic presuppositions and he even speaks in exactly the same terms as his Hellenistic environment of a transformation of men by the *Pneuma*.[1] A representative selection from the Pauline proclamation will give us all the material we need here for the investigation of such questions. We must first note carefully that Paul, in common with his contemporaries and rather in contrast to classical antiquity, has ceased to isolate human existence for observation; it is no longer something objective to be schematized and manipulated, to be divided up into reality and appearance, form and matter, interior and exterior, soul and body (with all the latter's manifold components). Human existence is for him no longer autonomous, it is determined by its involvement in its universe; it is both the object and the arena of the strife between heavenly and earthly powers. It is conditioned by the answer to the question: 'To which power do you belong? Which Lord do you serve?' Because man can undergo a change of lordship, the possibility of an existential transformation exists. And this is precisely what does happen in the sacramental event, when we are endowed with the gift of the *Pneuma*. Certainly Paul—and here again he is in agreement with his Hellenistic environment—does not conceive *Pneuma* as a mere disembodied force, but gives it a corporeal substratum. Thus it is for

[1] Cf. Rom. 12.2; II Cor. 3.18; Gal. 4.19; Rom. 8.29.

him the substance of resurrection corporeality and the dimension in which the Risen One exists. But this emphasis immediately disappears behind another, a dominant one. As we have already seen, the sacramental gift of the *Pneuma* is not for the Apostle some heavenly power, which enters man in some vague and impersonal manner. This gift brings with it its Giver; it is an epiphany of the exalted Lord, who becomes manifest in it. Through it we are brought into his presence and thereafter we stand 'before his face'. In the *Pneuma*, the *Kyrios* comes to us, takes possession of us and claims us for his own. This does not mean that a new element is added to our being which it did not possess before and which may now become the seed of a process of development. Such a view would separate the gift from the Giver and make of it an impersonal heavenly force, perhaps even a substance, a φάρμακον ἀθανασίας. In this particular matter it is Paul's *articulum stantis et cadentis ecclesiae* that, wherever he describes the *Pneuma* as a sacramental gift, there he is speaking most radically of the revelation of Christ himself, of his self-manifestation and his presence. Therefore Baptism is a putting-on *of* Christ and an incorporation *into* Christ. Therefore the Lord's Supper dispenses πνευματικὸν βρῶμα and πόμα from the spiritual rock which is Christ. Therefore the sacrament effects the transformation of man. Because my existence is not determined by myself but by whoever is my Lord at any given time, therefore the sacrament mediates the new existence by giving me the new Lord, the one true *Kyrios* beyond and above all the lordships of the world. And therefore we are entitled at this point to speak at last of incorporation into the Body of Christ. The Body of Christ is not a sociological structure, it is not merely the sum of his members. But neither is it for Paul, as it had been for the Gnostics, a metaphysical structure, accessible only to the techniques of mysticism: it is not therefore the homogeneity of all the elements of the world of light. The members do not constitute either the Body itself or its unity, because this Body receives its character as well as its unity from the *Kyrios* alone. He is the very *Kyrios* himself both in the diffusion of his universal power and in the recapitulation of all that belongs to him—in short, the dominion of the Christ. Wherever the *Kyrios* is present in the *Pneuma*, there he claims men for his dominion. But this is neither a natural process nor a mystical one. The *Kyrios* reaches out for me by claiming my will for himself, thus making me an instrument of *his* will and a member of his kingdom. Obedience is the new dimension in which the Christian exists and into which he is translated by the sacramental epiphany of the Christ. And this obedience is no *character indelibilis*, but the possibility of truly free decision and therefore also the possibility of apostasy. The sacrament does not guarantee salvation: it establishes both the possibility of obedience and the necessity for it. This new obedience is the gift of the *Kyrios* and the heavenly dimension, while earthly existence is rooted in disobedience.

Thus Paul shares the premises of his time and yet draws different conclusions from them. Hellenism already regarded the world and humanity as the arena and the object of the struggle between flesh and spirit, already held existence to be determined by its bondage to one or other of these two powers and was already familiar with cultic acts in which the heavenly realm, acting through *pneuma*, took possession of man and incorporated him into itself. Hellenism, however, knew only cosmic powers and could therefore only describe redemption as a species of natural process and, in so doing, reveal the fatalistic character of this process. But Paul knows the Lord, who does not reign as Necessity, but, according to II Cor. 3.18, dispenses freedom: the freedom to decide between obedience and disobedience. Therefore the sacrament mediates for him not Fate, but the possibility of obedience as *the* eschatological gift and, at the same time, as responsibility 'before the face of Jesus Christ'.

4

Will the results we have so far arrived at still stand if we are obliged to widen our field of observation and analysis to include I Cor. 11.17ff.?[1] What is immediately striking about this passage is the frequency with which juridical or legal concepts and turns of phrase occur: συνέρχεσθαι is the acknowledged term in antiquity for the official assembling of the *demos*, the 'people', and has obviously been taken over to denote the assembling of the Christian community for worship at the Lord's Supper. The antithesis between κυριακόν and ἴδιον δεῖπνον is so strongly emphasized

---

[1] I limit myself here to clarifying my interpretation of this passage in *Abendmahls-gemeinschaft*, 1937, pp. 81ff.; so far as possible I have avoided repetition.

that we are led to recall the constitutional use of the first adjective. Neither can we help noticing the stress laid towards the end of the passage on the verb κρίνειν and its derivatives; ἀναξίως (in its formal meaning—'not appropriate') and ἔνοχος are both surely to be understood in a legal sense. If καταγγέλλειν is to be translated 'proclaim', that fits in admirably with what has steadily come to be accepted as the meaning of διαθήκη—'decree' or 'ordinance'. God's eschatological ordinance must be proclaimed on earth, and this is exactly what the assembled Christian community does when it celebrates the Eucharist. παραλαμβάνειν and παραδιδόναι may safely be taken as the equivalents of the rabbinic terms *qibel* and *masar,* which connote the unbroken and legitimate succession of tradition and at the same time define the content of the tradition as authentic revelation. The account of the Last Supper is thus a formulation of sacred Law. Against this background, I should like to bring out two individual details in sharper relief than is usually the case. Since Lietzmann there has been frequent discussion of the question as to whether the command to repeat the actions of the Last Supper and with it the concept of ἀνάμνησις, which occurs in this command, are to be seen in the light of the usage customary in Hellenistic memorial feasts. In my judgment, even if this hypothesis is not rejected out of hand, it should only be applied within the most stringent limits and can at the most do no more than provide some justification for the derivation of the concept of ἀνάμνησις from the source suggested. If we take at all seriously Paul's ascription of a sacramental character to the Lord's Supper, it is plain that he cannot have regarded it in the light of a memorial meal of this kind. We must not overlook the further fact that the sense of ἀνάμνησις is so strongly determined by καταγγέλλειν which immediately follows that the translation 'remembrance' seems too weak. A good parallel to the usage here may be seen in εἰς μνημόσυνον αὐτῆς (Mark 14.9) which incapsulates in similar fashion a foreseen effect of the proclamation of the Gospel, but which can only have this effect if the 'memorial' alluded to is already a component part of this proclamation. In the same way, the 'memorial' of the divine act of salvation is perpetuated in Jewry by the recitation of the Passover *haggadah* during the festal meal. When the primitive Church inferred from the command to repeat the actions (and especially from the concluding words) the necessity of adding the so-called Anamnesis to the Words of Institution, it also gave expression to a conception of ἀνάμνησις which saw it as complete only when it issued in a confession of faith. Finally, the LXX version of Ps. 110.3f. lends support to this view in its use of ἐξομολόγησις and μνείαν ποιεῖν as parallel terms. From all this, I conclude that the command to repeat the actions does not merely bind the community to celebrate the Lord's Supper regularly and thus to keep alive in a literalistic way the meaning of the death of Jesus, but places upon it at the same time the obligation to proclaim the redemptive meaning of this death, as Paul himself lays down in his concluding gloss (v. 26) and as the liturgy of the Lord's Supper (no doubt already in existence by this time) effectually does.

The second consideration I should like to raise at this point is concerned with the introduction to the Words of Institution. As a purely historical reminiscence, the phrase 'in the night in which he was betrayed' appears somewhat threadbare. It can kindle a sense of 'being there' only in those to whom the details of the Passion narrative are already very familiar. Is that in fact what it is intended to do for the hearer? It seems to me that to interpret it in this way is to read overly modern shades of feeling into the text. Therefore I should prefer to adopt as a starting-point the thesis that here there is being handed on to the community an obligatory formula of sacred Law, the unimpeachable validity of which corresponds to its content and to the sacred nature of the action set in motion by this content. If this is so, it is reasonable to maintain as the next stage in the argument that the solemn naming of the Lord at the beginning is intended to establish without possibility of misunderstanding the authority on which the eucharistic action is based and from which the formula here being handed on receives its sanction. The expressly stated datum, which is an essential component of this sacred formula, would then be intended to define the *terminus a quo* of the validity both of action and formula; it would, in brief, bring out the character of the sacrament as something instituted and delimited by the Lord himself. Further support for this reconstruction is provided by the Apostle's use of the phrase ἄχρι οὗ ἔλθῃ in v. 26 as a *terminus ad quem*. It is all that remains of that eschatological expectation connected with the Supper, which we encounter in the Synoptists and in the *Didache*. Of course the rite has still an eschatological setting. But the balance has shifted. The sacrament is no longer primarily an anticipation of the eschatological banquet, but an ordinance appertaining to the Church and therefore tied to the 'time of the Church', which stretches from the death of Jesus to the Parousia. Because this is so, the shape of the eucharistic action is subject not to the unfettered judgment of the community, but to the ordinance guaranteed by the tradition, going back directly to the will of the Founder, valid until the Parousia and persisting in the form into which it has been cast by the formula. What purpose has this demonstration served? It has underlined the significance of the antithesis between the κυριακὸν δεῖπνον and any ἴδιον δεῖπνον. The Corinthians are obviously celebrating the Eucharist as an earthly anticipation of the banquet of the blessed in heaven just as, according to ch. 15, they hold that the day of ἀνάστασις has already dawned. They are conscious of themselves as the redeemed and fondly imagine themselves to be no longer *in via*. But now they are being called to order. They are being told that they do not yet stand where the banquet of the blessed may rightly be celebrated: they stand where the Lord's Supper has its appointed place, its clearly defined and obligatory shape and its unambiguous meaning —they stand between the death of Jesus and his Parousia.

What this means in concrete terms is now stated in vv. 27ff. Paul is speaking here out of the fullness of his apostolic authority, by virtue of which he is responsible for the ordering of the community and of its worship. Thus the decretal-like style of the passage cannot be called accidental. The introduction (v. 27) is in the form of a threat of judgment. But this description does not really convey the full force of the sentence. The Apostle is not merely threatening; he is formulating a law, the validity of which will be disclosed only on the Last Day. This is the sense of the eschatological future ἔσται. Bread and cup, body and blood of the Lord correspond to each other in strict analogy. These 'dimensions' are obviously identical, but the nature of this identity is mysterious and it may never be rationalized. Yet if the worshipper does not reckon with this identity, he is behaving ἀναξίως, that is, not so much 'unworthily' as, quite literally, 'inappropriately'. Paul surely employs the striking expression 'bread and cup of the Lord' in order to indicate how easily πνευματικὸν βρῶμα and πόμα can be confused with profane food and drink. This food and this drink can take on spiritual character and thus become identical with the body and blood of the Lord only because the *Kyrios* himself effects it. Following our earlier interpretation of the sacramental event, we may say: it is the presence of the Lord who is using this means to manifest himself. Therefore any worshipper is behaving himself inappropriately at the Eucharist who does not reckon with the self-manifestation of the Lord and therefore who is not in fact celebrating the κυριακὸν δεῖπνον. Further, he is guilty of 'the body and blood of the Lord'—which can have no other meaning than 'the death of Jesus'. In face of the self-manifestation of the Christ there are only two possibilities open—either to unite with the Christian community in proclaiming the death of Jesus or to unite with the world in bringing it about. And to fail to perceive this self-manifestation involves just this—becoming guilty, along with the world, of the death of Jesus. It is precisely at the Lord's Supper that this last possibility arises for the Christian and therefore it is essential to call the communicants to self-examination in v. 28 in the same solemn fashion as has already been done in 10.12. This warning must certainly seem paradoxical enough to those who think that they 'stand' and that they are already celebrating the banquet of the blessed *in patria*. But it is fully comprehensible within the framework of a *theologia crucis* in which a sacrament does not provide a guarantee of salvation but the possibility of obedience and with it a life of trial. And it is comprehensible also within the framework of a *theologia viatorum* which sees Christians as travelling towards the Parousia and therefore towards the Last Judgment. For this is now the direction of the thought of the passage, leading us on to vv. 29ff. Throughout the whole letter the Enthusiasts are being belaboured with two hard facts—the Cross and the Parousia (which involves the Judgment). Both are encountered in the sacrament in the closest proximity to each other. Verse 29 expresses this with such enigmatic brevity that later copyists felt bound to interpolate glosses into their readings, qualifying the subject by an ἀναξίως assimilated from v. 27 and adding a τοῦ κυρίου at the end of the sentence. However intelligible the reasons for these additions, the additions themselves only deprive the sentence of its point and make it into a flat repetition of v. 27. In fact, a warning is being uttered to those who are on the threshold of the danger area mapped out by ἀναξίως or who have already entered it. They are eating and drinking judgment to themselves. The progress of the argument in comparison with v. 27 is marked by the present tense of the verbs. The parting of ways which will be clearly revealed at the Last Day is already present in some measure in the sacrament. And to this extent the sentence provides both the grounds for the admonition about self-examination in v. 28 and the introduction to v. 30. For the last verse confirms the reality of what is stated in v. 29 by appealing to concrete examples which seem to be causing disquiet in the community. There are a number of illnesses and even deaths, and Paul ascribes these occurrences to the inappropriate behaviour of the Corinthians at the Lord's Supper. Are we compelled to understand by this that the spiritual food and the spiritual drink prove themselves to be poison wherever they are not respected and used as φαρμακόν ἀθανασίας? It can hardly be denied that this interpretation, for which massive verification can be found in the comparative study of religion, approximates closely to Hellenistic thinking and therefore to the views of the Corinthians. And indeed it is possible to maintain that Paul is himself arguing against the background of a philosophy of this kind. For 10.12 is also designed to show that the cult-meal sets the partakers in a dangerous field of force. The related concept of κοινωνία which is to be found there is introduced to convey the sense of falling into a sphere of domination; our translations 'participation' or even 'fellowship' are thus much too weak, because the concept is intended to describe the experience of forcible seizure, of the overwhelming power of superior forces.[1] And yet such an interpretation does not do justice to the Apostle's modification of the Hellenistic outlook. We have already seen that the Pauline doctrine of the sacraments is not determined by the view that impersonal, divine power is conveyed to man in the sacrament, but by the view that it is the locus of a self-manifestation of the Christ. This insight receives further confirmation here. It alone can account for the enigmatic brevity of v. 29. For that verse, rather in contrast to what is suggested by the eschatological future in v. 27, declares that judgment is already present and effective in the completed action of the Lord's Supper. And the later interpolation of ἀναξίως underlines the fact that Paul seems primarily to be making a generalization. The offence taken by

---

[1] *Abendmahlsgemeinschaft*, pp. 77f.

later critics at the verse ought to make us pay particular attention to this fact. How could Paul have expressed himself with such apparent ambiguity as to lend countenance to the view that every partaker of the Supper stands under judgment? Because, from a certain angle, that is, in fact, the case. The self-manifestation of the *Kyrios* is at the same time that of the universal Judge. Because his gift cannot be separated from himself, this gift does not merely convey impersonal death-or-life-bringing powers. Because, on the contrary, it brings with it the Giver himself, indifference towards it is impossible. His presence can never leave us unchanged. We do not, by our own lack of reverence, render his gift ineffective nor turn the presence of Christ into absence. We cannot paralyse God's eschatological action; salvation despised becomes judgment. Not to belong to the Christian community which extols the death of Jesus is to belong to the world which compasses that death. Wherever the Saviour is scorned, the Judge of the world nevertheless remains and manifests himself in that very place as the one from whose revealed presence we can find no way of escape. Wherever we do not truly partake of him and allow ourselves to be incorporated into his kingdom, according to 10.22 we are provoking the *Kyrios* to display his power of judgment and death and to meet us as the one stronger than we. It is of just this encounter that, according to v. 30, the frightened Corinthians are witnesses.

The significance of the accumulation of juridical and legal concepts and formularies in our text now becomes explicit. Their coincidence is not accidental but arises directly out of the Apostle's Christology. The sacramental self-manifestation of the *Kyrios* is not something which can be the matter of arbitrary human decision. It invariably sets men in the perspective of the Last Day and therefore bears within itself the marks of the divine action which will characterize that Day. It is thus a kind of anticipation of the Last Day within the community. What is happening here is certainly not a natural process on some higher metaphysical plane, but neither is it an historical event within the frontiers of cosmic immanence. Here we encounter him, in whom election and rejection encounter us; so that, according to our attitude to him, we choose one or the other for ourselves. And that means that, in the sacrament, while the Spirit is certainly given, at the same time a definite form of justice comes into operation, the justice of the Last Day, i.e. the justice of the Lord and Judge of the world in all places of his dominion. The Corinthians have to be reminded of this particular content of the Supper because in their enthusiasm they fondly imagine that they have been withdrawn from the jurisdiction of this justice and the tribunal which administers it. The self-manifestation of Christ calls men to obedience and this means that, at the same time, it calls them to account before the final Judge who is already today acting within his community as he will act towards the world on the Last Day—he bestows salvation by setting men within his lordship and, if they spurn this lordship, they then experience this act of rejection as a self-incurred sentence of death.

It is from this standpoint that the phrase $\mu\grave{\eta}$ $\delta\iota\alpha\kappa\rho\acute{\iota}\nu\omega\nu$ $\tau\grave{o}$ $\sigma\tilde{\omega}\mu\alpha$ in v. 29 must be understood. Every partaker of the Supper experiences the $\kappa\rho\acute{\iota}\mu\alpha$ to this extent, that he is confronted with the Judge of all. The concrete effect of this is that, according to v. 31, each man is subjected to an $\dot{\epsilon}\alpha\upsilon\tau\grave{o}\nu$ $\delta\iota\alpha\kappa\rho\acute{\iota}\nu\epsilon\iota\nu$. The presence of the Judge compels those who are thus confronted to judge themselves. For only the lost need salvation; and we can only lay hold of the Saviour as the one who has been crucified by our guilt. Not to judge ourselves means not to heed the Saviour and therefore to fall into the hands of the Judge and to be condemned with the world. By judging ourselves in the present, we escape the judgment which otherwise the Judge himself passes on us, as is already happening in Corinth. It is true that the fact that judgment is already being carried out in Corinth is not so exclusively related to the sacrament as punishment is to guilt. This judgment is carried out in the persons of members of the community and also on the basis of the sacrament and yet, even in its deadly seriousness, it still permits some of the grace revealed in the sacrament to appear. As in 3.15 and 5.5, grace gains through judgment itself a last chance of saving the guilty and preserving him from being condemned with the world. The judgment executed in the present is—although Paul says this expressly only in this one context—the 'pedagogical' work of grace which snatches us away from the judgment to come. The Apostle is obviously concerned to make clear to the Corinthians the dialectic which the sacrament brings into action. The play on the verb $\kappa\rho\acute{\iota}\nu\epsilon\iota\nu$ and its derivatives is designed to hint that we can only receive grace from the Judge alone and yet the Judge is he whom we encounter as our salvation in the sacrament. So great is this grace that, even when it is exercising judgment, it is still working towards its own proper end. And, conversely, so solemn a matter is this grace that it can condemn a man to death; and not only that, but a man can never encounter it at all without also encountering judgment and this is true above all of the communicant. When I conduct myself 'appropriately' at the Eucharist I receive salvation straight from the hand of the Judge himself and therefore as one who must 'examine' and 'judge' himself lest grace be turned in him to condemnation.

The words μὴ διακρίνων τὸ σῶμα show us where this last possibility becomes actuality. Here, too, Paul is obviously speaking dialectically. It is clear that διακρίνειν is not being used in the same sense as in v. 31, but means something like 'distinguish', 'differentiate', 'bring into relief'. And yet it is through the deliberate choice of the same verb that the essential relation of this verse to vv. 28 and 31 is brought out. Thus the body which is under discussion here is not being apprehended in its true nature if it does not impel the participant to the self-examination of v. 28 and the self-judgment of v. 31. It is this body which moves us to judge ourselves or else brings down upon us the κρίμα of the Judge. It does not seem to me to be possible to refer τὸ σῶμα to anything other than the sacramental element of the bread of the Lord's Supper. This makes it all the more striking that Paul does not include a mention of the blood of the Lord, as he does in v. 27. We may deduce from 10.16f. one reason for this omission. The element of the body in the Supper has a deeper significance for Paul himself than that of the blood because it affords him a better foundation for his own conception of the Supper. We can therefore tell that the Eucharist is regarded in this verse also as the gift of the exalted Christ, because in it the self-manifestation of the Judge follows immediately on participation. Yet we cannot be completely satisfied with these findings. Rather, the concise formulation of v. 29c urgently requires an exact interpretation of the Words of Institution themselves.

5

Let us begin from the words over the cup, since their meaning cannot be called into question.[1] For the sense of ἡ καινὴ διαθήκη in Paul is univocal. Καινός here is to be understood eschatologically as that which never grows old and is therefore final; the use of the expression itself undoubtedly goes back to Jer. 31.31ff. The new *diatheke* is synonymous with Christ's making of the kingdom of God into an already present reality. It can hardly be accidental that Luke 22.29 uses διατίθεσθαι as the verb to describe the establishment of the divine order and does so in close connexion with the idea of βασιλεία: the expression ἀποκαθιστάνειν τὴν βασιλείαν in Acts 1.6 must also belong to the same framework of reference. The death of Jesus therefore is the foundation on which the order of the divine kingdom is set up; as in II Cor. 3 this order is the antitype of the Mosaic *diatheke*. The eucharistic cup mediates participation in this divine order because it mediates participation in the death of Jesus on which the order is based. For however we may finally decide to interpret the ἐστίν of the Synoptists, about which disagreement has been so lasting and so violent, there is no problem in Paul, inasmuch as the Apostle has himself interpreted it in 10.16ff. by the use of the κοινωνία concept. Any purely symbolic interpretation is thus excluded *ab initio*. We have therefore no right to speak of 'figurative expressions', of 'imagery' or of 'sayings accompanying parabolic actions'. Indeed we can discover what kind of logical status this ἐστίν has within the framework of the Pauline view of the sacrament simply by inspecting the sentence ἡ πέτρα δὲ ἦν ὁ Χριστός in 10.4, where an inanimate object is similarly identified with Christ. Typology employs ἐστίν in the words of Institution, as well perhaps as in Gal. 4.24, to establish that a relationship or a person is represented by another relationship or person. By expounding the ἐστίν of the Words of Institution in terms of κοινωνία, Paul makes it quite clear that from his angle it is simply not possible to distinguish between the two dimensions in question in the way in which modern thought distinguishes between a thing and its image. According to the understanding of antiquity, the representing dimension does actually bring about the presence of what is represented and therefore mediates participation in it. Thus, whatever objections may be raised against the term 'Real Presence', it expresses exactly what Paul wants to say.

[1] Cf. *Abendmahlgemeinschaft*, pp. 84ff.

But we can no longer ignore the disparity between the words over the bread and those over the cup. This disparity, which is particularly striking in Paul, results from the fact that not only is the blood never mentioned without an interpretative gloss, but even then it is only used attributively. We shall only be in a position to solve the problem raised by this fact when we have taken account of the various possible interpretations of the σῶμα concept in the bread formula. For this purpose the procedure of exhuming some alleged Aramaic parallel is of very doubtful value, so long as no such parallel can be adduced with absolute certainty and the structure of the Pauline narrative of the Institution with its un-Aramaic turn of phrase τὸ ὑπὲρ ὑμῶν[1] stands in the way of the hypothesis of an original Aramaic text. Even if we did not want to rule such an hypothesis completely out of court, it would still not help us to understand Paul's own use of σῶμα. And this is precisely our concern at this point.

This means that we should do well not to accept so uncritically as is often the case today the translation of σῶμα by 'person' as being self-evidently correct. We may grant that the individual concepts of Pauline anthropology are not intended to designate different parts of man but the whole man with his various possibilities and relationships;[2] thus these concepts are frequently interchangeable with 'I'. But even while we grant all this, we may not, however, forget that the fulcrum of the personality in Paul may be expressed by καρδία but certainly not by σῶμα. In so far as the Apostle employs this latter concept in any special sense, he uses it to denote the corporeality of human life, organic to the creation, claimed by God as his own by right, yet threatened by the cosmic powers. That God does in fact lay claim to human bodies and their obedience is the burden of the baptismal instruction in Rom. 6.12ff. and is also brought up with great emphasis against the Enthusiasts in I Cor. 6.13ff. No New Testament writer stresses more than Paul that the resurrection of the body is the goal of all the divine action and that therefore to this extent corporeality is the end of all the ways of God. It is for this reason that when the Apostle wants to portray the new aeon created and ruled by Christ, he goes for his terminology not to the gnostic

---

[1] Dalman, *Jesus-Jeshua*, ET, 1929, pp. 144f.
[2] Bultmann, *RGG*[2] IV, 1930, cols. 1032f.

myth of the world-soul but to that of the Archetypal Man, who is also the Redeemer, with his immense body. The Body of Christ is the realm into which we are incorporated with our bodies and to which we are called to render service in the body, i.e. total service, service which embraces all our different relationships in and to the world. Bearing all these associations in mind, we can only para-phrase the bread formula as 'This is I myself' if we do not take τὸ σῶμά μου in the very exact sense in which it was intended. And if we do not do this, we shall certainly be misunderstanding Paul. Just because he is using σῶμα in this exact sense, he can afford to leave the interpretative gloss τὸ ὑπὲρ ὑμῶν hanging in the air, he can correlate σῶμα and αἷμα in the first and second formulae of Institution, finally he can think of our incorporation into the 'mystical' body of Christ as effected by means of the 'eucharistic' σῶμα Χριστοῦ in the Lord's Supper (I Cor. 10.17). If we take σῶμα as a really exact term and adhere to our own principles of interpre-tation, we can translate it in no other way than 'body'. The gloss then specifies that this body is the body of Jesus given over to death for us. The correctness of this interpretation is confirmed by the fact that an analogous reference to the death of Jesus is found in the correlative cup formula. The new *diatheke* is founded on this death, i.e. on the blood of Jesus, and for this reason the death of Jesus must, according to v. 26, be the content of the Christian proclamation.

The disparity which we discovered earlier to exist between the two sets of Words of Institution now takes on historical and theological significance. It is not merely a question of a different *form* of words. According to the first formula, the sacramental gift is participation in the death of Jesus, that is, in his crucified body; according to the second formula, the sacramental gift is participation in the new *diatheke*. That there is a connexion be-tween the two is not in dispute. It is precisely the death of Jesus which establishes the new *diatheke*. But equally the difference be-tween the two must not be ignored. This difference is already discernible in the fact that the background to Paul's cup formula is not Ex. 24.8 as in Mark and Matthew, but Jer. 31.31ff. Certainly we cannot reject out of hand the possibility that Paul found the motif of the new *diatheke*, which differentiates his version from the Marcan parallel, already present in his tradition and is here simply passing on this tradition. But it is very much more likely that the Apostle was deliberately reshaping in this passage the narrative of the Institution as he had received it. For while Mark's τὸ αἷμά μου τῆς διαθήκης can scarcely be derived from the Pauline formulation, and indeed in its deliberate assimilation to Ex. 24.8 bears all the marks of an original datum, the motif of the καινὴ διαθήκη must, on the other hand, be seen in the light of II Cor. 3 as a central Pauline theologoumenon. Further, this motif fulfils in our passage a function which is of the utmost importance in the perspective of the Pauline view of the Lord's Supper: it creates the possibility of assimilating the Pauline doctrine to the pre-Pauline tradition. The component parts of the latter are retained. But they are given a different sense by the change in the order and by the fact that the new *diatheke* is introduced from Jer. 31.31ff. For the objective content of the new *diatheke* is the Body of Christ which is the present form of the βασιλεία he has brought in. Just because this is so, we are justified in ascribing the variation as compared with the Marcan tradition to Paul himself. Even if this conclusion is disputed, it must still be acknowledged that the tradition enshrined in 11.23ff. touches directly on the special concern of the Pauline teaching about the Lord's Supper and can therefore, from this angle at least, be suitably incorporated into it. The new *diatheke* is certainly grounded in the death of Jesus; but as its content is the lordship of the Christ, he who partakes of the *diatheke* partakes at the same time of the *Kyrios*, that is of Jesus in his exalted state. The disparity between the two formulae of Institution thus consists in the fact that the sacramental gift is described in the first as participation in the crucified body, that is, in the death of Jesus; in the second as participation in the kingdom of the exalted Lord. These are not mutually contradictory, for Paul never separates the Cross of Jesus from his exaltation and presents the death of Jesus as the foundation of his lordship. But even then there is not an exact correspondence between them. Since we have inferred from 10.16 the existence (confirmed by Mark) of a pre-Pauline tradition which describes the sacramental gift as a participation in the body and blood of Christ (that is, in his death), we may therefore attribute the shift of emphasis to the Apostle who invariably understands the sacrament as the gift of the exalted Christ and corrects accordingly at this point the tradition he has received. In so doing, he has subordinated this received tradition to his own outlook or, if we do not find this historical analysis proven beyond doubt, we must at least say that, given his view of the sacrament, he may well have done so. The Lord's Supper sets us in the Body of Christ, in the presence of the Exalted One who, having passed through death, now reigns: it therefore places us under the lordship of this *Kyrios*. Thus our encounter with the *Kyrios* in the sacrament can be presented as an encounter with the Judge of all, as Paul presents it in his gloss in v. 26 on the command to repeat the actions of the Last Supper. A meeting with the exalted *Kyrios* means grace in the midst of judgment and judgment in the midst of grace. For such a meeting wrenches us out of the old aeon of the σάρξ and translates us into the new aeon of the πνεῦμα, of the body of Christ, of the *Kyrios* himself.

We must now consider one last problem. In I Cor. 10, Paul develops his doctrine of the Lord's Supper in its essentials out of the bread formula and appears to be picking up from that point in 11.29; but in ch. 11, conversely, he allows the weight of the sentence to rest on the cup formula. It can of course be argued that the tradition which Paul has received (11.23ff.) leaves the Apostle no choice. But this argument still does not settle the question as to whether in this passage Paul is simply passing on the first Word of Institution in its traditional form as he did the cup formula in 10.16.

The renewed allusion to it in 11.29 gives us sufficient grounds to answer in the negative. The element of the σῶμα Χριστοῦ remains important in I Cor. 11; how important, we must now see. Our best point of departure will be the assertion that our bodies can become members of the Body of Christ. This conception occurs in more than one form in the Apostle's thought. I Cor. 6.15f. states in the form of an exact antithesis the proposition that intercourse with a prostitute creates a single body out of two human beings and makes members of Christ into the members of a prostitute. To round off the argument, Paul quotes Gen. 2.24 and is forced by the Old Testament phraseology to speak of μία σάρξ and not, as previously, of ἓν σῶμα. We must conclude that σῶμα does not mean for the Apostle what it means for the modern idea of person or personality—it does not mean 'individuality'. We must bear this fact in mind all the time or else we shall be constructing for ourselves a false conception. In the anthropology of classical Greece, the essential characteristic of the body is that it experiences limitation and individuation through its form and proportions. For Paul, on the other hand, it is the possibility of communication. As body, man exists in relationship to others, in subjection because of the world, in the jurisdiction of the Creator, in the hope of the Resurrection, in the possibility of concrete obedience and self-surrender. And as the world is determined by the conflict of forces, so there is laid on man as a corporeal being the necessity of having a Lord, of being incorporated into a dominion, whether it is that of Adam as the representative of the cosmos or that of Christ as the representative of the world of the Resurrection. Because my existence is qualified by my present Lord, by my present allegiance, because the power of the cosmos in the σάρξ and the power of the Christ in the πνεῦμα are fighting over my body, therefore there is the double possibility: shall I become ἕν σῶμα with the prostitute or with the Christ? Shall I become a member of the one or of the other? This potential can only ever become act in the body, i.e. either by sexual intercourse with the prostitute or by that total concrete bodily obedience to Christ which is grounded in the sacramental transaction. In both cases I am laid hold upon existentially, i.e. absolutely, in and with my body and as the result of a bodily process.

Once these presuppositions of Pauline thought are clarified, the conclusions to be drawn from them with regard to our passage can follow without further ado. Just because he is the one who has risen in the body, there is for Christ both the potentiality and the actuality of communication with us. For what he now is, he is, not as a person in the sense of a separate individual, but in relationship to us and on our behalf, just as he acted 'for us' as the Incarnate and Dying One. The Risen One continues to do what the Incarnate and Crucified One has already done. He exists for us 'in the body', he gives us 'bodily' participation in himself. Thus he who is now exalted can, in the Lord's Supper, continually give us that which in his death he gave us once and for all: τὸ σῶμά μου τὸ ὑπὲρ ὑμῶν. The disparity between the two formulae of Institution does not, therefore, permit us forcibly to separate Cross and Resurrection, as though the exalted Lord were not the very one who had been crucified. The slight modification in the tradition, which comes to us through this disparity, is merely intended to convey that, according to Paul, it is not just by a 'something', not even by the sacramental act of eating and drinking, but only by the self-manifesting and present Christ himself that we can be made partakers in the death of Jesus and in the new *diatheke* grounded upon it.

But while it is the corporeality of the risen one which makes it possible for him to give himself to us in the sacrament, the real content of this sacramental self-giving of Christ is invariably described by Paul as the imparting of the πνεῦμα. To put this in a nutshell, we should expect Paul's version of the bread formula to run: 'This is my Spirit.' And indeed, in a second nutshell, this *is* Paul's view. For the corporeality of Christ is σῶμα πνευματικόν, just as he himself is the πνευματικὴ πέτρα and τὸ πνεῦμα. 10.3f. speaks in so many words of πνευματικὸν βρῶμα or πόμα, as the case may be, and I Cor. 6.17 says explicitly: 'Whoever cleaves to the Lord is one spirit with him.' Paul thus regards σῶμα Χριστοῦ and πνεῦμα Χριστοῦ as in certain respects interchangeable. According to I Cor. 12 the community only becomes the Body of Christ because the Spirit of Christ working within it makes it so; again, according to Rom. 8.9, we are those who have the Spirit of Christ because we are those who have been sacramentally incorporated into the Body of Christ. Paul's purpose in speaking of the Spirit as the sacramental gift has already been discussed. The Apostle is maintaining against every possible magical, metaphysical or mystical misinterpretation that it is the *Kyrios* himself in his self-manifestation who is dealing with us; and dealing with us in such a way as to lay hold on our will, lay claim to our obedience and set himself over us as indeed our Lord. It is all the more essential to establish that Paul took over the first Word of Institution in its traditional formulation and reinforced it by 11.29 because it is just at this point that the correspondence of σῶμα and αἷμα in the Words of Institution become important. The Apostle's clear intention here is to lay stress on the moment when the sacramental self-imparting of Christ becomes effective, just as in I Cor. 15, in contrast to the Enthusiasts who see the Resurrection as already accomplished in the reception of the πνεῦμα, he sees the actuality of the Resurrection as guaranteed only by the promise of the σῶμα πνευματικόν. Only in this 'bodily' actuality can the actuality of the death of Jesus, and indeed the actuality of the Incarnation itself, be preserved. As the divine action in Creation and Resurrection is directed towards us as 'body', so, too, is the sacramental action, the self-manifestation of the exalted Christ; it is by means of our actually eating the broken bread and drinking from the cup of blessing that he makes us partakers of his crucified body and of the new *diatheke* founded on his blood.

In the last resort, then, Paul's central tenet is this: the bodily self-imparting of Christ in the sacrament claims us for concrete obedience in our bodies within the Body of Christ. So concrete and effectual is this action of his that the disorder which has intruded into the Lord's Supper at Corinth is intolerable, and indeed brings judgment on the culprits, just as in I Cor. 10.5ff. it was the reception of a sacrament which formed the basis of the divine judgment on the ancient people of God. By claiming our bodies sacramentally for service in his body, Christ emerges as the Cosmocrator, who in our bodies takes possession of the present world as its Lord and in his own body inaugurates the new world.

Paul's doctrine of the Lord's Supper is thus part of his Christology and only if we treat it strictly as such can we fully appreciate its special concern and its originality.

VI

THE DISCIPLES OF JOHN THE BAPTIST IN EPHESUS[1]

TAKEN as an isolated passage, Acts 19.1–7 is the despair of the exegete. Almost every sentence presents its own difficulties and the whole section gives the impression of being contradictory and untrustworthy.[2] A short analysis may illuminate this judgment.

Paul encounters in Ephesus a circle of twelve people, who are described as 'disciples' and 'believers'. Exegetes are rightly agreed that these designations, used absolutely, can only apply to Christians.[3] But, against this, the phrase 'baptized into John's baptism' must indicate disciples of the Baptist.[4] It is possible, of course, to reconcile these two facts, as Dibelius does, by the simple explanation that these were former disciples of the Baptist who later became Christians.[5] Yet if this is so, it is not easy to understand why men who have already 'come over' should have to have explained to them the role of the Baptist as the forerunner of Jesus, and the significance of his baptism as merely a baptism of repentance; this would seem necessary only for those who were still disciples of the Baptist. Conversely, there could be no point in putting to the disciples of the Baptist the question 'Did you receive the Holy Spirit when you became believers?'[6] This question could only be meaningful if put to Christians, because the

---

[1] From the Essays presented to Walter Bauer on his 75th birthday, 8 August 1952.
[2] 'One of the most puzzling passages in Acts', says R. Knopf, *Die Apostelgeschichte* (Die Schriften des NT, 3rd ed., III), 1917, p. 105.
[3] J. Wellhausen, *Kritische Analyse der Apostelgeschichte* (AGGW, phil.-hist. Klasse XV 2), 1914, p. 39; Knopf, p. 105; E. Preuschen, *Die Apostelgeschichte*, 1912, p. 115; T. Zahn, *Die Apostelgeschichte des Lukas* II, 1921, p. 673; A. Loisy, *Les actes des apôtres*, 1920, p. 718; K. Lake, *The Beginnings of Christianity* IV, 1933, p. 237; M. Goguel, *L'église primitive*, 1947, p. 319; F. F. Bruce, *The Acts of the Apostles*, 1951, p. 353.
[4] H. H. Wendt, *Die Apostelgeschichte*, 1913, p. 272; A. Schlatter, *Die Geschichte der ersten Christenheit*, 1927, p. 193; O. Bauernfeind, *Die Apostelgeschichte*, 1939, pp. 228f.; Knopf, p. 106; *Beginnings*, IV, p. 237.
[5] *Die urchristliche Überlieferung von Johannes dem Täufer*, 1911, p. 88.
[6] So Loisy, p. 719.

New Testament lays it down quite firmly that it is the bestowal of the Spirit which distinguishes Christian baptism from that of the Baptist. Is Luke, in spite of this, portraying *Christians* being subjected to re-baptism, which might really have been done in the case of John's disciples? If we stick to the text, we thus find ourselves moving in a circle. The most remarkable thing about it is that what it says does not enable us to make a clear decision as to whether the incident in question really concerned Christians or disciples of John. The evidence for either view seems equally strong. The oddness of the narrative extends to the details. To the question 'Into what then were you baptized?' the catechumens reply not 'Into the *name* of the Baptist' (which we might have expected and which many commentators have understandably postulated as the original text)[1] but 'Into the *baptism* of John'. Because this seems vague or even meaningless—we are not baptized into anybody's *baptism*[2]—this phrase is usually interpreted as though it read 'with the baptism of John'. But the text seems to be avoiding the instrumental dative; and for the very reason that the construction with εἰς has a technical character, it is not permissible simply to assume that there has been carelessness somewhere and to substitute ἐν for εἰς[3] without further ado. Both emendations, in removing the ambivalence of the phraseology, by-pass the dilemma of the content which is inherent in the obscurity of the passage in question. 'Baptized into John's baptism' is descriptive of the rite as such, and not of the obligation entered upon. 18.25 shows that it was possible to differentiate in this way: for Apollos, certainly a Christian, only knows the baptism of John. Thus Luke is acquainted with the possibility that Christians may receive the baptism of John without therefore binding themselves to the Baptist. The curious construction of our text is designed to express this anomalous state of affairs. In other words, Luke wishes these disciples in Ephesus to be regarded as 'semi-Christians',[4] or rather as backward confessors of the Name of Jesus[5] or as representatives of an inferior and unapostolic

[1] Preuschen, p. 115; Wellhausen, p. 39; Loisy, p. 720.

[2] M. Barth, *Die Taufe—ein Sakrament?* 1951, p. 225, speaks without evidence or meaning of 'an abbreviated mode of speech'.

[3] As against A. Steinmann, *Die Apostelgeschichte*, 4th ed., 1934, p. 230; Bruce, p. 354.

[4] Dibelius, p. 90.

[5] Zahn, p. 676.

brand of Christianity.[1] We ourselves cannot be satisfied with this. It is, indeed, Luke's solution which is our problem. Wellhausen[2] has justifiably described as a *contradictio in adjecto* the portrayal of the twelve 'rogue' disciples who, being Christians, are yet baptized into the name of John. Its incomprehensibility is emphasized yet again by a final stumbling-block which our passage places in our way. In answer to Paul's question, these disciples declare that they have never heard of the Holy Spirit. The harshness of this assertion is palliated by the emendation of the Western Text 'never heard that anybody has received the Holy Spirit'; it is removed altogether by modern exegesis which almost unanimously agrees with the sense of this emendation and assumes that it is not the existence of the Holy Spirit but his manifestation on the first Whit-Sunday which is alluded to here. But it was precisely this harshness which was the important thing in the eyes of the writer. He was trying, in however exaggerated a fashion, to depict the disciples in question as completely unacquainted with the Christian message of the Spirit. Yet his intention is carried out in a way which makes no sense whatever historically. For in the Hellenistic epoch every pious Jew *and* Gentile knew of the existence and of the self-manifestation of the divine Spirit, because ecstasy and inspiration were universally accepted phenomena.[3] And, according to the Synoptic tradition, which is of course presupposed by the writer, the Baptist himself had pointed forward to the coming baptism with the Spirit. These Ephesian disciples seem to be living in a vacuum. Paul certainly stumbles upon them but otherwise they are in no kind of communication with the outside world. They know neither Apollos, who would at least have been able to enlighten them about the gift of the Spirit, nor the Christian community in Ephesus, which was nevertheless sufficiently influential (according to 18.27) to send letters of commendation to Corinth.[4] If we ask how this state of ignorance came about and even if it is historically possible that it existed, Luke has absolutely no answer to give us.

It is true that Bauernfeind maintains that the question itself is

[1] Loisy, p. 717.
[2] *Kritische Analyse*, p. 39.
[3] *Beginnings* IV, p. 237.
[4] Knopf, p. 106; Wendt, p. 270 n. 3; J. Weiss, *The History of Primitive Christianity* ET, 1937, vol. I, p. 318 n. 3.

not a legitimate one.[1] According to him, Luke has simply taken over in its essentials an existing self-contained and independent tradition which assumes some knowledge of the community of the Baptist's disciples; possibly he has abbreviated it, in order not to digress too far from his own plan. But this hypothesis is unacceptable. It merely capitulates before the problems raised by our passage, after having first exonerated Luke from any responsibility for them. In the face of all the various difficulties we have enumerated, only two possibilities remain. Either we have here historical fact of so remarkable a nature that we shall be bound in the light of it to revise drastically the version of early Church history current among us; or else the real history of primitive Christianity has in this passage been painted over by Luke (or rather, by his source) in the pursuit of some apologetic interest. If the latter is the case, we have to separate by critical analysis the historical core from the later tendentious re-writing. We can describe the exegetical situation best by saying that in general it is the first road by which the exegetes have travelled. Let us briefly recall the different variations on the theme.

Preuschen[2] and Wendt[3] declare themselves unreservedly for the historicity of the passage, although they stress more strongly than Bauernfeind the paucity of the knowledge at our disposal, while Zahn, Steinmann[4] and Lohmeyer[5] are in the happy position of having no doubts about the reliability of the narrative. J. Behm[6] also holds that behind the passage there lie dependable primitive reports which were taken over by Luke, although not fully understood by him, and which set us insoluble puzzles. Dibelius[7] postulates an unofficial, syncretistic Christianity, speaking of 'the last outposts of the Baptist's movement'; W. Beyer[8] suggests that these men were probably pupils of Apollos, knowing only of the baptism of repentance and of the coming Messiah. Loisy[9] and Goguel,[10] on the other hand, plump for remnants of the

---

[1] *Op. cit.,* pp. 228f.

[2] *Op. cit.,* p. 115.

[3] *Op cit.,* p. 270 n. 3.

[4] 'Disciples in the wider sense, believers in Jesus who have not yet received the Spirit' (p. 230).

[5] *Das Urchristentum* I: *Johannes der Täufer,* 1932, p. 26.

[6] *Die Handauflegung in Urchristentum,* 1911, p. 19.

[7] *Die urchristliche Überlieferung,* p. 90.

[8] *Die Apostelgeschichte* (NTD), 1933, pp. 112f.

[9] *Op. cit.,* pp. 719f.   [10] *L'église primitive,* p. 320.

original Jewish Christianity for which the Gentile Christianity of the end of the first century could feel no sympathy and which it therefore regarded as having remained at the stage of John the Baptist, ignorant of the Church's worship and not viewing as axiomatic the connexion between baptism and the Spirit. According to Lake,[1] the passage provides evidence for an 'evolution of Christian baptism'. M. Barth[2] sees here the baptism of John ecclesiastically legitimized and rehabilitated and the neophytes received into the Christian fellowship. This thesis can naturally only be maintained if the account of the re-baptism in v. 5 is set aside. This is done simply and elegantly by attaching v. 5 to v. 4 without the full stop and thus making it a statement within the framework of Paul's speech. Finally, mention must be made of H. Preisker's article 'Apollos und die Johannesjünger in Ephesus',[3] in which historical investigation is most obviously subordinated to theological interest. The two stories belong together in so far as they both point to a stage in Christian history 'when neither cultus nor official ministry is the decisive element but the possession of the Spirit is everything'. According to Preisker, we are to conclude from the differences between them that at that point 'inner unity without uniformity' was the order of the day. We must be all the more grateful to Luke 'for preserving vestiges of tradition which give us information about that era of origins' because in his own time 'uniformity in baptismal practice had already been established'.

This conspectus has brought before us every even barely conceivable variety of naïveté, defeatism and fertile imagination which historical scholarship can display, from the extremely ingenuous on the one hand to the extremely arbitrary on the other. A defect common to almost all these attempted solutions is that the question of the historicity of what is narrated is not raised sharply enough and therefore the question of the part played by the writer himself is not given proper consideration. The textual difficulties do not lead on to methodical criticism but tempt the various scholars to baseless reconstructions of the history. For the hypothesis that there was ever a Christianity without cultus or official

[1] *Beginnings*, p. 231.
[2] *Die Taufe—ein Sakrament?* pp. 167ff., 171ff.
[3] *ZNW* 30, 1931, pp. 301–4.

ministry is not only incapable of proof but contradicts directly the role of apostolate and prophecy on the one side and of the sacraments on the other, as far back as we are able to see. Luke himself does not depict either Apollos or the disciples in Ephesus as representatives of primitive Christian freedom but of an immature form of Christianity. The bestowal of the Spirit in our passage is already tied to baptism and the laying-on of hands as actions of the organized Church. Similarly, Paul's introductory question and the rest of the narrative based upon it are orientated in this direction. The living context of the passage is the reception of ecclesiastical outsiders into the *Una sancta catholica*. Only after we have brought out in sharp relief this concern of Luke's in writing can we rightly go on to enquire about the historical circumstances underlying his source. From this point of view, Preisker's thesis can be seen for what it is—the superimposition of a modern liberal-idealist outlook on the primitive Christian past. For the Spirit bestowed upon the Ephesian disciples is precisely *not* the mark of a community without cultus or ministry but the seal of incorporation into the organized Church. The reference to the bestowal of the Spirit is thus an essential component in the structure of the Lucan composition, and the question of historicity does not dovetail with it. Similarly the identification of these disciples with Jewish Christians of the primitive 'use' can only be regarded as a piece of whimsy unsupported by anything in the text and quite incredible so far as this particular author is concerned. For even if Luke at the time of writing was no longer in a position to have a true understanding of the dynamic of Jewish Christianity, still its history cannot have been an unintelligible religious fossil to the man who wrote the Gospel and Acts 1–12. Once again exegesis has begun at the wrong end. Both our analysis of the text and our exegetical conspectus have shown clearly that the problems of the passage arise out of its characterization of the Ephesian disciples as immature Christians. That makes it probable that the most likely explanation is an overpainting by Luke of the tradition he had to hand.

There remains thus only one possible point of departure for an adequate historical investigation: the hypothesis that these disciples had been baptized into John's baptism. This hypothesis can hardly lead to any other conclusion than that it is disciples of the

Baptist who are the subject of the passage; the Gospels themselves presuppose the existence of a Baptist community in competition with the young Church. These disciples have naturally no contact with the Christian fellowship, know nothing of the Spirit which has been bestowed on Christendom and therefore have to be enlightened about the place of the Baptist as the forerunner of Jesus and be subjected to re-baptism, which incorporates them into the Church and imparts to them the Spirit. This gives us a consistent and historically intelligible situation at which, on any other hypothesis, we cannot arrive.

But what reason can Luke possibly have had to complicate and obscure this situation in his presentation of it? The answer is simple: the existence of a community owing allegiance to the Baptist could not be admitted without endangering gravely the Church's view of his function. For such a community would be bound to put John in the place which Jesus occupied in Christendom, making him Messiah and *Kyrios* and thus the rival of Jesus; it would thus run counter, in the most concrete and thoroughgoing fashion, to the Church's tradition of the forerunner of Jesus. Criticism of the Synoptic narrative concerning the Baptist has actually shown that this tradition is a dogmatic construction in which the forerunner of the Universal Judge has been made into the forerunner of Jesus. This was possible because Jesus was held to be the future Judge of all. Neither can we overlook the fact that this construction has a polemic intention—the refutation of the claims of the Baptist community. Jesus himself had been baptized by John and had in some sense appealed to his authority; parts of very early Christendom had sprung from the circle around the Baptist; thus it was not easy to regard John as a rival of Jesus and to attack him as such. But conversely, any idea of competition had to be resisted. Our Gospels, like the tradition underlying them, have escaped from this dilemma by presenting the claims of the Baptist community as a misunderstanding of the Baptist's message and by depicting John himself as pointing forward to the Christ who should follow him. Verse 5 shows that Luke is here making use of his way out of the difficulty, and in a form more akin to that of the Fourth Gospel than that of the other Synoptists.[1] But he has not stopped there. As his tradition made

[1] Lake, pp. 237f.

John into the herald of Jesus, so Luke has gone on to make John's disciples into an odd species of Christian and thus he has radically eliminated any suggestion of real rivalry. Such a presentation can certainly only have been possible if Luke knew of the existence of a Baptist community by hearsay alone and was not obliged to attach to it any real significance because, for him at least, it belonged to a past already remote. Only in such circumstances as these could he dispense with concrete polemics and content himself with painting over the tradition.

But what grounds have we for holding Luke himself responsible for this re-shaping? One immediate answer is that the restricting of the Spirit to the *Una sancta*, the bestowal of the Spirit through the laying-on of hands and the performance of this action by Paul are characteristic themes of the Lucan view of Church history. But it would be well to enlarge the horizon of our considerations and take into account some related passages in Acts. The parallel with 18.24ff., which has been so often remarked, will be found especially helpful. This narrative also is in itself contradictory and incredible. Apollos is portrayed first as inspired by the Spirit, secondly as being accurately instructed in the history of Jesus, thirdly as a teacher in the Church and a propagandist in the synagogue of the Diaspora. But none of these points are compatible with the statement that he was only acquainted with the baptism of John, which can only mean that he had been baptized into it. There have certainly been attempts to minimize the first three of these assertions in the interest of the last. We ought, it is alleged, to translate not 'inspired by the Spirit' but 'of a fiery temperament'.[1] But against this suggestion it must be said that the use of the expression 'fervent in the Spirit' is unambiguously defined by Rom. 12.21 as a phrase current in the language of Christian edification; and its position between two clauses concerned with Apollos as a Christian establishes its meaning.[2] Nor can we any more easily agree with Steinmann[3] in his attempt to limit the Alexandrian's familiarity with the history of Jesus to the knowledge that Jesus was the promised Messiah and that the baptism of repentance was of obligation. The text postulates

---

[1] So Wendt, p. 270; Zahn, p. 669; Loisy, p. 712.
[2] So J. Weiss, *op. cit.*, vol. I, p. 316; Dibelius, p. 95; Preisker, p. 301; Bauernfeind, p. 229; Lake, p. 233.
[3] *Die Apostelgeschichte*, p. 222.

expressly that Apollos was insufficiently informed only so far as the necessity and character of Christian baptism was concerned; in all other matters it ascribes to him the full knowledge proper to a mature Christian. How are these to be reconciled? It is utterly inconceivable that anybody could be well informed about Christian origins without being aware of the line of demarcation between Jesus and his community and the Baptist and his baptism; that anybody could be 'inspired by the Spirit' without seeing that the advantage of the Christian over the disciple of the Baptist lay precisely in his being endowed with the Spirit; that a primitive Christian teacher could differ from the whole New Testament in failing to connect the possession of the Spirit in the closest possible way with baptism; and, finally, that an evangelist could end his preaching without the call to Christian baptism. It is true that the distinction between 'babes' and 'the full-grown' is a very early one. But 'babes' never meant 'the unbaptized'. According to the unanimous witness of the New Testament, anyone who has not received Christian baptism does not belong to the community at all. Baptism is the inescapable presupposition of membership in Christ and his Body. There is no evidence whatever for the idea that once Easter had happened, baptism was not always and everywhere the universal custom.[1] From these facts we can draw only one conclusion: 18.25c must also be regarded as a Lucan fabrication.[2]

What was the motive for such a fabrication? Acts 8.14ff. and 10.44ff. supply the answer. Frequent attempts[3] have been made to combat the idea of a necessary connexion between baptism and the Spirit by appealing to these passages, but this is a quite unjustifiable procedure. True, it is easy to be misled by the picture painted in 8.16ff. and particularly by the μόνον βεβαπτισμένοι in 8.16 which is so strikingly reminiscent of the expression 'knowing only the baptism of John' in 18.25 and which seems even more unlikely. For, quite apart from the significance of baptism for primitive Christianity, the sub-apostolic era and the rise of early Catholicism saw an increase rather than a decrease in the value

---

[1] Dibelius, p. 96 n. 1.
[2] So also Wendt, p. 270 n. 3; R. Bultmann, *The History of the Synoptic Tradition*, p. 247 n. 1.
[3] Behm, p. 165; Preisker, p. 302; M. Barth, pp. 167ff.

placed upon the sacrament.[1] If then, in spite of this, a writer can venture to use phraseology such as that of 8.16, he must have overwhelming reasons for doing so. These reasons are not far to seek. Philip has begun upon the evangelization of Samaria on his own initiative and without express authorization, and has been highly successful. The result of his efforts has been the emergence of a church almost entirely independent of Jerusalem. In the eyes of later Christendom this is an intolerable state of affairs, threatening to disrupt the unity of the Church. Solidarity must be shown with the claims to primacy which have certainly been put forward in Jerusalem by this time. Peter and John must therefore be portrayed as going to Samaria to visit the community which has come into existence there and to receive it into the fellowship of the apostolic Church. Only so can the Samaritans, and, farther on in the book, the Ephesians, receive the Spirit, who is accessible solely within the boundaries of the apostolic fellowship. The turn of phrase '*only* baptized' thus becomes intelligible. The Church of a later day could not admit the existence in the sacred past of primitive Christian free-lances and communities resting on any other than apostolic authority: because otherwise it would have granted letters patent to the Gnostics and other heretics by whom it was being menaced. Generally speaking, Acts is silent on the subject of this threat, although we know from the Pauline epistles how early it made itself felt throughout Hellenistic Christendom. It is one of the basic convictions of Luke's day that schisms and heresy had been unknown in the very earliest days of Christianity. The whole plan of Acts is conditioned by this view. Only in one passage, which certainly receives unusual emphasis, does Luke fail to uphold this otherwise strictly observed convention. In Paul's farewell speech delivered, according to Acts 20.17ff., in Miletus, the Apostle can be reported as referring to the dangers and difficulties of his own time and contrasting with them the ideal of the *Una sancta*, the integrity of which is guaranteed by the teaching office of the Church resting upon the apostolic succession. For all practical purposes Luke's general picture is shaped by this presupposition, which can be illustrated by the narratives of the Hellenists, of the conversion of Paul and Cornelius, of the emergence of Barnabas in Antioch and of the apostolic Council. These

[1] So also Behm, p. 28.

narratives are the pillars of Luke's historical edifice. 8.14ff. must also be placed in this context. The password '*Una sancta*' remained ineffectual unless it could be deduced from the history, or rather read back into it. There could only be a place in the reconstructed past for free-lance evangelists like Philip or free-lance apostles like Paul if they had at least retrospectively received the apostolic blessing and been legitimized by Jerusalem. Luke was faced with the necessity either of admitting Philip's administration of baptism to be fully valid and thus acknowledging the existence of an independent ecclesiastical structure in Samaria or of maintaining at all costs the unity of the apostolic fellowship by stigmatizing Philip's baptism as defective; he chose the latter course. The Samaritans are therefore described as 'only baptized' and their real incorporation into the Church is ascribed to the apostolic laying-on of hands. Thus the shape of 8.14ff. is determined by a dogmatic theory.

10.14ff. presents us with a similar case. Cornelius and his circle receive the Spirit prior to their baptism and this serves naturally to emphasize the ruling theme of the narrative, namely that it is not man but God who has initiated the Gentile mission with continual signs and leadings and even in the face of apostolic reluctance. He maintains the initiative by sending the Spirit before baptism and thus giving his sanction to the action of the Church which for her part immediately opens her doors to the Gentile world and, by apostolic command, baptizes the representative of this world. Once again, therefore, what we have before us is not the report of an historical happening designed to prove the possibility of separating baptism and the bestowal of the Spirit, or at least of driving a wedge between them. The passage is orientated in the direction of the whole Lucan interest and goes back to Luke the writer or, even more, to Luke the theologian who is concerned by this means to hammer yet again into the heads of his hearers: 'This is the will of God.'

After this digression we can draw a line under our working and arrive at certain well-defined conclusions. First: if in Luke alone of the New Testament writers there is sometimes a disjunction between baptism and the bestowal of the Spirit, we cannot properly make any inferences from this concerning the history of Christian origins or even a very early view held within the

Christian community. On the contrary, these passages provide evidence only for Luke's conception of Christian history and its main dogmatic convictions and constructions. It is unfortunate that the exegesis of Acts has treated the Lucan presentation of events as a narrative compiled from sources rather than as a composition of Luke the writer and theologian. This procedure has resulted in the postulating of happenings that, historically speaking, are extremely odd and in a failure to discern the basic Lucan presuppositions which alone make sense of the presentation.

Secondly: the problem in 18.25 is automatically solved by what we have established about 8.14ff. The cases are very similar. Apollos suddenly appears before us out of complete darkness and Luke has already had to deal with an exactly parallel situation. He could not integrate the Alexandrian into the Jerusalem church or even subordinate him to it as he had already done with the Seven, with Barnabas and with Paul. But equally he could not allow him to appear as an authorized teacher of the Church until he had in some way incorporated him into the apostolic fellowship.[1] Otherwise he would immediately have provided all those who in his own day were breaking away from the bond of the Church with a figure out of primitive Christianity as a prototype and as an example to which they could appeal. He has escaped from the dilemma by making Apollos receive at least supplementary instruction from Aquila and Priscilla, the companions of Paul. Luke has obviously not dared to report the re-baptism of one known to be inspired by the Spirit and a celebrated missionary into the bargain. The question was, at which point the instruction could best follow. The disciples at Ephesus came in useful here. If they had only received John's baptism, Apollos could at least be associated with them.[2] Thus the fabrication of 18.25 was born.

Thirdly: the connexion between the two narratives in 18.24ff. and 19.2ff. now becomes clear. The second has influenced the first, but the reverse process has also taken place. We have tried to show why Luke could not give a satisfactory rationale of the existence of a Baptist community. By previously linking Apollos to the disciples in Ephesus, he created for himself the possibility of

[1] Only Wellhausen (p. 38) and Loisy (pp. 701ff.) have seen this clearly. Preisker (p. 303) wrongly brings in from I Cor. the rivalry with Paul, which does not interest Luke.

[2] So also Wendt, p. 270 n. 3.

portraying all disciples of John as standing to Christians in the relation of embryos. A regular *communicatio idiomatum* could now take place. The Spirit-filled Christian became a man who knew only John's bpatism; while, to compensate for this, the disciples of John became immature Christians. Luke may have translated them to Ephesus so that this exchange could take place in the locality where Apollos was known to have operated. For, apart from the passages in question, we have no evidence for Baptist communities outside Palestine and Syria.[1]

Fourthly: if the above reconstruction is accurate—and it does solve the problems of our text in an unforced and complete way— the whole presentation of the narrative has been very strongly moulded by Luke the writer and theologian. Further, we can from this example penetrate his method of procedure and the motives lying behind it. Our narrative betrays, in common with all those allied to it, an ideological theology of history. Its characteristic feature is this: it reads back into the past as an historical reality the postulate of an *Una sancta* grounded on the apostolic fellowship and then, conversely, uses this postulate to validate the claims of the orthodox Church of his own times. Luke has over-painted and re-shaped history in order to defend the *Una sancta apostolica* against the assault of the Gnostics and other heretics of his day. We can only understand him as an historian, if we have first understood him as a theologian. As a theologian he can only be understood from his doctrine of a legitimate Church.

[1] Preuschen, p. 115; Goguel, p. 318.

VII

A PRIMITIVE CHRISTIAN BAPTISMAL LITURGY[1]

THE hymnic character of Col. 1.15–20 has long been recognized and generally acknowledged. But the purpose served by this hymn within the framework of the whole letter has remained obscure. In what follows, an attempt is made to solve this problem.

1. THE STRUCTURE OF THE HYMN

E. Lohmeyer is the most recent writer to have made it his business to investigate very thoroughly the structure of the hymn; he has come to what at first sight seems a very impressive conclusion which, for the sake of clarity, may be set out for further examination as it appears in his translation of the text, vv. 13–20.[2]

13 'He who delivered us from the power of darkness
and transferred us into the kingdom of the Son of his love,
14 in whom we have redemption, the forgiveness of our sins.

15 For he is the image of the invisible God,
First-born before all created things,
16 For in him were all things created
in heaven and on earth,
visible and invisible,
Thrones or Princes,
Powers or·Authorities.

All have been created through him and for him.
17 And he is before all things,
and all things subsist in him.

---

[1] First published in *Festschrift Rudolf Bultmann zum 65. Geburtstag überreicht*, ed. E. Wolf, Stuttgart, 1949, pp. 133–48.
[2] *Die Briefe an die Philipper, an die Kolosser und an Philemon* (KEKNT 9, 8th ed.), 1930, p. 41.

18 And he is the head of the body, the church,
   he the beginning, the first-born from the dead,
   that in all things he might have the primacy,
19 for in him by God's own will the fullness of God dwelt,
20 and through him God reconciled all things,
   made peace on his account through the blood of his cross,
   peace through him on earth as in heaven.'

Two seven-line stanzas are thus placed in juxtaposition and opposition, each introduced by a three-line stanza. Now if this analysis is correct, we have before us a classic example of hymnodic form, unparalleled in the New Testament. But unfortunately the analysis is not supported by the facts; the apparent regularity is only an artificial construction and violence is done to the content of the hymn for the sake of this particular articulation of the form. We can see even at first glance that the last line of v. 16 belongs, according to its content, to what has gone before and picks up 16a. Once the symmetry of this whole analysis is thus shattered, no justification remains for the separating of v. 17 from what precedes it. That is where it belongs by content, inasmuch as the second series of Christological statements begins with v. 18; and by form, because the key phrase τὰ πάντα, which dominates 17a and b, links this verse with the last line of v. 16, in which the same phrase is so placed that the stress falls on it. Finally, v.18a should also be assigned to the first stanza. For surely we cannot possibly fail to see that the relative clause 18b corresponds exactly and of set purpose in its emphasis on the predicate πρωτότοκος as applied to Christ to the parallel relative clause 15a, which is itself so characteristic[1] of the style of oriental prayers and hymns. The second stanza begins by setting 'first-born of all creation' over against 'first-born from the dead'.[2] It is true that this observation is in contradiction to the content of v. 18a, in which Christ is addressed as the head of the Body (the Church) and thus the series of statements concerning the mediator of creation is broken off.[3] Thus, in the division of the text which is suggested to us, the

---

[1] Cf. E. Norden, *Agnostos Theos* (cited from the 1st ed. of 1913), pp. 201ff.; Lohmeyer, pp. 42, 54.
[2] So, too, Norden, p. 252.
[3] M. Dibelius, *An die Kolosser* (HNT 12), 1927, p. 6 and Lohmeyer, *op. cit.*, pp. 41f., for this reason attach v. 18a to what follows.

formal and the material beginnings of the second stanza do not coincide. But if we subject the facts of the case to this kind of minute examination, it immediately becomes obvious that this divergence is caused by the two words τῆς ἐκκλησίας in v. 18a, which must be understood as an epexegetic genitive, i.e. an elucidatory expression in apposition to τοῦ σώματος. The associations (which we shall have to investigate later) of the theologoumenon 'Body of Christ' in the setting of the comparative study of religions make it legitimate for us to see this Body, of which Christ is here called the Head, not as a soteriological entity confined to the Christian community, but as a 'cosmological' entity in creation. Such an interpretation would fit excellently with 2.10, where Christ is described as the head of all powers and authorities, and these latter are thus thought of as at least component parts of his body. Such an interpretation would fit equally well with the first stanza, which culminates (17b) in the statement (almost[1] unparalleled in the New Testament): 'all things subsist in him.' Here the idea of the Body of the Christ is already indirectly anticipated. The whole passage requires this conclusion, more especially as 2.10 shows that Colossians is familiar with a philosophy of this kind. Lohmeyer has also noticed that the expression τῆς ἐκκλησίας imparts a certain clumsiness to the construction of v. 18; in his case, it leads him to speak of a gloss by Paul himself.[2] The traditional reading, quoted by Lohmeyer from Oecumenius, 'head of the body and of the church',[3] is no improvement; it reveals the offence which the original formulation gave to a later generation, and also the still continuing understanding of the fact that the Body of Christ could also be seen in creation. The hypothesis[4] that the text was glossed in post-New Testament times by the insertion of τῆς ἐκκλησίας is not supported by any variant reading. And yet the correspondence in form between v. 15 and 18b, dividing the hymn as it does into two parallel and antithetic stanzas, must carry such weight that we are bound to declare τῆς ἐκκλησίας to be a gloss on these grounds alone; the other considerations we have mentioned clinch the issue. We are left

---

[1] The one parallel is Acts 17.28.
[2] *Op. cit.*, p. 61 n. 2.
[3] *Ibid.*
[4] So Max-Adolf Wagenführer, *Die Bedeutung Christi für Welt und Kirche*, 1941, pp. 18f., 62ff.

with only one conceivable solution: these words are to be seen as a Christian redaction of a pre-Christian hymn.

This hypothesis is admittedly only tenable if we are prepared at the same time to maintain that the expression 'through the blood of his cross' (v. 20) is also a Christian interpolation into the earlier hymn. Are we justified in doing this? It is not a question of justification, but of compulsion. It is no accident that the exegetes have found our passage a stumbling block.[1] In the hymn the predicates of Christ are those of Mediator in creation and Risen or Exalted One. These belong together; they complement and elucidate each other. This relationship is sensibly disturbed when the connexion of creation and eschatological new creation is broken by the reference to the event of the Cross—a reference for which the way is totally unprepared and which has immediately an anachronistic effect. There is another consideration. The cosmic peace, of which v. 20 speaks, is obviously the fruit and the goal of the ἀποκαταλλάξαι τὰ πάντα εἰς αὐτόν and directs our attention back to the beginning of the hymn. Where paradisal peace is reigning over a reconciled new world, the original creation is, in a certain manner, restored. But in classical antiquity, as the Fourth Eclogue of Virgil shows, cosmic peace as the characteristic of the new aeon is both the sign and the result of the Universal Saviour's entry into his kingdom. Since it is impossible to divest our passage of this kind of historical connexion, we may rightly see, in this association of the peace of the cosmos with the event of the Cross, a modification of an original reference to the enthronement of the Redeemer. And this original reference stands out clearly in our text if we place the words 'through the blood of his cross' in brackets. For then the last line becomes quite self-contained, reading thus: εἰρηνοποιήσας δι' αὐτοῦ εἴτε τὰ ἐπὶ τῆς γῆς εἴτε τὰ ἐν τοῖς οὐρανοῖς.

Once we accept the hypothesis that we have here a Christian redaction of an already existing pre-Christian text, we can make the link with vv. 13f. For there should be no doubt that these verses belong to the hymn in its present form.[2] The striking change of person in v. 13 is only comprehensible if the writer is here harking back to a confession of faith already current in the com-

[1] For example, Dibelius (p. 13) and Wagenführer both feel the tension between the reference to the Cross and the general orientation of the passage towards the exaltation of Christ.
[2] Cf. Norden, p. 252; Lohmeyer, p. 41; Wagenführer, p. 17.

munity. The introductory relative clause with ὅς bears a liturgical stamp (cf. vv. 15, 18b; Phil. 2.6; I Tim. 3.16; Heb. 1.3). This is further supported by the fact that the concepts which are used here can by no means be described as typically Pauline. The writer of the epistle has evidently found vv. 13-14 already associated with the hymn. In that case, the interpolations in vv. 18 and 20 go back not to him but to the tradition which he had to hand. We may go even further than this and ask whether v. 12, too, may not come from this tradition. At any rate, a critic with so expert a knowledge of classical prose writings as Norden has voiced this opinion.[1] The participial construction τῷ ἱκανώσαντι and the heaping-up of relative clauses are both equally characteristic of hymnal texts. Very influential texts have ἡμᾶς instead of ὑμᾶς, so that the use of the other person here is no counter-argument.[2] On the one hand, the verse is clearly stylized in liturgical fashion; on the other, equally clearly it cannot rightly be said to have a specially Pauline construction. Even the expression τῷ ἱκανώσαντι, which is certainly genuine,[3] has not the same shade of meaning as it has in Paul, who uses the verb in II Cor. 3.6 to characterize apostolic authority. Again, the expression τῷ πατρί used without any further qualification only in this one place, would fit especially well into a liturgy.[4] But the connexion between v. 12 and what follows becomes nothing less than mandatory if we interpret the introductory εὐχαριστοῦντες along the particular line opened up by G. Bornkamm.[5] Lohmeyer[6] had already called attention to the remarkable fact that nowhere else does a Pauline intercession pass into a thanksgiving or a summons to thanksgiving, and had asked what motive the Apostle could have had for altering his custom here. Dibelius[7] answered that Paul was familiar with the idea of *oratio infusa* precisely as applied to thanksgiving and that, on this assumption, the co-ordination of this particular thanksgiving prayer with the rest of the context became easier to understand. But this suggestion only

---

[1] *Loc. cit.*

[2] Lohmeyer (p. 30 n. 3) assumes that the reading 'us' has been influenced by the following verses, but there is an equally strong case for saying that 'you' has been influenced by the preceding ones. The evidence for this is perhaps stronger still.

[3] The more usual κολέσαντι should be rejected as a copyist's error (with Lohmeyer, p. 30 n. 4).

[4] The later qualifications in a number of MSS testify to the rarity of this usage.

[5] 'Das Bekenntnis im Hebräerbrief', *TB* 21, 1942, col. 61.

[6] *Op. cit.*, p. 38.

[7] *An die Kolosser*, p. 5.

took on real significance in the light of Bornkamm's thesis. This was as follows. *Eucharistia* here has the concrete meaning of homology; the community's confession of faith in Christ[1] rendered in hymnic form, 'which later acquired its settled, although, within wide limits, variable liturgical form in the prefaces of the ancient liturgies.' If this thesis is correct, as it well may be, we should merely have to insert a semi-colon and quotation marks after εὐχαριστοῦντες and all would be clear. There then follows the community's confession of faith, which we have already recognized as such on other grounds; its beginning would be in v. 12. The structure of the hymn now becomes clearly visible. The pre-Christian hymn has been worked over by Christian hands and provided with a liturgical introduction; it now embodies a community homology, which is cited by the writer of the epistle as a pendant to his proem. It remains for us to ask what purpose is served, first, by the liturgical redaction and, secondly, by the introduction of the community homology.

2. THE GENESIS OF THE HYMN

Before we turn to this question, we must state the reasons which lead us to conjecture that behind vv. 15–20 there lies a pre-Christian hymn.

How near to the surface the material for this conjecture is can easily be seen by simply placing within brackets eight of the total of 112 words in the text; this is all that is needed in order to eradicate every specifically Christian motif. For even the title 'First-born from the dead' can no longer be put into this category by anyone who has to some extent familiarized himself with gnostic terminology, in which the Redeemer, acting as the pathfinder and leader of those who are his, makes a breach in death's domain.[2] Similarly, creation and new creation are invariably linked together in the myth of the Archetypal Man who is also the Redeemer.

All this becomes even clearer from a comparison with vv. 12–14. True, the concepts which are used in these latter verses hark back

---

[1] G. Harder, *Paulus und das Gebet,* 1936, pp. 38ff., underlines this from the other side when he demonstrates that εὐχαριστεῖν supplants εὐλογεῖν in Paul, but that this is not a new expression coined by the Apostle, nor does it signify merely the personal thanksgiving of the believer. It may well mean an already formulated liturgical act of thanksgiving, as in Judaism and in Philo.

[2] Cf. E. Käsemann, *Das wandernde Gottesvolk,* 1938, pp. 98ff.

throughout to the language of the LXX and revive many of its liturgical and cultic formulations, as might be expected in a passage which has itself been shaped by liturgical practice. But the whole breathes an atmosphere of rejoicing—possible only in a Christian milieu—over the eschatological act of salvation once and for all completed in the turn of the aeons, to which vv. 21ff. with their πότε . . . νυνὶ δέ also point back. In contrast, vv. 15–20 contain, apart from the Christian interpolations, the supra-historical and metaphysical drama of the gnostic Redeemer,[1] which only gains a new eschatological significance from the Christian redaction and framework.

Merely to postulate older traditions behind a passage is not satisfactory by itself when the hymnic construction is so clearly revealed in the fully rounded-off shape of the passage in question and in the way in which its lines are distributed so as to form stanzas. Only the hypothesis of a pre-Christian hymn remains.

The discussion of the concrete religious background of the hymn has been carried so far by Dibelius[2] in particular (in his excursus on the passage) that it is no longer possible to mistake[3] the contours of the gnostic myth of the Archetypal Man who is also the Redeemer. Indeed, the myth is present in a form characteristic of Hellenistic Judaism.[4] Speculations concerning the Archetypal Man and Sophia or Logos are combined, as is the case also in the parallel passage in Philo, *De confus. ling.* 146: καὶ γὰρ ἀρχή καὶ ὄνομα θεοῦ καὶ λόγος καὶ ὁ κατ᾽ εἰκόνα ἄνθρωπος καὶ ὁ ὁρῶν, Ἰσραήλ, προσαγορεύται.

It is sufficient for our purpose to disentangle the most important themes far enough to gain from them a perspective on our text.

Wisdom, which in Wisdom 9.4 is described on the basis of very primitive Near Eastern traditions as πάρεδρος τῶν σῶν θρονῶν, is, as

---

[1] This fact provides some justification for Lohmeyer's interpretation, which presents us with one of the most attractive contradictions in modern exegesis. For while, from the angle of the comparative study of religion, he tries throughout to reach an understanding of the passage on Jewish presuppositions, so far as its content is concerned he does not draw the logical conclusion that it is to be seen in strictly historical terms; phenomenologically, his interpretation gets no further than the uncovering of supra-historical-metaphysical 'facts' and his thought therefore starts in practice not from Judaism but from Greek philosophy.

[2] *An die Kolosser*, pp. 9ff., 14f.

[3] For what follows, cf. Käsemann, *Leib und Leib Christi*, pp. 138ff.; *Das wandernde Gottesvolk*, pp. 61ff.

[4] So, too, Norden, p. 254; Dibelius, pp. 7, 9ff.; Lohmeyer, pp. 46f., 53, 60.

such, the mediator in creation[1] (Wisdom 7.21; 8.6; 6.9); it is characteristic of these passages that creation is spoken of (as in Col. 1.15ff.) in terms of the Stoic formula τὰ πάντα.[2] Wisdom or the Logos, which is identified with Wisdom, is therefore called ἀρχή[3] in the sense precisely defined by W. Staerk,[4] viz. that its epiphany constitutes the beginning of the new aeon and determines its nature. At this point, the doctrine of Wisdom coincides with that of the Archetypal Man; this coincidence is repeated when the predicate πρωτότοκος is used both of Sophia[5] and Adam[6] and again when both are described as the image of God.[7] This last piece of terminology, which has never yet been subjected to a satisfactory analysis, is particularly important. As a title of the Archetypal Man who is the Redeemer, it cannot be understood from Palestinian Judaism alone, since the latter, having always held[8] that it is man as such and without qualification who bears the image of God, cannot therefore see in this attribute a significant mark of the Redeemer. But once the attribution of the image of God to the Archetypal Man had been taken over, certainly no time seems to have been lost in reading it back into Scripture. The earliest testimony to this process is to be found in the LXX translation, which in Gen. 1.27 is still saying of man as such that he was created κατ᾽ εἰκόνα θεοῦ, but in Gen. 5.1 is applying the expression to Adam only. The same rabbinic tradition comes to light again in I Cor. 11.7, which ascribes—though in rather qualified fashion—the possession of the image of God to the man only. This is only comprehensible on the premise that in the primary sense it is Adam, and Adam alone, who possesses it. The combination of the 'image' predicate with Sophia, or Logos, has a complicated origin. In Philo, Plutarch and the Hermetic Corpus, it is the cosmos which is thought of as the first-born and the image of God, and therefore as the Son of God and δεύτερος θεός.[9] This was the starting-point which enabled Hellenistic Judaism to take over the predicate for

---

[1] Cf. Philo, *De ebriet.* 30; *Leg. alleg.* III 96; *De cherub.* 127.
[2] Prov. 8.22ff.; Wisdom 7.21ff.; 8.1, 5–6.
[3] Prov. 8.22ff.; Ecclus. 1.1ff.; 24.8f.: referred to the Law, Strack-Billerbeck II, pp. 353ff.
[4] *Soter*, 1933, p. 134.
[5] Philo, *De conf. ling.* 146.
[6] Cf. W. Staerk, *Die Erlösererwartung in den östlichen Religionen*, 1938, p. 14.
[7] Wisdom 7.26; *De conf. ling.* 146.
[8] Cf. Kittel, *TWNT* II, pp. 380f.
[9] Cf. Dibelius, pp. 9ff.; Kleinknecht, *TWNT* II, pp. 386f.

Sophia and Logos, inasmuch as the former was similarly 'the first-born' and, as πάρεδρος, was in practice also δεύτερος θεός. Thus when, as in the Philo passage quoted at the beginning of this discussion, the doctrines of the Logos and the Archetypal Man who is the Redeemer meet and mingle, it is precisely the 'image' concept which emerges as the link between the two. Furthermore, it is again I Cor. 11.3, 7 which demonstrates from Jewish tradition that εἰκών and κεφαλή can be used synonymously. These two concepts belong together to this extent, that both of them imply the possibility of εἶναι ἐκ the same magnitudes whose archetype or head they are.[1] It is a characteristic mark of the *eikon* to stand within a series and, in its capacity as archetype, to throw off 'copies'; it is this notion which Paul is reproducing when he uses the phrase 'to be shaped to the likeness of his Son'.[2] For, in contradiction to Judaism, Paul has given up the idea that man as such has retained the image of God.[3] The *eikon* concept in his writings has already and invariably a soteriological function.

Instead of the εἶναι ἐκ of I Cor. 11.8, Col. 1.17 has τὰ πάντα ἐν αὐτῷ συνέστηκεν. The former is undoubtedly contained in the latter, since it is only through the creation that the ἐν αὐτῷ (so characteristic a phase in our particular context) comes about. But the latter has a wider range. If, as regards the content, the continuing existence of the world is referred back to the mediatorial function of Christ in creation, the mythological garb in which this content is clothed can only be understood by recalling the cosmic scope of the idea of the Archetypal Man. Adam is not only 'Microcosmos' but at the same time, as Staerk[4] puts it, 'Macro-anthropos'; or, put more clearly, he is the aeon itself. The world is Adam's body, he is its soul or its head.[5] Thus the first stanza in its original conception concludes logically with the predication: 'He is the head of the body.'

Sophia also had some soteriological content for Judaism. Otherwise, it would not have been possible to substitute for this figure that of the Law or, in Philo, the Logos. It is almost superfluous to refer expressly to passages in which this is done, such as we have

[1] I Cor. 11.8; cf. Schlier, *TWNT* III, p. 678.
[2] Rom. 8.29; II Cor. 3.18.
[3] Sometimes Philo also does so, e.g. in *De conf. ling.* 147.
[4] *Erlösererwartung*, pp. 15ff.
[5] *Ibid.*; Dibelius, pp. 9ff.; Käsemann, *Leib und Leib Christi*, pp. 65ff.

in Prov. 8.34; Wisdom 7.27ff.; Odes of Solomon 33. Yet in the second stanza of our hymn Sophia retreats into the background in favour of the doctrine of the Archetypal Man because it is only on this basis that a sufficiently strong emphasis can be given to the mythical concept of the body of the Redeemer; this, in turn, is the starting-point·from which to reach the desired culmination— the picture of peace reigning over the cosmos. In the same way as the Archetypal Man who is the| Aeon is not only ἀρχὴ but τέλος and the first Adam is orientated towards the second in the Redeemer,[1] the words εἰς αὐτὸν ἔκτισται in v. 16 anticipate this eschatological orientation which then receives concrete expression in the soteriological statements of the second stanza. When the first-born from the dead appears in ch. 39 of the *Epideixis* of Irenaeus as head and pioneer of the divine life and, at the same time, as the deliverer of his followers from hell,[2] this is not merely a very remarkable parallel to our text. Much more important, this parallel obviously stems, independently of our text, from the same gnostic tradition, in which man's existence in the cosmos is seen as imprisonment in hell and death and the saving act is seen in the event of resurrection.[3] The Redeemer, as ἀρχηγός,[4] is at the same time πρωτεύων, and for this very reason the first-born from the dead. His sovereignty as head of the body is defined by his drawing the redeemed after himself and offering to them anew the possibility of the εἶναι ἐκ from him as centre.

As the clearest expression of the mythological character of the hymn in the first stanza was the phrase πάντα ἐν αὐτῷ συνέστηκεν, so in the second it is the parallel ἐν αὐτῷ εὐδόκησεν πᾶν τὸ πλήρωμα κατοικῆσαι (v. 19). This expression, which has been such a bone of contention among exegetes, is only properly comprehensible in a gnostic setting. It is not permissible to interpret the sentence as an accusative and infinitive dependent on εὐδόκησεν and thus to make God the subject. Not only is God no longer actually being spoken of; there is no thought of him at all, because the Redeemer is to appear as the divine epiphany. The subject, therefore, is Pleroma, the all-embracing, all-uniting fullness of the new aeon.[5] This inter-

---

[1] Cf. Staerk, *Erlösererwartung*, pp. 21ff.
[2] *Ibid.*, p. 22 n. 1.
[3] *Ibid.*, pp. 23ff., 30ff.
[4] Cf. Käsemann, *Das wandernde Gottesvolk*, pp. 79ff.
[5] Cf. Dibelius, p. 13.

pretation is shown to be possible, and, indeed, justified, by the parallel in 2.9. This second passage makes clear at the same time what is the point here: the new aeon has become incarnate in the Redeemer. Thereby the All is 'reconciled', its conflicting elements are pacified. They are pacified in that they have found their Lord, the Cosmocrator, to whom the universal subjection in Phil. 2.11, the worship of the powers in Heb. 1.6ff. and the 'believed on in the world' in I Tim. 3.16 are also ascribed. The restored creation is his work; and inasmuch as it now forms his body, he is himself the 'redeemed Redeemer'. The hymn does him homage as it is done in heaven and on earth.

3. THE PURPOSE OF THE LITURGICAL REDACTION

The pre-Christian hymn has been transformed by a liturgical redaction into a Christian homology. Is it possible to establish the original *Sitz-im-Leben* of this homology? G. Bornkamm[1] has attempted to draw a line connecting Heb. 1.3 with the primitive Christian liturgy of the Lord's Supper (Lohmeyer[2] has done the same with Phil. 2.6ff.) and it is his opinion that all parallel homologies—and therefore our passage—are to be seen in this light. But there is certainly no real foundation for such an assumption in this particular context. There is no allusion to the Lord's Supper in the epistle as a whole. The hymn itself in its present form contains nothing that could be construed as a reference to it. We cannot base any interpretation of this kind on the term εὐχαριστοῦντες in v. 12, however firmly it may establish what follows as an act of praise used in the cultus. The most we could do, since Lohmeyer's thesis has remained pure supposition, would be to lean heavily on Bornkamm's suggestion about Heb. 1.3 and argue from the parallelism between our own passage and that one. But there is a less far-fetched alternative.

Bornkamm himself has demonstrated[3] in illuminating fashion that the 'Son' predication of the Christ has its real roots in the primitive Christian baptismal profession of faith. It is just this very predication which appears in v. 13 in the unique formulation 'Son of his love'. When the striking objective genitive is taken in conjunction with the other genitives of our epistle (remembering

[1] *TB* 21, cols. 6of.
[2] *Kyrios Jesus* (SAH, phil.-hist. Klasse), 1927/28, Abh. 4, pp. 65ff.
[3] Cols. 57f.

particularly 'the blood of his cross' in v. 19) and with the parallel in Ps. Sol. 13.9, where 'Son of love' and 'First-born' are similarly interchangeable, it is shown to be an Hebraism; and this is perhaps rather characteristic of liturgical style. Be this as it may, we have here a paraphrase of the proclamation of Jesus as υἱὸς ἀγαπητός at his baptism.[1] Is it then possible to incorporate our text into the framework of primitive Christian baptismal liturgy? In actual fact, a wealth of indications tell in favour of this suggestion and we must now go into them in detail.

So far as content is concerned, deliverance from darkness and translation into the kingdom of God's Son are unquestionably thought of as following from baptism. The other associated terms also suggest this relationship. Baptism represents a gulf between the two spheres of power such that only a μεταστῆναι can bring a man out of one into the other. Heaven and hell are face to face with each other here, so that the idea of displacement significantly defines the sacramental action of incorporation into the new sphere of jurisdiction. The condition created by baptism is characterized by the use of the expression 'inheritance of the saints in light' (v. 12) as heavenly existence. For light is the environment of the heavenly world or, as Lohmeyer[2] prefers to call it, paradise. The motif of the occupation by God's people of the promised land, which is expressed in the conjunction of μερίς and κλῆρος[3] (this conjunction itself having ready-made liturgical associations from the LXX), is transposed into the key of the transcendent. In this liturgical context we may understand the 'saints' as angels, that is, those who have been perfected.[4] The phrase 'he delivered us out of the power of darkness' is made to bear, in the interpretation of Lohmeyer,[5] a particular shade of meaning, which is not exegetically unassailable but which is by no means impossible within the framework of our total understanding of the passage. He establishes that 'he who delivered us' is almost a standing attribute of God in the LXX and that the deliverance from Egypt, and especially the incident of the crossing of the Red Sea, had become the prototype of all divine ῥύσασθαι for Judaism. Rev. 15.2ff. shows

[1] Mark 1.11.
[2] Commentary, p. 39 n. 3.
[3] *Ibid.*, n. 2.
[4] *Ibid.*, p. 39, against Dibelius p. 5; Procksch, *TWNT* I, pp. 108f.
[5] *Op. cit.*, p. 48.

how this constellation of images was taken up into the liturgical material of primitive Christianity. Its association with ideas about baptism can be seen from I Cor. 10.2. From there we may go on to ask whether we ought not to connect the heavenly sea, on which the conquerors in Rev. 15.2 stand, with the waters of baptism, especially as a parallel is obviously being drawn between it and the Red Sea. It is upon these waters that those conquerors wax strong, who have left Egypt behind them and have been delivered from the power of darkness. If this hypothesis is right, Lohmeyer's interpretation would be even more probable.

We do not need to produce proof that ἄφεσις τῶν ἁμαρτιῶν, as the message of baptism,[1] came to belong to the Church's Gospel of salvation[2] and to the kerygma of the Last Supper.[3] Ἀπολύτρωσις also bears not a specifically Pauline, but surely a liturgical, stamp (Rom. 3.24; I Cor. 1.30).

The adoption of the pre-Christian hymn into the Christian baptismal liturgy is particularly illuminating. The sense of Rom. 6 stands and falls with the evaluation of baptism as the calling forth of the καινὴ κτίσις.[4] In Judaism the deliverance from Egypt was understood as a new creation.[5] Philo identifies Noah with the Archetypal Man,[6] because he concludes antediluvian history as its *telos* and appears after the deluge as δευτέρας γενέσεως ἀνθρώπων ἀρχή.[7] Noah can also be called ἀρχηγέτης νέας ἀνθρώπων σπορᾶς[8] or, together with his family, παλιγγενεσίας ἡγεμόνες καὶ δευτέρας ἀρχηγέται περιόδου.[9] These few quotations may focus attention on the point at which mythology and the Christian image of baptism were bound to meet and to combine. Redemption in mythology is essentially 'always *restitutio in integrum*'.[10] Similarly, in baptism, the eschatological orientation of the original creation towards the new creation is laid bare and redemption as the beginning of the new aeon is referred back to the first creation. Because of its eschatological character, redemption can also be understood (as it is in

---

[1] Mark 1.4; Luke 3.3; Acts 2.38.
[2] Luke 24.47; Acts 5.31; 10.43; 13.38; 26.18.
[3] Matt. 26.28.
[4] II Cor. 5.17.
[5] Cf. Staerk, *Erlösererwartung*, p. 58.
[6] *Ibid.*, p. 44.
[7] *De Abr.* 46; *Vita Mos.* II 60.
[8] *De Abr.* 46.
[9] *Vita Mos.* II 65.
[10] Staerk, *Soter*, pp. 134f.

myth) as a resurrection of the dead; the most impressive testimony to this is the short baptismal anthem in Eph. 5.14: 'Awake, thou that sleepest, and arise from the dead, and Christ shall give thee light.'

The total context of the epistle supports our thesis equally strongly, and puts it beyond question. It is no accident that 2.10 speaks of baptism in schematic fashion; for it is from this perspective that Colossians should fundamentally be understood. Especially important here is that view of the Cross of Jesus (also to be found elsewhere in the New Testament) which sees it as the beginning of his exaltation;[1] in the light of it, the apparently anachronistic interpolation in 1.20 becomes more easily comprehensible. The exaltation which begins on the Cross is called Christ's circumcision, inasmuch as he has 'put off' his flesh (2.11) or the powers and authorities (2.15); or, in other words, the Adamic body tyrannized over by the demonic rulers of this aeon.[2] The strength of the cosmic powers collapses with the collapse of their form of existence. From being terrible despots, they become conquered and derided captives in the train of the triumphant Christ. This circumcision of the Christ is reproduced sacramentally in the members of the community by baptism. They also lose their old form of existence and are 'translated' into a new one—that of the body of the Christ; they make the successful journey from the power of darkness into the kingdom of God's dear Son, the inheritance of the saints in light.

For Christianity as for Gnosis, the primary significance of any form of true existence is not 'Here is a sharply individuated and independent animate being realizing its potential' but 'Here is a being determined by a particular sphere of influence.' Even when 'flesh' or 'matter' is under discussion, the real reference is not to the physical substance but to the enslaving cosmic power. In baptism the Christian changes from one jurisdiction to another. Henceforth he belongs not to the cosmos, but to the Cosmocrator. He has cast off his dependence on the forces which govern this world and is subject from now on solely to the Son, whose empire is defined by the forgiveness of sins. He has returned to the place

[1] Cf. the dialectic of the Johannine 'lifted up'; Käsemann, *Das wandernde Gottesvolk,* pp. 140ff.
[2] Käsemann, *Leib und Leib Christi,* pp. 140ff.

where the world stood at the beginning and will once again stand at the end, the place where the light of creation and resurrection shines. For he lives within the body of Christ and therefore within the possibility of the εἶναι ἐκ from Christ, its Head, who is the revelation both of Creation and of Resurrection. His life within this body is so orientated that he does not only come from Christ and go to Christ, but he is 'in Christ' because the new aeon has incorporated him into itself in order that he may abide with Christ and under Christ's sway.

This condition which has thus become sacramentally for the Christian the new reality of his existence is at the same time one in which he is the object of an unremitting claim. Such is the presupposition of the paraenesis in 3.5ff., which also clearly harks back to baptism. The putting off of the old man (v. 9) is the parallel to the putting off of the body of the flesh in Christ's way of circumcision. The putting on of the new man in v. 10 is the complement of this process, and therefore takes place, like it, in baptism. But what has already happened sacramentally must be unremittingly repeated 'ethically'. The gift is also a task; or, better put, the gift includes the task. Because baptism translates us into the jurisdiction of Christ our Head, at the same time it posits the obedience which confirms that we belong to this jurisdiction. As the tyranny of the cosmic powers was dissolved by the kingdom of the Son and thus the fear of the elementals is now abolished, so the πράξεις of the old man (v. 9) are done away with by the ἐπίγνωσις (embracing understanding and action) of the new man who is made in the image of God (v. 10); asceticism and the worship of angels are replaced by the perfection of *agape* (3.14).

Finally, the old Law with its guilt-creating decrees (2.14) is dissolved by the Law of Christ, represented by the Household Code of 3.18ff. It is logical that the Law of Christ should appear in this form. For a passage in which the foundations of Christian life are being discussed against the background of baptism cannot pass over the re-ordering of earthly relationships within the Christian community.

In what has been said, I have tried to bring out those themes which are to the epistle as corner-pillars to a building. They all point us back to baptism. A properly finished exegesis would further supplement this finding. Here we shall have to be content with what we have so far established: the sense of the liturgical redaction of the pre-Christian hymn is to convert it into a baptismal liturgy.

4. THE REASON FOR THE INTRODUCTION OF THE BAPTISMAL LITURGY

Some of the problems which have hitherto occupied exegetes in their treatment of our text have solved themselves incidentally and of their own accord, so to speak, as our investigation has proceeded. Above all, our interpretation has put out of court Lohmeyer's[1] attempt to see the whole passage in the light of the Jewish Day of Atonement. The evidence for this thesis rested in any event on very insecure foundations, apart from the occurrence of the term 'reconcile' in v. 20.[2] The liturgical character of the passage is to be explained by the character of the baptismal homology. 'The summing-up and the reality of the Jewish atonement-cultus'[3] is just what we do *not* see in Christ—only its fulfilment and consequent abolition. Cultus, in the true sense of the word, is only to be found in the 'sacred precinct', not in the world-wide body of Christ; it is to be found only where Law still reigns and the demons still oppress men,[4] i.e. in the dimension of repetition. But where the forgiveness of sins is vouchsafed once and for all with eschatological finality, there cultus is to be found no longer.

The alleged allusions to the Colossian heresy, which some[5] claim to have found in our text, are also rendered untenable by the interpretation of it set out above. The only correct piece of observation in this theory is the close contact (set up by the appropriation of the gnostic hymn) between the gnostic doctrine of redemption and the baptismal liturgy of our epistle. We thus arrive at the peculiar fact that heresy in Colossians is combatted by a confession of faith, the formulation of which has itself been very strongly conditioned by heterodox views. The danger arising from this state

---

[1] Cf. pp. 43ff., 66.

[2] Lohmeyer himself is obliged to hark back to mythology (pp. 46f.). Even he cannot deny that the Day of Atonement is orientated primarily towards the Jewish people, not towards the world. If creation and reconciliation meet there also, it is because they do so in the idea of a chosen people. The world is judged.

[3] So Lohmeyer, p. 45.

[4] This is the purpose of the sacrifice for Azazel, cf. *ibid.*, p. 46.

[5] *Ibid.*, pp. 40f., 58f.; Dibelius, pp. 6f.; Wagenführer, pp. 17f.

of affairs is obvious. The wind may be taken out of the enemy's sails for the moment. But who can guarantee that it is not precisely the heterodox origins of the confession which will be the rallying-point of future generations? This unquestionably happened in the early Church when she constructed her dogmatic edifice on liturgical material stemming from primitive Christianity, giving it dogmatic weight simply because it was already available in packaged form and enjoyed liturgical sanction. The doctrine of justification very quickly sank under the weight of a dogmatic development which sprang originally from the liturgy and was therefore particularly liable to become subordinated to outside influences. This danger must be recognized from the outset and exegesis recalled, in the light of it, to its duty of exercising criticism on the content of this development.

Finally, if our interpretation is adopted, certain difficulties experienced by exegetes in dividing up the text disappear; there are the difficulties caused by the fact that, while the proem concludes at 1.11, the attack on the heresy which has invaded Colossae does not begin until 2.4. Attempts have been made[1] to remove these difficulties by pointing out that the Apostle was not very well acquainted personally with the Colossians and that this might explain his reluctance to come to the point. But this explanation could not give final satisfaction because it left the exegetes with a really monstrous proem. Here also progress was made by Lohmeyer,[2] who at least made a unity out of 1.13–29 by treating it as an exposition of the Pauline gospel and dividing it up according to the respective viewpoints of Christ, community and Apostle. Our understanding of the passage, however, as against his, gives us the citation of the primitive Christian baptismal liturgy in 1.12–20 following immediately on the proem.

The reason for grafting this liturgy into the epistle at this particular point can no longer be in doubt after the above argumentation, more especially as there is an exact parallel to hand in Heb. 1.3ff., the sense of which has already been laid bare.[3] The Colossian community is threatened by false teaching. This false teaching must be repelled. This is done by anticipating antithesis

---

[1] Cf. Dibelius, p. 5; Lohmeyer, p. 40.
[2] *Op. cit.*, pp. 40ff.
[3] Cf. Käsemann, *Das wandernde Gottesvolk*, pp. 105ff.; Bornkamm, *TB* 21, cols. 63ff.

by thesis, polemic and paraenesis by the confession of the community. But the confession of the community is contained in the baptismal liturgy. This provides both a base for the necessary battle and at the same time the authority under whose banner the battle is to be fought. The field on which the issue is to be decided is excellently chosen. Since baptism is the foundation of the Christian's standing, all false teaching represents an attack on the baptismal state. Conversely, it is in the light of baptism that heresy is stripped of its false attraction, because in baptism the fundamental saving acts are declared and the once-for-all separation is made between the domains of light and darkness, of the Body of the Christ and the body of the flesh, of the cosmic powers and the Cosmocrator. By reminding the community of its baptismal confession, the writer calls it to order and makes it proof against false teaching which obliterates the frontiers of these spheres of influence. The confession of faith is already, to the Colossians, 'the rampart which surrounds baptism'.[1]

We must concede that what we have so far established about the confession of faith has not yet explained in what relationship it stands to 1.21–2.3. Now that we are clear as to the nature of 1.12–20, Lohmeyer's arrangement of the passage is not, as a whole, tenable. His second section runs on into vv. 21–22, as can be seen by the fact that v. 23 begins the treatment of the apostolate. This section is obviously only a transitional summary of the content of the key word 'reconciled' in the baptismal confession; this word is now made into a matter of personal appeal to the Colossians. Only the third part of Lohmeyer's division now remains; and the perfect title for this section, which, according to content, also embraces 2.1–3, is 'Apostle'. According to our analysis, it stands alongside the baptismal confession between the proem and the actual paraenesis. The only meaningful explanation is that the section somehow shares the exposed position of the baptismal confession and is being used with it to establish a base and a sanction for the battle which has to be fought. Thus we arrive at the following thesis, for which we cannot produce any further evidence here but which, simply as a thesis, should be illuminating in the total context of our passage: the community is bound not only to its confession of faith, but, at the same time, to the apostolic office

[1] Cf. E. Schlink, *Theologie der lutherischen Bekenntnisschriften*, 1940, p. 14.

as guardian of the truth. The apostolate expounds the truth of the Gospel, as the confession of faith fixes it. We may justly doubt whether it is in fact Paul who is relating confession and apostolate in this way and thus making the apostolate in practice the explication of the confession. This is the voice of the sub-apostolic age.[1]

For us, another insight is of greater importance. Wagenführer,[2] whose essay in general only takes up and refines the ideas of others, is bold enough to make the following judgment (the content of which is already to be found in Dibelius):[3] 'The Colossian syncretists felt that they were in the hands of cosmic powers and authorities. If the forgiveness of sins had been proclaimed to them as the sole soteriological act of Christ, that would not have been enough; for the menace from the cosmos would have continued in being. Full redemption can only be assured in the moment of living faith in Christ as him who before time was, while time lasts and at the end of time fills the cosmos, the *Kyrios* who is mightier than the cosmic powers and holds sway over them.' He thus understands the hymn to be a 'cosmic vision in which Christ is the central figure'.[4] To him, the Church is 'essentially a cosmic dimension',[5] a part and a function of the cosmos,[6] to which it brings the message that Christ is Lord of the cosmos.[7] It is in Ephesians that, for the first time, Christ is declared to be the Head of the Church.[8] Wagenführer therefore rejects 'that one-sided judgment, which sees in the New Testament only soteriology and ecclesiology and nothing more'[9] and states categorically: 'Only a cosmic Christ, who is at once the soul of the world and its Creator, could satisfy and overcome the religious concern of the Colossian syncretism. . . .'[10] The Colossian syncretism would certainly have been satisfied by a Christology of this kind. For this was in fact its religious concern—to incorporate Christ into its cosmology and, what is

[1] Paul also did, in fact, in both Rom. 1.3f. and Phil. 2.5ff., have recourse to a formulated confession of faith and, in many passages, to the liturgy. But this was a matter of occasion, not of principle, as Phil. 2.5ff. well illustrates; he did it of his own free choice, not out of respect for developing dogma.
[2] *Die Bedeutung Christi für Welt und Kirche*, p. 72.
[3] *An die Kolosser*, p. 15.
[4] *Op. cit.*, p. 80.
[5] *Ibid.*, p. 97.
[6] *Ibid.*, p. 97 n. 70.
[7] *Ibid.*, p. 98.
[8] *Ibid.*, p. 27.
[9] *Ibid.*, p. 82.
[10] *Ibid.*, p. 19.

more, as the Head. The sole object of its practices, its dogmas, its philosophies, its minute prescriptions was to find the way to Christ. For between Christ and it there now stood the cosmic powers which would only allow access and suffer themselves to be reconciled at the price of acts of voluntary self-humiliation. It is precisely to counteract this state of mind that the Colossians must be spoken to about baptism. For baptism proclaims: 'You are reconciled and the cosmos is pacified, because the powers which swayed it have been despoiled and now follow in the train of the triumphal progress of Christ. They have lost their lordship and their position as mediators. For you are "translated", you have entered into an immediate relationship to the Christ, you are his body.' The introduction of τῆς ἐκκλησίας in v. 18 has dogmatic significance. It illustrates the condition of being 'translated' into the kingdom of the Son and makes the cosmological statement into an eschatological one. Christ is also head of the powers and authorities. But they are not his body in the strict sense. They are 'in him', inasmuch as he is their creator and has authority over them. The community is his body, inasmuch as it lives from the resurrection of the dead and marches towards the resurrection of the dead. But that means, in the here and now, that it stands within the forgiveness of sins. It neither means, nor indeed can mean, anything else at all. Because it stands within forgiveness, it is a new creation, the cosmic powers have nothing more to say to it, to give to it or to ask of it. There is no way through to the original creation other than the way which passes through, and continues in, forgiveness. Every immediate attempt to break through, every attempt, that is, which does not derive from eschatology, turns into cosmology, into apostasy from forgiveness, into renewed slavery to the cosmic tyrants, who then take on the aspect of demonic powers. One thing only is necessary for a community which is menaced by false teaching of this kind; it must hear the message of baptism, which is the message of forgiveness, through which Christ alone is exhibited as its Lord and the claim of the cosmos upon it is seen to be extinguished, because it is the new creation and the body of Christ. 'For where there is forgiveness of sins, there also is life and salvation.'

VIII

AN APOLOGIA FOR PRIMITIVE CHRISTIAN ESCHATOLOGY[1]

THE Second Epistle of Peter was written as an apologia for primitive Christian eschatology. This is what gives it meaning and actuality. If, however, it receives strikingly little attention, this attitude can only constitute a declaration that the apologia does discredit to its object. For the Second Epistle of Peter is from beginning to end a document expressing an early Catholic viewpoint and is perhaps the most dubious writing in the canon. This in itself ought to be an inducement to make a thorough investigation of it. For theological work is always carried on by means of critical cross-examination. It is just the extreme types of doctrine which are particularly apt to produce clarity of perspective and mind. We might thus call it almost symptomatic that, apart from dutiful treatment in the various commentaries, almost complete silence has shrouded our epistle. In any event, we can see from this that we are still very far from thinking through in any thorough-going fashion our position either on the canon or on eschatology. The following investigation will at least raise the problem afresh.

I. THE CIRCUMSTANCES OF WRITING

(i) *The Occasion.* 3.3–4 expose the situation out of which the epistle has grown. 'In the last days there will come men who scoff at religion and live self-indulgent lives, and they will say: "Where now is the promise of his coming? Our fathers have been laid to their rest, but still everything continues exactly as it has always been since the world began." ' The whole context shows that this pronouncement has now come true. Prophetic speech here replaces simple statement; first, in order to characterize the existing state of affairs as not accidental but, seen within the framework

[1] A lecture given at the Beinrod Convention on 10 September 1952, and also at the Berlin Society for Evangelical Theology on 10 October 1952. First published in ZTK 49, 1952, pp. 272–96.

of salvation history, as necessary; secondly, in order to contrast it with that which obtained in the apostolic age. For it is a basic conviction of the latest New Testament writings that serious schisms or heresy were unknown in the hallowed days of Christian origins and that, on the contrary, they are manifestations of decay. The use of the traditional formula 'in the last days' should also be understood in this light. For however unambiguously it brings the happenings described within the framework of the logical necessity of salvation history, it marks with equal clarity the difference between the sacred past and present conditions. The primitive Christian view that the End had already dawned with the coming of Jesus is no longer strictly adhered to. 'The last days' are now a phase following on the coming of Jesus and the apostolic proclamation. But this means that eschatology is now orientating itself along the line of the current secular conception of time.

To the anger of the writer, the rejection of the primitive Christian hope has sunk to the level of derision. So far as material arguments still play any part, they are based reasonably enough on the evidence of the eyes: those fathers of the first Christian generation who still fervently expected the Parousia are dead, and the world goes on in the same old way. Rhetorical questions seem to be quite enough to produce a consciousness of the ridiculous nature of the hope which has been cherished. If a discussion can reach this point, very little resistance can have been offered to the confident attack. Just because of this, the writer of the letter must now intervene as *defensor fidei*. According to 2.2f. many have been impressed by the agitation and the speeches of the heretics; in particular, the newly converted have fallen victim to their seductions (2.14, 18). The whole community is embarrassed and disturbed by the fact of the delay of the Parousia, a fact naturally used by the adversaries to bolster up their argument (3.9). (ii) *The Adversaries.* In spite of the relatively comprehensive polemic in the epistle, we gain comparatively little direct knowledge of those who are in conflict with the primitive Christian eschatology. This corresponds to the tactics employed by the sub-apostolic age in the fight against heretics. Those who are immediately involved do not need to have their adversary described to them. Explanation to a wider circle has the disadvantage that in certain circumstances it may draw attention for the first time to the heretical modes of thought and thus drive insecure members of the community into the arms of the opposition. Finally, the greater skill in debate very often lies with the gainsayers and it is therefore preferable to cut off the discussion at its source. It is, however, clear from what is said that it is a question of a more or less clearly defined group, which may still be exercising a certain influence on the Church and maintains contact with individual adherents of orthodoxy but which is organizationally quite separate, having its own assemblies for worship in the form of love feasts—called by the writer 'mock love-feasts' (2.13). We may conclude that the writer is dealing with Christian sectaries and this is expressly confirmed by the accusation of apostasy and of the denial of the Lord who bought them (2.1, 15, 20f.; 3.17). More precisely, we have to do with Gnostics. As Gnostics, they proclaim the message of redemption under the slogan 'Freedom from the transitory', to which allusion is made in 2.19; they know themselves to be superior to the angelic powers (2.10f.) and also, as the whole chapter gives us to understand, to be exempt from every ordinance of Church and civil community, because they are no longer subject to the old aeon and its powers. It is just because they are Gnostics that the primitive Christian eschatology has no longer any meaning for them.[1] For, as far as we can see, the Gnostics had always adopted a critical attitude to it, whether directly or indirectly. The Enthusiasts at Corinth had already felt themselves lifted above temptation and thus above responsibility to any earthly ordinance because they were convinced that baptism had endowed them with a heavenly nature and the freedom of the truly spiritual man. They celebrate the Eucharist as those who have been translated out of the old aeon—it is for them the banquet of the saints in bliss—and deny (we must surely interpret I Cor. 15 thus) the necessity of a bodily resurrection in the future, because they wrongly believe that they have already experienced the resurrection in the sacrament. The error of the false teachers in II Tim. 2.18, who say that the resurrection has already happened, also springs from this conviction; and the modification of the view which we find in the Fourth Gospel, the deutero-Pauline epistles and the baptismal paraenesis of the New Testament at least harks back to this same

[1] So G. Hollmann and W. Bousset, *Der zweite Petrusbrief* (Die Schriften des NT, 3rd ed., vol. III), 1917, p. 314.

origin in gnostic tradition. All Gnosis testifies to the present nature of salvation and, in so doing, diverges from apocalyptic. It was in vain that Paul, although likewise very deeply concerned for the present nature of salvation, even to the extent of making extensive use of gnostic motivation and terminology, passionately defended the primitive Christian eschatology. Circles infected by Gnosticism, as in Corinth, persisted in appealing to his teaching. According to 3.15f., they were still doing it when our epistle was written and it is not unlikely that the efforts of the heretics to quote Paul in their own support partly called forth the vindication of him at the close of the document.[1]

(iii) *The Position of the Writer.* From all that has been said so far, it emerges that the epistle is a piece of documentation of the process of demarcation between right belief and heterodoxy; that, according to the almost unanimous verdict of criticism, it is the latest in date of all New Testament documents and in any event not written by the Apostle Peter.[2] There is no necessity today to marshal detailed proof of this from style and argumentation,[3] although the analysis which follows will touch at least indirectly on these points. Similarly, we do not need to undertake any accurate attempt at dating, but can content ourselves with the general assumption that we can settle for the middle of the second century. It is more important to remind ourselves that the epistle nowhere addresses itself to a limited circle of readers, but, rather, sets out to be a catholic writing. The circumstances which it presupposes are therefore characteristic of the ecclesiastical conditions over an area comprising at least a province—I have in mind Asia Minor. It is particularly illuminating to find that the writer is familiar with *a*, if not *the*, canon of Scripture[4] which coincides to a considerable extent with the one we know. It includes—obviously—the Old Testament; then the corpus of Pauline writings, mentioned, but not exactly defined, in 3.16, and the 'other scriptures' also referred to there. From 3.1 we can hardly draw any other conclusion than

---

[1] R. Knopf, *Die Briefe Petri und Judä* (KEKNT 12, 7th ed.), 1912, p. 326, enumerates the points which the Gnostics found ready to hand in Paul; H. Windisch, *Die Katholischen Briefe* (HNT 15, 3rd ed.), 1951, p. 99, even maintains that the heretics in question were 'radical Paulinists'.

[2] Against this, see G. Wohlenberg, *Der erste und zweite Petrusbrief*, 1915, in which he sees Peter as turning to the Jewish Christians of Galilee and North Palestine.

[3] On the Hellenization of various concepts, cf. Knopf, p. 253; Windisch, p. 85.

[4] Cf. A. Jülicher, ed. E. Fascher, *Einleitung in das Neue Testament*, 7th ed., 1931, p. 222; Hollmann and Bousset, p. 317.

that I Peter is already thought of in this light. Chapter 2 is, without any doubt, partly an extension and partly a revision of Jude,[1] which thus does not seem to have gained circulation or standing on any considerable scale. The reference to the Transfiguration story in 1.16ff. and a reminiscence such as 3.10a betray familiarity with the Gospel tradition. There may be a further allusion to this in 3.2, where the predictions of the prophets are joined in a remarkable combination with 'the commands given by the Lord and Saviour through your apostles' and the whole is made to offer scriptural proof for the continuing validity of the primitive Christian eschatology in the Church. If the apocryphal literature of Jewish apocalyptic, which is freely quoted in Jude, is obviously and deliberately suppressed in ch. 2, this shows that, on the other hand, the canonical collection of Scriptures is already subject to critical sifting.

What is the significance, in these conditions, of the fact that the author of the epistle writes not merely anonymously, but, with the utmost deliberation, pseudonymously? We cannot answer this question without first having paid due attention to the conception of apostolate and tradition which it presupposes. The introduction to the epistle throws the first light on the subject. It describes the addressees as those 'who through the justice of our God and (of the?) Saviour Jesus Christ share our faith and enjoy equal privilege with ourselves'. *Pistis,* which is clearly used here to define the estate of a Christian, is not merely the gift of revelation and grace and, as such, the link with the heavenly world. It also establishes communication between the apostolate, to whom this gift was originally and peculiarly vouchsafed, and the members of the community. This line of communication is in no way self-evident;[2] rather, there is revealed in it also divine grace, that justice which in its capacity of *aequitas* bridges already existing differences.[3] If this interpretation is correct, we are faced with a proposition

---

[1] Against Wohlenberg, p. XXIX and commentary ad loc.

[2] Knopf, p. 259, speaks of the faith of the community as the 'precious deposit entrusted by the Lord Jesus to the Apostles'. This view, represented also by Hollmann and Bousset, p. 303, and Stählin, *TWNT* III, p. 350 n. 32, is supported by Wohlenberg (p. 167) on the basis of the Catena edited by Cramer, VIII 85. Windisch (p. 84) puts forward the other possibility that the Gentile Christians were here being associated with the Jewish Christians, but that goes beyond the scope of the passage and indeed of the whole epistle.

[3] Wohlenberg (p. 169) rightly sees this as a barrier erected against 'arbitrary and capricious action' and 'all too human standards'.

unique in the New Testament—at least, in this stark form: *pistis* is no longer the act of becoming a believer or of obeying in faith, but the saved state of the citizens of heaven which primarily belongs to the Apostles of Jesus as the specially elect, but which overflows from them on to all other Christians on the basis of renewed divine action. God bestows the gift of access to the apostolic privilege on the community also and thereby demonstrates his justice as the source of order in the realm of the Church. Justice has here a good Greek meaning—the possibility of levelling out inequalities. Only it is directed no longer now merely at the world of social distinctions, but at the world of salvation history, which has its own internal differentiations. But the Christian community, as the fellowship of those who believe and have been apprehended by Jesus, is the host which is under the command of the Apostles. This is the peculiar criterion by which it is judged and which validates it as the community of faith, the community of the Word, the community of the Lord.

If we go on to ask in what sense this is meant, we come upon the passage 3.2, already mentioned above, which speaks with untranslatable compression of the τῶν ἀποστόλων ὑμῶν ἐντολή τοῦ κυρίου καὶ σωτῆρος. If we remember the forthtelling as well as the foretelling of the holy prophets, this phrase cannot refer to a single commandment. Thus, the adversaries are also characterized as those who have fallen away from the holy commandment which was delivered to them; parallel with this, they have abandoned the knowledge of the way of righteousness (2.21). Thus by 'commandment' we are to understand here revelation in its character of a claim on man. Admittedly, this is not a sufficient definition. We think of revelation, commandment, the will or demand of God as an event, while to the writer of our epistle it is obviously the result of an event. For this reason he can speak of the παραδοθεῖσα ἀγία ἐντολή (2.21) and, in identical terms, of the παροῦσα ἀλήθεια (1.12). Revelation has come to the community in the manner of an object which is handed over; further, it is now available within the community on the same basis. Expressed in an exaggerated fashion, but with the truth in question brought out by the caricature: revelation is now a piece of property which is at the community's disposal; it is 'the Christian religion',[1] just as *pistis*

---

[1] Knopf, p. 274: 'The Church's truth available in the congregations.'

meant the state of being a Christian. But the correctness of this proposition depends on the interchangeability of its component parts. For the Christian religion *is* as such the divine truth and revelation, the will of the Lord and Saviour, the gift of salvation come down from heaven and mediated in the community by the Apostles. This is most clearly visible in the formula ἅπαξ παραδο- θεῖσα τοῖς ἁγίοις πίστις (Jude 3), which is known to our epistle and is modified by it. As faith clearly means here the Christian doctrinal tradition, so the original purpose of ἅπαξ in the New Testament was to emphasize the once-for-allness and finality of the eschato- logical event. But this means that now an eschatological character is being ascribed to the Christian doctrinal tradition as such. Hitherto there stands inscribed over it the 'once for all' which denotes divinely posited irrefragibility and completeness. The formula of Vincent of Lerins, '*quod ubique, quod semper, quod ab omnibus creditum est,*' is only the reflection of what was already implied in Jude 3 and is now taken up again by the use of the phrase 'the truth you possess' in II Peter 1.12. The tendency which has led to this kind of phrase and outlook is ultimately directed towards removing the *fides catholica* from the influence of all arbitrary individual interpretation. It may be explicated, but, being once for all delivered and made available, i.e. entrusted to the Church as the instituted means of salvation, it cannot now be altered or supplemented. This is naturally a form of polemic against the enthusiasm of the Gnostics who ascribe their πλαστοὶ λόγοι (2.3) and σεσοφισμένοι μῦθοι (1.16) to the Spirit. Against them, the orthodox Church defends at the same time the historical nature of existence and the historical reality of revelation. She does this by opposing to the Gnostics' boastings about the Spirit (which are designed to conceal the whims of novelty and speculation) her own doctrinal tradition as the unique and self-contained revelation. And she upholds the historical reality of revelation, the particu- larity of the eschatological event, by putting in the forefront the apostolicity of her doctrinal tradition. The apostles, therefore, are to her not primarily models of piety but essential organs of her being, because it is they who have conveyed to her the commands of the Lord and Saviour. It goes without saying that in an outlook of this kind some of the primitive Christian motifs are retained. Paul, too, laid the strongest possible emphasis on the eschatological character of his apostolate and required that all apostolate should be understood solely in the light of revelation and the Apostle himself seen as the embodiment of the Gospel. True, to establish this is to define at the same time a decisive distinction: the correlation of Apostle and Gospel is replaced in II Peter by the correlation of Apostle and the Church's doctrinal tradition. The effect of this is that the Apostles no longer appear as those subject to the eschatological temptation (as for instance in I Cor. 4.8ff.; II Cor. 4.7ff.; 11.23ff.; 13.4) nor do they need, as in I Thess. 2, to defend themselves against the suspicion of being spongers. Peter is certainly depicted in our epistle as a man who is about to die, but this is only in order that he may set out for the community his last will and testament. It is no accident that the pseudonymous writer shelters behind the authority of the Prince of the Apostles. The passage 1.12f. shows clearly that, as in Luke, it is the fact of having been a witness of the words and deeds of Jesus which is really seen as setting the seal of authenticity on an apostolate. There is an inner logic in this. Only one who has been an eye-witness and hearer of this particular history can be a guarantor of the tradition of the Church, which is based on salvation history. Only he can maintain the continuity and the validity of the Church against the Enthusiasts who appeal to the Spirit and to individual revelations. It is thus the Twelve who are the real Apostles, however great the services which Paul may have rendered. He may be reckoned in our epistle as a writer of canonical Scriptures and be dubbed by Peter 'our beloved brother', so that his status approaches that of the Twelve very closely. He, too, on his part, confirms the doctrinal tradition of the Church, which goes back to the beginning. But he cannot be a founder of it; this is the sole prerogative of the original companions of Jesus. His apostolate stands, as in Acts, in a unique twilight. The Church of the Gentiles cannot deny that it is essentially his work. Conversely, orthodoxy cannot make him out to be one of its own foundation stones because, unlike the Twelve, he does not preserve that continuity with the historical Jesus in which orthodox belief sees the guarantee of its doctrinal tradition.[1] The conception of an Apostle has

---

[1] Thus Windisch's verdict (p. 89) is that Paul was strictly excluded. 3.15f. shows that orthodoxy both appealed to the authority of Paul and found him an embarrassment.

therefore changed. The messenger of the Gospel has become the guarantor of the tradition, the witness of the resurrection has become the witness of the *historia sacra,* the bearer of the eschatological action of God has become a pillar of the institution which dispenses salvation, the man who is subject to the eschatological temptation has become the man who brings *securitas*. And this transformation does not stop at the conception of the apostle. It determines no less the doctrine of the Church, which from being the *creatura verbi* becomes the guardian of the truth it 'possesses'; the doctrine of the Spirit, who is dissolved into the doctrinal tradition and is thus no longer in any position to exercise criticism on the letter; the doctrine of faith, which becomes a decision for the integrity of the tradition; and the doctrine of the Word of God, which, according to the primitive Christian view, is never ruled off as completed but is revealed anew from day to day—cf. the Johannine 'a little while'—*ubi et quando visum est Deo*.

We can now say what it was that drove the writer to pseudonymity. Where apostolicity is the criterion of the legitimate doctrinal tradition, the defender of this tradition stands in the shadow of the Apostles. The ancient world was not so finicky about pseudonymity as we are, nor did it place the same value on originality as we do; and so, for the *defensor fidei* the pseudonym was an expression of the fact (which seemed to him incontestable) that his message preserved the apostolic teaching. If, with rather less modesty, he hides under the disguise of the Prince of the Apostles, that says less about him than about the esteem and the standing which, at the time of writing, Peter enjoyed. According to the contemporary view, the whole doctrinal tradition of the Church, humanly speaking, flowed from him. It is thus more than just the employment of a current Christian usage when 1.13ff. characterizes the epistle as Peter's last will and testament. The writer feels himself really to be the executor of this will. This is the reason for the appearance in 1.12ff. and 3.1f. of the keyword 'recall', which enshrines the main concern of the document. The Christian truth now lies before men whole and complete and needs only to be handed on from one generation to another. Certainly this must be done in such a way that, in the face of attacks from outside and of human imperfection within the community itself, this truth is always being freshly expounded, explained and related to the existing situation. But meanwhile the Church holds fast the truth which is hers and, according to 1.12, the Apostle lives on 'for all time' in the apostolic witness.

2. THE COMPOSITION OF THE EPISTLE

(i) *The Arrangement.* The structure of the epistle is simple and to the point. The introduction in 1.1f. is followed in vv. 3-11 by a kind of proem, reminding the community of the promise which has been made to it and calling it to a corresponding transformation of life. Verses 12-18 base the certainty of the promise on the revelation which the Apostle encountered, vv. 19-21 on the appeal to Old Testament prophecy. Chapter 2 destroys the credit of the Gnostics who are attacking the Church's eschatology and thus provides support *via negationis* for the proof which is being built up. The way is now open for a treatment of the main subject matter in 3.1-13; this sketches an outline of the primitive apocalyptic as a way of rebutting the heresy in question, and attempts at the same time to dispel the doubts which have been engendered in the community by the delay of the Parousia. 3.14-18 contain the concluding paraenesis.

(ii) *The Content of the Eschatology defended by the Epistle.* An apologia for the primitive Christian eschatology cannot be vindicated merely by clinging to what has been handed down or by defending, on however good and logical grounds, the perspective of revelation over against Enthusiasm. Such an apologia must necessarily be measured by the standard of its own eschatological kerygma. How does our epistle come out of a test of this kind? The result of a critical analysis may immediately be anticipated in a negative formulation: The real theological problem of the epistle we are considering lies in the fact that its eschatology lacks any vestige of Christological orientation. It is true that formal allusions are made to 'the powerful Parousia of our Lord Jesus Christ' (1.16) to his 'eternal kingdom' (1.11), to 'the day of the Lord' (3.10, 12) or 'of judgment' (2.3f., 9; 3.7), so that the thesis we have laid down seems to be untenable. But conventional turns of phrase have little meaning unless their object of reference is clearly identified. This is done for us by the significant passage 1.11 in which the purpose of the proem—the description of the promise made to the faithful —is accomplished and the starting-point for the next stage in the argument is reached. Windisch has a good translation: 'For thus will a lavish entry into the eternal kingdom of our Lord and Saviour Jesus Christ be arranged for you.' In the background lies the conception of the classical Chorus, which a prosperous citizen has fitted out.[1] But, as the context shows, there is another picture combined with this one. The term ἐπιχορηγεῖν points back to the same word in v. 5 and to the admonition to make every effort to maintain the Christian way of life. There then follows (vv. 5-7b) a catalogue of virtues consisting of eight members, linked together by the rhetorical device of a chain syllogism and together describing the eightfold path of heavenly life. As in Ignatius, *Eph.* 14.1, faith and love are the first and the last links in this chain; they form a framework for that Christian demeanour which expresses itself outwardly in moral power, in the acknowledgment of the divine demand, in an attitude of reserve towards all that is meant by 'the world', in patience under temptation and in the maintenance of piety and brotherly love, issuing finally in *agape* as the bond of the Church's solidarity.[2] Verse 10 looks back to this with the admonition 'Exert yourselves to clinch God's choice and calling of you. If you behave so, you will never come to grief.' An ideal picture is being drawn here, depicting the Christian as a gladiator in the arena of virtue; the diatribe had done the same for the wise man. The prize is proportionate to what is at stake; it is the solemn entry of the victors into the eternal kingdom with full pomp and circumstance, with God himself as the master of ceremonies.[3]

1.4 similarly confirms that this, and nothing less, is the real content of the expectation of the Parousia so passionately defended in our epistle, for in it the writer once again makes explicit in unambiguous terms his eschatological hope. The great and glorious promises which have been made to us are all aimed at making us partakers of the divine nature. The writer really means what he says here, as can be seen from what follows: 'after we have escaped the corruption which reigns in the world through lust.' It would be hard to find in the whole New Testament a sentence which, in its expression, its individual motifs and its whole trend, more

[1] Cf. Knopf, p. 272; Hollmann and Bousset, p. 305.
[2] Knopf (p. 267) rightly emphasizes that the structure of this chain of virtues is not a logical one. But, as the interpretation which follows shows, neither is it purely arbitrary. In any event, it has a purpose (although Knopf disputes this).
[3] Bengel: *quasi cum triumpho.*

clearly marks the relapse of Christianity into Hellenistic dualism.[1]
Two worlds confront each other; the first is characterized by
corruption as the greatest of all evils and by sensual lust, which is
for ever being seduced by what is corruptible and thus delivering
man over to it; the other is characterized by an incorruptible, i.e.
divine nature. Man is called to emigrate from the one in order to
arrive in the other. Only then does he become what he is meant to
be—not merely man, but a partaker of the divine *physis*. Apotheosis
is his true destiny. This is what the mystics and Gnosis promise
him. But, according to our epistle, this is exactly what the
Christian kerygma promises him also. This is the end for which
the divine power has endowed us with everything that makes for
life and true religion (v. 3). To this end we must exert ourselves
and do battle in the arena of virtue (vv. 5 and 10).[2] This end
becomes reality with our entry into the eternal kingdom (v. 11).

The critic will object that this is not the whole story. He will
point to 3.13: 'We have his promise, and look forward to a new
heaven and a new earth, the home of righteousness.' Granted; but
we have to ask ourselves how the writer intends this formula,
probably drawn from some older material, to be taken. The
question can be easily answered, because here, too, the context
makes sure that we do not remain in any doubt. 3.10ff. contain a
'little apocalypse' which paints in lurid colours the dissolution of
the universe. The point of these verses emerges in the rhetorical
question in v. 11 and is paraenetic: just because the cosmic catas-
trophe is imminent, in which everything will dissolve into its
component parts, it is vital to preserve every possible form of
devout conduct and piety. In this way the Parousia of the day of
the Lord will be hastened (v. 12, picking up a Jewish theologoumenon). Good works also have their contribution to make
to this hastening of the End, obviously because they provide proof
of a break with the world and thus make easier the divine work of
final separation. Within this framework, v. 13 looks forward to
that state in which the definitive separation has already taken place,
the old aeon and the wicked who were at home in it have gone
down to destruction and the pious only remain. The new heavens

---

[1] So also Knopf, p. 264; Hollmann and Bousset, p. 304.
[2] 'For this very reason' v. 5. As παρεισφέρειν cannot imply secrecy, the passage
must mean: 'In addition, you must exert yourselves.' Syncretism is then unmistakable.

and the new earth, which are the home of righteousness, are thus the stage for the just, now delivered from their enemies and rewarded for their pious works. The whole cosmic drama, in which we actually see only the universal disintegration and the roar of the stars as they come crashing down, serves the single end of giving the pious peace from their adversaries at last. This is exactly what the threats against the heretics in 2.9, for instance, are saying: 'The Lord is well able to rescue the godly out of trials, and to reserve the wicked under punishment until the day of judgment.' Verse 12 declares even more plainly that the false teachers are like brute beasts, destined by nature simply for destruction; this doubtless was intended for the thoroughgoing satisfaction of those who, like the righteous Lot in v. 8, were being afflicted on earth by having day after day to be eyewitnesses and hearers of the godlessness of their environment. According to vv. 5ff., Sodom and Gomorra are a type of what happens at the End, summarized briefly in the formula: the rewarding of the righteous, the destruction of the wicked.

We have now looked at all the passages which can throw any light on the content of the eschatological hope in our epistle. The thesis with which we began should by now be fully vindicated. This whole eschatology has only one link with Christology, namely, that the future Judge of the world is the court which puts into effect reward and punishment. In reality, it is purely man-centred. The pious man wants to know what is going to become of him and of his adversaries. This is the only question which is gone into expressly and circumstantially: otherwise, we hear only of a cosmic spectacle which the writer goes so far as to describe in onomatopoeic fashion (cf. the use of the word ῥοιζηδόν, 3.10). But this means that, in fact, this eschatology only presents us with a straightforward doctrine of retribution. Can we then really call our letter, in all seriousness, an apologia for the primitive Christian eschatology? It seems to me that we must return a negative answer to this question. True, the hope here expressed does take up, in a way, what Paul was trying to say in his doctrine of the σῶμα πνευματικόν. In that doctrine, too, the real point at issue is that the Apostle cannot imagine a redemption which does not include the cessation of temptation. The spiritual body is for him that state of existence which is free from the tension between life in obedience and life under the threat of the powers of the old aeon. All creation waits with the Christian for this deliverance. But once that becomes clear, we can see immediately the characteristic difference between the two views. It is not only that II Peter substitutes for existential language the Hellenistic and naturalistic phraseology of the θεία φύσις and thus alters the Pauline statement of the doctrine in a materialist sense. The most important consideration is that the Pauline statement must not be taken out of its context. The hope of the spiritual body is only one factor, if an integral one, in a more comprehensive expectation which is equally concerned with the sighing of created being for the liberty of the children of God and with the restoration of Israel. If we ask how such disparate elements can be held together, we find that here, too, the heart and the motive force of the Pauline proclamation is the doctrine of justification, in the framework of which Rom. 9–11 is expressly set. It is unthinkable for Paul that the God who brings that which is into existence out of nothing, who effects the *justificatio impii*, the obedience of the children of Adam, the *resurrectio mortuorum*, should be faced with an endless fight against sin and death as the powers sovereign over this world; that he should not finally overcome all his enemies and reign as unquestioned Lord of his creation. A God so limited would not be really God. But this faith has also implications for the doctrine of man. It is equally unthinkable for Paul that Christian existence should remain permanently in that state of conflict between flesh and spirit which determines it today. Such a redemption would not be total redemption, it would not be *redemptio mundi*. Certainly, in the tribulation of the Christian the possibility of the new obedience is given. But it proves also that God's sovereignty is still being contested. Pauline eschatology, like that of the Apocalypse and of the whole of primitive Christianity, centres round the question whether God is indeed God and when he will fully assert himself as such. It proclaims the sovereignty of God in the doctrine of justification: equally, it proclaims the sovereignty of God in its apocalyptic. 'Yet Christ must triumph' is its central theme, as the enthronement of the Lamb is that of the Apocalypse. The manward-orientated eschatology is only one section of this proclamation, its radical penetration into the depths of individual existence and its concrete expression there. The *Kyrios* comes to take possession of his creatures and his world

—this is the meaning of salvation. But if we state the doctrine in these unqualified terms, we can see that II Peter has lost all real understanding of this 'He comes in triumph'; it is determined by the expectation of something impersonal—the divine nature. The sub-section has become the main subject; the Judge of the world has become the instrument of the apotheosis of the pious man. This is to abandon the peculiar theme of the primitive Christian eschatology and to re-establish that form of apocalyptic which Jews and Greeks also treasure and preach.

(iii) *The Significance of Eschatology for the Theology of the Epistle.* Eschatology may be the theme of the epistle but we are struck by the fact that it is not the central point of the theology propounded therein. This is another difference between the writer and primitive Christianity, the history and theology of which can be comprehended and described only in terms of eschatology. The findings of the last section provide proof of this. A non-christologically orientated eschatology can only lead to a Christology which is only half-heartedly and partly eschatological. Again, this thesis is not materially affected by the fact that our epistle uses primitive Christian christological predicates and formulae—such as *Kyrios, Soter,* the Lord who bought us—and speaks of Christ's Parousia and eternal kingdom. For all these phrases are no longer used to characterize him who has brought in the turn of the aeons but the divine being,[1] or, better still, the God of the Christian cultus, in his various capacities and manifestations, among which is included that of universal Judge. It is for this reason that the predicate applied to Christ runs, in stereotyped fashion, 'our Lord and Saviour'[2] and 1.3 can speak of the divine power which is essential to life and piety, as something impersonal. Similarly, in the same passage, the writer stresses as characteristic of this Lord his property of δόξα and ἀρετή, i.e. his power of working miracles; in 1.16 it is his δύναμις and μεγαλειότης; while the predicate *Kyrios* is applied sometimes to Christ, sometimes, as in 3.9, 15, to God. The Cross has disappeared from the Christian message; the *gloria Christi* dominates all else. The vocabulary of being has replaced

---

[1] Similarly Hollmann and Bousset, p. 304.
[2] Because of its consistent use elsewhere, it is hardly legitimate to draw together the expression 'our God and Saviour' (1.1) into a Christological predication, as Knopf does (pp. 259f.). Even then, however, we must still concede that v. 3 establishes that Christ is being spoken of as a divine being.

that of soteriological function; where there is mention of the latter, it is quite overshadowed by the former. Ontology and metaphysics press forward into the foreground.

The same is true of the ethics of the epistle. After what we said above, we need not go into detail. There is no longer any link with justification. This means that the *nova oboedientia* is no longer seen as primitive Christianity saw it—as life under the sign of the Resurrection. Let us concede that here, too, there is still some reference to eschatology. But now the point of it is to provide a basis for a doctrine of rewards and punishments. The man who struggles for virtue wins for himself the promised prize. In the place of the obedience of faith, effected in us by the Spirit, the new Christian morality appears. But it is new only in the sense that it is countersigned by a new authority. For both in content and in structure it is really very little different from what was possible and, indeed, already available in any form of Judaized Hellenism. Its concern is the flight from corruption with its stranglehold of lust, and its goal is the impassibility of a world without death, desires, error or falsehood. Here also the anthropocentric character of the whole system is manifest. The motivation 'to be . . . to the praise of his glory' (cf. Eph. 1.6, 12, 14) is hardly to be found. Man's imprisonment in sensuality, rather than his self-assertion, is thought of as the real evil. It is not the sovereignty of God which is seen as salvation, but rather the world of divine being, to attain to which brings apotheosis. Correspondingly, the Parousia no longer brings the judgment to which even the pious are subject but the death of the cosmos, in which corruption comes to an end; this is the same promise which the mystery religions make in respect of the existence of the individual. In fact, orthodoxy took over at this point the distinguishing mark of its gnostic adversaries: it became the preacher of a dualistic religious philosophy. But its Jewish heritage is betrayed by its conception of righteousness as life lived according to the divine norm. The new religion brings the *nova lex* and, in following it, emerges as ἐυσέβεια, as religiosity. Because the heretics offend against the moral code, they are children of the curse (2.14), slaves of corruption (2.19), they do not know the way of righteousness (2.21); thus they can have no idea of the ἀλήθεια of God as the true religion.

We have seen where the real centre of gravity in our epistle lies; it is in what is said about the apostolic doctrinal tradition. Apocalyptic eschatology is part of this and is therefore dutifully defended by the writer. But it is no longer, as it was in primitive Christianity, the bond of unity holding the whole kerygma together; rather, it has a relatively autonomous existence alongside the other articles of Christian doctrine. It is already what it has customarily been ever since in Church history—the concluding chapter of dogmatic theology, the 'doctrine of the Last Things', as it is so elegantly called. As such, eschatology can naturally arouse only mild interest. Indeed it would arouse no interest at all if its help were not needed in giving a clear-cut solution to the problem of theodicy and in encouraging Christian morality by directing the eye towards reward and punishment. It is enlisted in the service of the Church's task of education, as when baptism is seen as the beginning of the discipline of virtue (1.5ff.). We are compelled to see that the protest of the Gnostics against such an eschatology is not wholly unjustified, in so far as Enthusiasm, in its own way and with its own characteristic distortion, is emphasizing, on the other wing, both the *sola gratia* and the present nature of salvation. Both adversaries have destroyed that tension between present and future salvation which was peculiar to primitive Christianity. They are nearer to each other than they themselves know or wish to acknowledge. Both feel themselves to be the legitimate Christianity and both are relatively right and relatively wrong. Their strife is hopeless, so far as the content of faith is concerned.

3. THE ARGUMENT OF THE EPISTLE IN DETAIL

We must now embark on one final reading with the object of assembling the evidence of the epistle in some detail. As a result of this procedure, our finding will not be altered but illuminated and powerfully underlined.

(i) *1. 12–18.* The general sense of this passage is clear. The Apostles are, in an extremely personal way, the guarantors of the Christian hope. This is proved by the pretended Peter with the help of the Transfiguration story. It was essential to lay very strong emphasis at this early stage in the epistle that proof is possible in this matter. For it is precisely in this that orthodox Christians know their faith

to be different from the fabricated myths in which the Gnostics
traffic. The Apostles, and therefore also, of course, the doctrinal
tradition founded by them, do not follow mere fancy. They hand
on facts and are able to do so because the Apostles were ἐπόπται.
This term comes from the vocabulary of the mysteries and combines the motif of the eyewitness with a second, namely, that what
has been apprehended is a mystery accessible only to the elect.[1]
The story of the Transfiguration is recounted in a notably abbreviated form and clearly according to a tradition which is secondary
to that of the Synoptists. The writer is concerned solely with the
perfected Transfiguration as an established fact and with the voice
from heaven. In what the tradition has to say about the latter,
there is a mixture of the phraseology of the Transfiguration and
the Baptism stories. The predicate ἀγαπητός has become a mere
ornamental qualification of υἱός and is thus no longer understood
in its original sense of divine election. Verse 17 ends as an anacoluthon. There are two possible reasons for this. True, the writer
has begun with what happened to Jesus; but he is more concerned
to get on to what the Apostles experienced, because it is they who
stand in the foreground of his interest. Secondly, he has begun by
portraying what could actually be seen in order to bring out the
status of the Apostles as eyewitnesses. But it is equally important
to him to emphasize that they were hearers.[2] In other words, if
they have received the content of their witness from heaven itself,
then the doctrinal tradition which stems from them is of divine
origin. The transition between these two distinct motifs is marked
by the anacoluthon. The whole narrative serves to display the
glory of the earthly Jesus. The content of the revelation to the
disciples in the Transfiguration is precisely this, that he has been
walking the earth in his hidden divinity all this time. There remains
the question whether the writer has gained anything for his
argument by establishing this. The answer must be, that the
Transfiguration demonstrates not only the possibility but the
accomplished reality in the past of that to which the Christian
hope looks forward—participation in the divine nature. God has
given an example in Christ of what he promises to believers. It is

[1] So Knopf, p. 279; W. Bauer, *Greek-English Lexicon of the New Testament* (ET),
p. 305.
[2] So also Windisch, p. 89.

striking that this proof is not established by means of the Easter narrative; this is contrary to the usual procedure of primitive Christianity which treats the Resurrection of Jesus as the foundation of the future glory of Christians. There can surely be only one explanation of this remarkable fact. The Easter narratives must be so strictly and exclusively associated in the writer's mind with Christology that he does not dare to draw from them any conclusions concerning the doctrine of man. In the first place, he sees the Resurrection of Christ as something which affects only Christ himself and no longer as that eschatological event which brings in the general Resurrection. Against this, the Transfiguration is something which happened to the earthly Jesus and can therefore be used as an example of what awaits us also. If this interpretation is correct, all the individual statements fit without any forcing into the pattern of our investigation: the apostles are guarantors of the *historia sacra* and, because they are witnesses to the facts, founders of the doctrinal tradition of the Church, the content of which is the heavenly mysteries. Wonders which have already occurred provide justification for Christian hope which is, in essence, directed towards the apotheosis of man. Christology and eschatology are already divorced from each other. They are only connected in so far as the content of the Church's eschatology can be explicated by reference to the typical experience of the earthly Jesus. We are now at the stage when to believe means to accept the tradition of the apostles. But this is a safe option because the testimony of the apostles to the facts should bring immediate illumination. *Theologia gloriae* triumphs all along the line.

(ii) *1.19–21.* The apostolic guarantee of the Church's hope is complemented by that given in the Old Testament prophecy; or, rather, in the Old Testament itself, because the whole of it is to be understood as prophecy. The phrase πᾶσα προφητεία γραφῆς (v. 20), which takes up the introductory προφητικὸς λόγος, makes it clear that it is Old Testament prophecy, and that alone, which is envisaged here.[1] We might well wonder why all mention of primitive Christian prophecy has disappeared. But there is a simple solution to this problem. It is very evident that primitive Christian prophecy was one of the most dangerous instruments, if not indeed the determining factor, in the increasing hold which Gnosticism

[1] Cf. Wohlenberg, p. 201; Knopf, p. 282.

187

was gaining on the Church. It was in order to meet this danger that the Church adopted the Jewish institution of the presbyterate, out of which the monarchical episcopate grew. A ministry conferred by ordination is bound to be the natural opponent both of Gnosis and of primitive Christian prophecy. Thus it was no accident that the latter either died out gradually within the ranks of orthodoxy or was crowded out into the sects. II Peter has lost all knowledge of it; prophecy is now confined to written prophecy as recorded in the Old Testament. This is further reflected in the fact that 2.1 speaks only of false teachers, although the context expects a reference to false prophets. Verse 21, in what must be called a classic formulation of the strictest possible doctrine of inspiration, declares the Old Testament in its totality to be inspired. Men of God spoke as the Holy Ghost dictated. This statement represents an essential step in the writer's argument. For the Old Testament, too, bears witness to the hope of the Parousia. If it is God himself who is addressing the community in the Old Testament, then that hope is thereby characterized as a divine summons which cannot be ignored.

Verse 19 combines this proof with the previous one, but not by mere conjunction. In what the Apostles have experienced, a piece of Old Testament prophecy has already been realized.[1] Thus prophecy is no longer only promise: already it is being at least partially fulfilled. This fact provides justification for adhering to it even more closely and seeking enlightenment from it. In what follows, the writer is unquestionably employing material from the tradition of primitive Christian apocalyptic. Features of it are the simile of the light shining in a dark place, the use of ἡμέρα absolutely for the day of the Parousia and the phrases about the dawning of this day and the appearance of the morning star, a metaphor which was originally applied to the return of Christ. Wohlenberg[2] and J. Boehmer[3] have challenged the eschatological orientation of the text, not without grounds. For it is very noticeable that the writer is no longer really at home with the traditional material he is using. He may end his paraenesis with the sentence 'until the day breaks and the morning star rises in

---

[1] So also Windisch, p. 90.
[2] *Op. cit.,* pp. 203ff.
[3] 'Tag und Morgenstern', *ZNW* 22, 1923, pp. 228ff.

your hearts'; but this is not to be interpreted, as it is by Knopf:[1] 'The day of the Parousia will shine forth and then the darkness, the uncertainty in your hearts, will disappear.' Rather, language which was originally intended in an apocalyptic and cosmic sense has here been given a psychological twist. The writer is speaking of the inner illumination given by the word of prophecy. A trivial example such as this shows, perhaps better than many others, how little the writer of the epistle is qualified to defend the primitive Christian eschatology of which he himself has only a fragmentary grasp and which he deprives of its real point.

His true position is expressed in v. 20, probably the most significant utterance of the whole epistle. ἐπίλυσις means exposition, interpretation; γίνεσθαι τινός means to become someone's property, to fall to someone's share; in this case, to appropriate to oneself. The sense of ἰδία ἐπίλυσις[2] is a matter of dispute among Protestant exegetes because they do not take proper account of the antithesis. Knopf[3] completely misses the polemical point of the passage when he interprets: 'With awe, with restraint and with humility—this is the right way for Christians to approach the prophecies of the Old Testament.' And when he attempts to ascribe the interpretation of these prophecies to great 'men of the Spirit' and to new prophets, it must be pointed out in reply that, in the sense in which these words were used by the Enthusiasts and which is presupposed here, such people had ceased to exist in orthodoxy by the middle of the second century. Equally dubious, however, is the view represented by Wohlenberg[4] and Schlatter,[5] according to which prophecy receives its interpretation and its fulfilment from within history. Quite apart from the fact that this is not what the text says, we should always beware of any exegesis based on *kairos*. This, too, would inevitably fall a prey to Enthusiasm. O. Holtzmann's[6] comment is very much to the point: 'Our epistle already considers an ecclesiastically authoritative interpretation to be essential.' He thus declares his adherence to the

[1] *Op. cit.*, p. 283.
[2] There are careful summaries of the various attempts which have been made to give the true sense of this expression in Wohlenberg, pp. 206f., and Knopf, p. 284.
[3] *Loc. cit.*
[4] On the basis of an appeal to the Catena, p. 207.
[5] *Erläuterungen zum Neuen Testament*, 3rd ed., Vol. III, 1923, p. 82.
[6] *Das Neue Testament nach dem Stuttgarter griechischen Text übersetzt und erklärt*, 1926, p. 261.

Catholic mode of exegesis which has not been infected by Protestant Liberalism. Even Windisch and Knopf cannot entirely disassociate themselves from this view, for they, too, set authorized interpretation over against ἰδία ἐπίλυσις. It receives further support from the Jewish parallels cited by Billerbeck:[1] 'He (Moses) said to them "I do not speak to you of myself, but out of the mouth of God:" ' and: 'If one should say: "The whole Torah comes from God with the exception of this one verse, which was not spoken by God, but by Moses out of his own mouth"—on him the judgment is passed "The Word of God has he despised".' As the last sentence, taken together with v. 21, makes clear, 'not of myself' and 'out of his own mouth' give us the sense of ἰδία ἐπίλυσις It denotes an interpretation which one has discovered for oneself and by one's own efforts.[2] Here the logical conclusion from the struggle with Enthusiasm is drawn. There is no longer any living prophecy within orthodoxy. Only scriptural prophecy is admitted. But the danger is not eliminated, only delayed. For even exegesis, which now takes the place of prophecy, is exposed to the threat of error, as the example of the exegesis of Paul's letters shows (3.15f.). It must therefore be regulated; this is done by tying it to the Church's teaching office. Feine's[3] statement of the position is therefore accurate: 'Thus the Church is here the possessor of the correct interpretation of the Scripture, just because she is the possessor of the correct teaching.' In the same breath with which the Church is called to hear and obey the Scriptures, it must be impressed upon her that personal exegesis, undertaken by the individual, not authorized or prescribed by the official teaching ministry, is not permitted.

Now we can see the full implications of v. 21. The Scriptures are wholly and totally inspired. But Spirit can only be understood and interpreted by Spirit. The exegete must therefore have the Spirit if he is to comprehend the Scriptures. But it cannot now be guaranteed that every Christian *ipso facto* possesses the Spirit, although Paul could still say in Rom. 8.9: 'Whoever has not the Spirit of Christ is none of his.' In early Catholicism the Spirit is

---

[1] Strack-Billerbeck III, p. 769; cf. also Philo, *De vit. Mos.* I 281, quoted by Knopf and Windisch.

[2] W. Bauer, *Wörterbuch zum Neuen Testament*, 4th ed., 1952., col. 670: 'on one's own authority' (cf. ET, p. 370); Büchsel, *TWNT* IV, p. 339: 'as one likes'.

[3] *Theologie des Neuen Testaments*, 7th ed., 1936, p. 413.

bound to the official ministry. The community is seen, not only organizationally but theologically, as the generality of the laity. Exegisis cannot be given over into its hands. Its proper activity consists in hearing and obeying what the teaching ministry says to it. And so faith is transformed unmistakably into *fides implicita*: I believe what the Church believes.

(iii) *The Polemic against the Heretics in ch. 2.* I do not want to weary you too much and must therefore hasten on to my conclusion. So I shall only deal with one or two problems arising out of this section. We have already said that this chapter is a recasting of the Epistle of Jude. Even if it was not the Prince of the Apostles but only a teacher from the ranks of orthodoxy who thus plagiarized his colleague, that in itself is sufficiently illuminating. *Repetitio* is not only *mater studiorum*, but equally it is the curse and the tedium of all traditionalism. The well-worn tracks are always being travelled just once more. Where truth is regarded as a disposable possession, it is only a question of administering the correct dose in the right package. Unlike Wohlenberg,[1] I am unable to discover in II Peter ideas 'full of originality' or 'displaying a gift for acute observation.' In particular, the attack on the heretics has taken on a stiff and stereotyped character, because the writer is no longer conducting the campaign on the basis of his own experience. The enemy is disposed of in very primitive fashion; first, by accusing him of moral depravity, then by showering him with well-chosen proverbs (as in v. 22) and, thirdly, by painting the punishment of the heretic in lurid colours. Our chapter is a classic example of these tactics, which obviously found ready hearers then as now. The disadvantage of this method is that historical reality is always threatening to blot out the stereotype. Thus, for example, it is by no means a foregone conclusion, although a highly probable one, that the false teaching in question is some kind of Gnosis practised by the Libertines. Indeed, we know that even Paul had been accused of Libertinism by his enemies and we have therefore every reason to be cautious here. What the writer calls debauchery might easily turn out to be no more than the ecstatic state of those who believe that they are celebrating the banquet of the blessed. This assumption is strengthened by the wording in v. 13, where the writer reproaches the adversaries with carousals in broad daylight,

[1] *Op. cit.*, p. XXXV.

for immediately afterwards there is an allusion to false Agapes. It is a matter for particular anger that the heretics do not treat the angelic powers with proper respect. But this argument becomes very dubious if we look at Jude 8f., by which our passage has unquestionably been inspired. For there it is even forbidden to curse Satan and an unashamed veneration of angels is a component part of the faith. II Peter retouches Jude at this point because the use of apocryphal writings already seems offensive to him, although this does not mean that he would necessarily have had any objection to the story of the dispute over the body of Moses. In any case he shares Jude's veneration for the angels and, according to the end of v. 10, he even considers insults offered to the fallen powers to be a blasphemy of the Gnostics, who on their part see in it little more than an expression of rejoicing at being liberated from necessity and the power of darkness. The reproach of covetousness made against the enemy in vv. 3, 14ff. can be explained from the obvious fact that both sides are trying to retain the well-endowed members of the community within their own ranks, so as not to be deprived of their donations. To sum up, apart from the very general complaints, there is not much left which does not reflect equal discredit on both the conflicting parties. The theological disagreement does not range as widely as the moral disparagement. Apart from the differences over the eschatological problem, we can detect only a divergent attitude to the veneration of angels.

It is only indirectly that we become aware that, in spite of what has been said, the conflict does have deeper roots and that two incompatible theological conceptions are here at war. Verse 12 compares the heretics with brute beasts and v. 20 speaks of their relapse into the μιάσματα τοῦ κόσμου. These passages constitute a refutation of their claim to be men possessed by *Pneuma*; this claim is replaced by the assertion that they are controlled by *psyche* and by *sarx*. Thus each part makes the same accusations against the other. At bottom, their dispute concerns the nature and the locus of *Pneuma*. The conflict is really about the third article of belief and the things that are actually said are only superficial manifestations or logical implications of this conflict. A very good expression of this is the completely stereotyped way in which *epignosis* is stated to be the distinguishing mark of the community. The implication is that the community is really the assembly of the Gnostics—of those who truly know. Thus, when 1.12 addresses them with the words 'although you are familiar with, and grounded in, the truth you already possess', this is not merely intended as a 'polite compliment'.[1] Its opposite occurs in 3.16, where the gainsayers are described as ἀμαθεῖς. Only the Spirit can bestow this knowledge as it is possessed by orthodoxy under the influence of the Spirit and out of the riches of the apostolic tradition of doctrine.[2] It then becomes clear from 1.8f. that *epignosis* is bestowed in baptism; correspondingly, the antithesis of receiving *epignosis* is apostasy from Christianity (2.21).[3] Thus it is not a mere coincidence that both the salutation (1.2) and the conclusion (3.18) wish the community growth in knowledge. This *epignosis*, which, according to Windisch,[4] is the 'basic conception of personal Christianity' in II Peter, has the exact meaning of *fides catholica*, the orthodox doctrinal tradition. According to our epistle, to acknowledge its authority is to be a Gnostic in the true sense of the word; to possess it is the same as possessing the Holy Ghost; to apostatize from it is to embrace the very essence of heresy and to plunge into the depths of every kind of corruption.

(iv) *3.5–13*. It remains for us to take a last look at the arguments which are put forward in the face of the delay in the coming of the Parousia—an undeniable fact and one which is disturbing the community. Verses 5–7 presuppose the apocalyptic scheme of beginning and end, creation and judgment. The world which was created through the Word has already been destroyed once, sc. through the Flood. The false teachers are thus wrong when they say that all things continue the same for ever. As there is a correlation between beginning and end, so the Flood will repeat itself, although modified to this extent, that it will be replaced as a judgment on sin by a universal holocaust. In this all the ungodly will be destroyed so that space is created for the new world in which only the righteous will remain. Verse 8 bases the argument on a conception of God. Ps. 90.4 is called in to help. But this is done in a way which is not legitimate, because the lament over the

---

[1] Against Knopf, p. 273.
[2] *Ibid.*, p. 327.
[3] Knopf (pp. 270f.), Wohlenberg (pp. 184f.) and Windisch (p. 87) also consider that the context is baptismal.
[4] *Op. cit.*, p. 84.

transience of all things earthly is made the starting point of a philosophical speculation about the being of God, to which a different conception of time is made to apply from that which applies to us. It is certainly possible to relativize the delay of the Parousia on this basis. But if this is done, at the same time that very apocalyptic expectation which it is the writer's concern to defend is robbed of all meaning.[1] If we ascribe to God a time-scale different from our own, we are no longer in a position to maintain seriously the 'soon' of the apocalyptic believer, but are compelled to refrain from any utterance about the time of the Parousia. For we should then have begun to trespass in the realm of metaphysics in which the writ of primitive Christian apocalyptic does not run. In v. 9 the writer fends off the reproach that God is tardy in fulfilling his promise by speaking of the long-suffering which gives to all time for repentance. But this contradicts what is said in all the rest of the letter to the effect that the ungodly are predestined to destruction, and means in practice only that the present is the time when the Church keeps open its doors by missionary activity. Finally, v. 10 picks up the motif, which is found in the Gospel tradition, of the coming of the Day of the Lord like a thief in the night, and then fades into the 'little apocalypse' which we have already discussed. The verse is obviously designed to be a warning against a false sense of security, as v. 9 is against impatience.

This cursory glance reveals that the arguments in question are disconnected and not without internal tensions nor without tensions in regard to the epistle as a whole. The writer has obviously placed together material which had previously been current as individual units. The way in which he has assembled it betrays embarrassment rather than force. There can and could be only one result—each man reads out of the section what suits him. The truth is, then, that our epistle closes with the admission that the doctrine of the Last Things is already landing the Church in difficulties, and her apologia is in fact the demonstration of a logical absurdity.

I, too, have come to the end of what I have to say. It was my intention that my analysis of the epistle should pose acute problems. Perhaps, at least, it has shown us our own reflection in the mirror of history; if so, I shall be satisfied. For the promise is only

[1] So also Windisch, p. 102.

for those who see its logical absurdity. And it is not only theological problems, but untheological catchwords, which are the danger. We have to find an answer to the following questions:

What have we to say about an eschatology, which, like that of our epistle, is concerned only with the hope of the triumphal entry of believers into the eternal kingdom and with the destruction of the ungodly?

What have we to say about the canon, in which II Peter has a place as the clearest possible testimony to the onset of early Catholicism?

What have we to say about a Church, which is so concerned to defend herself against heretics, that she no longer distinguishes between Spirit and letter; that she identifies the Gospel with her own tradition and, further, with a particular religious world-view; that she regulates exegesis according to her system of teaching authority and makes faith into a mere assent to the dogmas of orthodoxy?

INDEX OF NAMES

INDEX OF BIBLICAL REFERENCES

EXTRA-CANONICAL BOOKS